THE
GOLDEN AGE
OF
TELEVISION

THE
GOLDEN AGE
OF
TELEVISION
Notes from the Survivors

MAX WILK

MOYER BELL LIMITED
Mount Kisco, New York

Let this be dedicated to all those who helped to create this book in deed and word . . . and are no longer here to take their proper bows.

Published by Moyer Bell Limited
Copyright © Max Wilk, 1989

**LIBRARY OF CONGRESS
CATALOGING IN PUBLICATION DATA**

Wilk, Max.
    Golden age of television.

    1. Television broadcasting—United
States—
History I. Title.

PN1992.3.U5W5   1989   791.45′0973   89-13285

ISBN 1-55921-000-1

Manufactured in the United States of America

CONTENTS

CONTENTS

Illustrated with photographs

ACKNOWLEDGMENTS

Having labored for more than a quarter century in and around show business, I am keenly aware of the value of screen credits. And since there's an old, pragmatic rule about the importance of getting the name up there—*in front*—rather than after "The End" (where, if the show runs overtime, there's a good chance the credit can be chopped), here are some very important credits.

In the past two years of compiling this work, I have often relied on the kindness of strangers as well as of friends. Herewith I recognize their assistance.

Arthur Tourtellot and Helen Brown, of CBS, both of whom have opened doors, unraveled network red tape, and enthusiastically expedited my requests, both on the East Coast and out West.

Larry White, late of NBC, and John Kasmire and Owen Comara, of that network, for similar open-door treatment.

Two remarkable gentlemen, truly dedicated to their work: Mr. Joe Ricciuti, of NBC, and Mr. Iz Seigal, of CBS, keepers of the network photography files. Respecters of history, knowledgeable, and tolerant of my most ridiculous request. Gentlemen, may your networks decorate you for your cooperation in this project.

Steve Allen, Marc Daniels, Franklin Heller, and Ralph Levy, philanthropists all, who have supplied photos from their precious private collections, as well as old clippings, reviews, and documents.

Eric Sevareid, of CBS, George Heinemann, of NBC, Lucille Kallen, Reginald Rose, Jack Paar, and Pinky Lee, who interrupted busy personal schedules to share their reminiscences and experiences. If space does not permit inclusion of all their contribution, it is not to minimize its worth one whit.

Lois Porro, of Westport, who has for two years now never failed to transcribe hours of audio tape with skill and good humor, and always on time.

The staff of the National Broadcast Pioneers Library, in Washington, who cheerfully tolerated all sorts of vague questions from a wandering author.

Messrs. Ross Claiborne and Ellis Amburn, a tandem of enthusiasts from Delacorte, who have never lost faith in this project, even when it began to appear that it would run on longer than *Love of Life.* Judith Sachs, of Delacorte, who has never flinched in the face of endlessly revised pages.

My wife, Barbara Wilk, who has spent all these years with me and never complained about being a television widow, and is still willing to listen to her husband's latest story line.

Most of the people who were interviewed in the past two years for this book are either friends or acquaintances of mine. (I hope they will remain so after publication.)

Among those you will meet are producers, network executives, writers, directors, and performers. There is one, alas, who will be conspicuous by his absence from these pages. His name is John McGiver. He was a schoolteacher in the Bronx who was launched on an acting career in the cast of a *Kraft Television Theatre* live hour show twenty years ago. In a short time, John became one of the most successful comedy character actors in the business. He made many films, appeared in numerous plays on Broadway and in Los Angeles, and did dozens of TV shows.

He was not only a remarkable actor and comedian but also a witty raconteur, a man possessed of an enormous appetite for the life he led, and a true friend to many of us.

John died suddenly in the summer of 1975, a few days before we were scheduled to meet. It was my plan to make a chapter out of his often riotously amusing reminiscences of an actor's life in the frenetic days of live TV. McGiver's saga would have enriched this work enormously.

ACKNOWLEDGMENTS

Some years back, John bought a copy of one of my novels, unbeknownst to me, and read it. He presented the book (*A Dirty Mind Never Sleeps*) to the library of our club, the Players, with a note that read: "Since this book is obviously unfit for the eyes of my small children, please accept it from my shelf to yours, as a token of my esteem for its author."

To the memory of my late good friend, John McGiver, then—as a token of my esteem for him.

Westport, Connecticut

PREFACE

"They call television a medium," said the late, great Fred Allen, "because nothing on it is ever well done."

Thank you, Fred, for supplying us with the opening. *The grabber.*

For those of you who don't know what that means, a brief explanation: the grabber is what producers contrive to say—or to do—in the first twenty-odd seconds of a television show. The hook that will impale the audiences, and paralyze their fingers, to keep them from flipping over to see what's on the other channels.

Mr. Allen spoke the truth, but King Canute he wasn't.

Television came. We saw. It conquered.

Back in 1947 or so, the RCA genie presented us with the first seven-inch-wide magic lamp. We rubbed it, and ever since, we've become a nation of myopic viewers. Which is a switch on the old Aladdin syndrome . . . for where was it ever ordained in the legend that we, not the genie, should become slaves?

Hooked on television.

What's the most popular magazine on the stands? Why, the one that sits on your table and contains a Michelin tour of next week's TV programs. The timetable of all that oncoming drama, films (old and new), news (local and national), talk shows, commentary, daytime serials, sports events, sitcoms, game shows, special events, award shows, tributes-to and put-downs . . . all those twenty-odd hours a day times seven of living wallpaper whose grand design is held together by a system of commercials and station breaks.

Split seconds after all of it has paraded past your eyes, it's gone. Vanished, and we are left with disembodied voice-overs spieling the arrival of tomorrow's smorgasbord, which will begin promptly at 7 A.M., after this brief message from . . .

Way, way back in the early days, Fred Allen also said, in one of his mellower moments, "Television is a triumph of equipment over people, and the minds that control it are so small that you could put them in the navel of a flea and still have room beside them for a network vice-president's heart."

It was in 1949 that one of those same vice-presidents (who wore CBS stripes and whose name shall be spared for obvious reasons) burbled euphorically in the public prints: "Television is growing, changing, adjusting. It's a field where there is no established taste, no formula. While its audience is untrained and still developing, television is a challenge to creative imaginations to learn the basic characteristics of the medium and then devise suitable material for it."

(In his somewhat misty crystal ball, was he envisioning *Let's Make a Deal, Celebrity Bowling, Hollywood Squares*, or did he have dreams of such future breakthroughs in dramatic concepts as *McHale's Navy, Hogan's Heroes*, and / or the *Mod Squad?*)

Any art form so temporal, so available—how can one seriously survey it as a type of history? Didn't savant Bertrand Russell say it all when he scornfully referred to television as "chewing-gum for the eyes"?

And that's far from all that's been said. TV has been fair game for every commentator, psychologist, senator, critic, and beer drinker since that first Admiral or Philco was installed in your neighborhood bar and grill.

Say what you will (and you will) about television, it has been, and is, undeniably our history. A peculiar sort of culture, a strange hodgepodge of artifacts, true. Nothing at all like the ceiling of the Sistine Chapel, or the Pyramids, the Elgin marbles that decorated the Parthenon, or the walls of the caves at Lascaux. No, the past quarter century of what we've sat and stared glassy-eyed at, or glanced at while we ironed, sipped booze by, placed our *kinder* in front of, gobbled our TV dinners to, or blinked at between our feet as we lay dozing in bed, is a unique and evanescent record of our own times. What's left of the electronic artifacts of the mid-twentieth century tells a lot about ourselves.

Don't ask exactly what.

Certainly, some archaeologist of the future may not be able to make too much of a good portion of a society that lived by *Broadway Open House, Songs for Sale, Racket Squad,* or *Captain Video* and his adventures. But, hopefully, he will learn something about our culture if he takes a look (provided there's still a kinescope around then) at the Army-McCarthy hearings from Washington, some episodes of *Omnibus,* any of the original dramas from *Philco Television Playhouse, Studio One, Your Show of Shows,* or *Mama,* or even the legendary "Ford Fiftieth Anniversary" celebration of 1953. (In the process of selection that poor man who's working on his Ph.D. may incur quite a few headaches, nagging backaches, irregularity, and stomach distress.)

Whether we accept it or not, the medium is a reflection of our own times. Pity the poor psychologists who continually try to evaluate television's massive impact on all of us out there. And pity us, trying to remember everything we've watched. All too much of it was so eminently forgettable; it's a fairly safe bet that we can't remember what we were watching back then . . . or even last month. The parade's been too long, and the gaudy floats move by so rapidly.

Try thinking about *Garroway at Large; Wide, Wide World; Danger; The Arthur Murray Dance Party; Martin Kane, Private Eye; Kay Kyser's Kollege of Musical Knowledge; Mr. Peepers;* or *The Goldbergs,* and what, if anything, do you remember? (This may be an unfair question: what do you remember about last week's *Tony Orlando and Dawn?*)

All right, then, evoke such ghosts of your own viewing past as Jerry Lester, Faye Emerson, Carmel Quinn, Hal March, Dagmar, Uncle Miltie, Wendy Barrie, Vivian Blaine and Pinky Lee, Renzo Cesano (the Continental), Ed Sullivan, John Cameron Swayze, and Ted Mack. . . .

For a while there, they were cult figures. And now—disappeared. Vanished, along with dozens of others, some of whom couldn't even sustain through their scheduled thirteen weeks before they dropped off the tube. Oh, certainly there are still a few survivors around: Lucille Ball; Dinah Shore; Art Carney and his friend, the Great One, Mr. Gleason; Jack Paar; and Perry Como. But their scant number is proof positive that no medium has ever engorged talent, chewed it up, and tossed it onto the refuse heap with more ruthless abandon than has your Zenith seventeen-incher.

Tonight you may be paying your weekly homage to Cher, Archie Bunker, Rhoda, Mary Tyler Moore, Chico and the Man (and we shall not attempt to make any value judgments on their lasting impact), but before all the artifacts of live TV, those scratchy 16 mm. kinescopes, are locked away as history, might it not be rewarding to find out how television all began, back in 1947? And to trace its first awkward steps, its flowering, and its departure, in the mid-fifties, with the advent of videotape?

That's the era we'll attempt to re-create and to explore. So switch off the set for a bit (it's only a rerun they're doing, anyway) and let's return to the Twilight Zone . . . not as archaeologists, but as bemused browsers, veterans of 1,001 nights long since gone.

TEST PATTERN–
THE FORD
TELEVISION THEATRE

It was a humid summer afternoon, a quarter century or so ago, when I sat in a fitfully air-conditioned suite of meeting rooms atop the New Weston Hotel, on Madison Avenue. Not exactly the sort of setting where one expected to follow the moving finger as it wrote a *mene, mene, tekel, upharsin* on the wall. Especially a message about television.

A cadre of authors and playwrights had come together that day, under the auspices of the Authors League, the stated object being to design and implement a new guild, one that would eventually deal with the networks and the advertising agencies and the sponsors in that brand-new, uncharted area of entertainment which loomed up on our horizons, could be bought for $179.95 for a seven-incher at Macy's, and called itself television.

The guest list read like a volume of Who's Who in American Literature. Present were such sachems as Elmer Rice, Lillian Hellman, Rex Stout, John Hersey, Dorothy Fields, Oscar Hammerstein; there were others there far less well known but no less determined to band together for a mutual purpose, i.e., self-preservation of authors' rights to their own material in the face of this squalling new electronic brat.

Throw any two authors together and they'll instantly find something on which to disagree. Make it forty-odd solo performers, and the decibel level will rise with such intensity as to make the Jets' locker room at half time of a losing game sound positively pastoral.

★ 1 ★

The late Moss Hart was chairman of that particular afternoon's long and arduous group encounter. Tall, saturnine, unruffled by the claims, counter-claims, motions from the floor, and longish periods of emotional harangue, Moss never lost his cool, neither that warm afternoon nor in the many sessions that were to follow. As the president of the Dramatists Guild, and as a veteran of years of playwriting, rehearsals, out-of-town hotel-room hassles, and opening-night tension, he was well equipped to steer us through the bramble bushes of internecine alarums and excursions that cropped up through that afternoon, as the steamy gathering of playwrights, authors, and radio writers sought to find some common ground in which to bury their arsenal of ego-engraved hatchets.

What were the arguments about? Jurisdiction, mainly. It boiled down to logistics. We were all agreed on the terms we wanted for our work. But who would represent authors in the years to come when it came to negotiating contract terms with the potential buyers for TV?

There were many successful authors in the room who found it difficult to take television seriously. Remember, in 1948 we were in the horse-and-buggy days of the medium, when NBC and CBS and DuMont were staffed by struggling pioneers who labored mightily in makeshift studios to bring forth perhaps two hours' worth of sporadic programming most evenings. Truly, it was hard to accept their output as much more than a joke; what flickered across that seven-inch screen those nights was ill-conceived, awkward, and just plain dull. "Amateurs playing at home movies," grumbled one veteran Broadway playwright.

Mr. Hart would not accept that criticism. "Maybe what they're doing now is painful, but please believe me, it's not going to remain at that level," he warned, a moody Cassandra. "You'll see—the network people will start to expand their schedules as fast as they can find sponsors, and then they'll never stop. And as far as material is concerned, this medium is going to be voracious!"

"I wouldn't write for television"—another virtuoso sniffed—"and I don't know anyone else who would."

"You wouldn't have written for Sam Goldwyn when *he* first started making films," Hart pointed out, "but I'm certain you wouldn't hang up on him to-day. Believe me," he said, "the time will come when they will be telecasting twelve, perhaps fourteen hours a day. Now there are already six licensed channels here in New York. That means those stations will need seventy-two hours or more of *something* to send out to the viewers."

His arithmetic was correct, but his vision seemed highly speculative.

Hart warmed to his thesis. "Consider," he said. "We write one play, it takes months to put it on, and then, if it's a success, we play it eight performances a week, two hours a performance. When we sell out, we reach a weekly audience of perhaps nine thousand customers . . . *if* we sell out."

The room echoed with a repressed titter. We all knew the odds on that particular gamble. They went with the territory.

"But," continued Hart, "the day is coming when that two-hour play can be seen once—by millions of people. And when that happens, the networks will have to be looking for people to supply them with thirty-six of those plays—or seventy-two hour-long plays—*each week!*"

No one spoke as we grappled with Hart's prediction.

Those gates he'd opened, that vast, demanding maw of the future gaped at us, but it was too huge, too inexorable, too terrifying. No single typewriter, no phalanx of twenty authors, not even a regiment of ink-stained wretches, all pounding away full time as their calloused fingers typed out stage directions, dialogue, comedy lines, and dramatic climaxes, could ever serve to stroke such an insatiable entertainment engine. Perhaps, if we closed our eyes, the specter would simply go away.

"Where was it ever decreed that man had to have so much entertainment?" someone finally demanded.

"Nowhere, friends," agreed Hart. "And it scares the hell out of me, too. Why, in the days when I was growing up, people found a few hours each week to read a book, or to play the parlor piano. Then there was vaudeville and the theater, and that took up maybe a couple of your hours. Even the double-feature movie houses only change their bills twice a week. Since when should we be overwhelmed with entertainment all day long and maybe most of the night?"

"And for free!" pointed out one of his confreres.

That dreaded word sparked further controversy. Say "free" to an author, and he or she will instantly fix bayonets.

But Hart quieted the ensuing discussion about pay television. (Oh yes, even then it was being suggested.) "*Whatever* form the medium takes," he warned, "we writers must get together on common ground. My friends, there's that box standing in the living-room corner with its glass eye staring out at us—and unless we build our ark now, what comes out of it will wash us all away!"

A prophet in pinstripes, immaculate shirt, and tie, Hart paused to allow his

Eddie Albert and Janet Blair, *Joy to the World* (Courtesy CBS)

warning to take effect. Then he smiled. "But if we can retain control of our material," he soothed, "*if* television is handled properly—by creative minds— it could become the most exciting medium we've ever had! Think of it—with one twist of the dial, you can bring great drama, music, ballet, education, poetry, everything in the arts, right into everybody's living room!"

"The way *radio* did?" scoffed one curmudgeon.

"But this isn't radio!" insisted Hart. "Remember—this is a *visual* medium."

Alas, poor Moss. He hadn't dealt with network executives, with advertising agency people, with Nielsen program surveys, with slide-rule ratings and mass market audience statistics, with demographics and computerized programming theories, and all the rest of the Orwellian machinery that moved in so swiftly and took over the commercial development of television.

If he had, along with the rest of us he might have been less sanguine. As it was, he was relatively fortunate. For the rest of his career, he had little to do with television.

★ 4 ★

And the rest of us: since 1948, when all of those earnest, optimistic, creative minds sat in the New Weston, trying to blueprint television's future, it's been downhill for most of the arts. The tube in the corner *has* engulfed it all. The movie audience that was once counted in the umpteen millions per week has shrunk by two-thirds. Hart's own turf, the theater, his Fabulous Invalid, in which twenty or thirty solid dramatic hits once flourished each season, now manages to deliver perhaps nine or ten plays each year, if that. How many people can afford twelve-dollar Broadway seats when there's a two-hour film of the week on tonight for free? Where once a dozen or so national weekly magazines adorned the local newsstand, now two or three still publish. Short-story writers and nonfiction article specialists have no markets left. Situation comedies and news programs have supplanted them. A best-selling novel which once could be counted on to sell by the tens of thousands of copies is now considered to be a smash if the publisher unloads several hundred copies per week. True, there remains such a mass market for writers as the paperback, but more and more that field concentrates on its block-buster titles. And as for newspapers, well, outside the New Weston in 1948, the stands carried eight metropolitan New York newspapers. Today there are three.

We did build ourselves an ark; we even erected a few contractual dikes to protect working writers. But the electronic floods overwhelmed us. The glass eye in the corner of the living room, plus the two or three others scattered around the rest of your home—they're thriving, operating eighteen or twenty hours each day, seven days a week.

Television has more than accomplished what Hart warned us it would, that warm afternoon years back. It has come to dominate our waking hours beyond his most dire predictions. If ever old Mr. Gresham's law—that bad inexorably drives out good—needed to be proved out, the networks have provided the proof positive.

And as we survivors of that early era sink slowly beneath the remorseless waves of giveaway shows, old movies, game shows, staged quizzes, commercials, interviews, taped situation comedies, and all the rest of that living wallpaper, turn down your set for a moment, please, to hear us as we cry out—somewhat vainly, perhaps, but none the less fervently—how did it all happen?

The great Duke Ellington, who spoke from years of experience, said that success is a matter of being in the right place, with the right people, at the right time. Those three elements must certainly have collided in my life back in 1948, for how else could I have so abruptly become, in one day, a full-fledged television writer?

That morning in April I'd dawdled over coffee and *The New York Times*, just another one of the many semipro writers around Manhattan, with a few short stories and a couple of screenplays to my credit. By 8:30 that night I had spent most of the day up on the eighth floor at the NBC studios in Radio City. In those days the rooms were still populated by radio actors emoting into mikes, but in one such studio there was a newly improvised set, and a group of somewhat bewildered improvisers milling nervously about beneath blazing-hot lights, in front of the NBC cameras, trying to produce a fifteen-minute television show.

During the morning the producers sent out an SOS for a writer—someone who could supply a few lines of so-called dialogue for the performers. The name of the show was "Home on the Range," and behind that somewhat heavy-handed pun of a title lurked a cooking show, one which featured a cheerful Broadway actor named Hiram Sherman, and which purported to take place in his dining room. Several of his guests were habitués of Mr. Vincent Sardi, Sr.'s, Forty-fourth Street theatrical boardinghouse; and for a climax to the quarter hour's worth of entertainment, Mr. Sardi himself demonstrated how to produce tasty crêpes from a chafing dish.

The world will little note nor long remember that quarter hour, which flickered light years before Dione Lucas, Julia Child, and the Galloping Gourmet began to chop, peel, baste, and braise in front of the TV lens. In those elemental pioneer days, the chances are excellent that NBC's presentation of chitchat cum crêpes made no impact whatsoever on what viewers there were assembled in Brooklyn and Bronx taprooms. (That's where most of the existing TV sets were installed back then.) But when the closing credits flashed across the screen, they bore my name as the writer. The desperate producer, by no coincidence whatever my sister, Ruth Nathan, having nepotically press-ganged me into this shaky enterprise that morning with an offer of payment for my services of taxi-fare to and from NBC (plus all of Mr. Sardi's crêpes I could eat) had with that one bold stroke propelled me into a new career. That night when the show was finished (an apt word) I had, although I did not know it until later, acquired, along with heartburn from all those crêpes, instant panache. Yesterday I might have been unemployed, but tonight I was an unemployed television writer.

But there's nothing unique about my experience. If I was dragged headlong into television as abruptly as if I'd been inhaled by a giant vacuum cleaner, then so it was with most of the writers, directors, and producers who broke into the medium in the following early years.*

For the production brains at the networks were baffled by their new electronic machine, and they approached programming with fear and trembling. Would that they were as respectful of it today.

To remind you of what you might expect to see on the mighty seven-inch screen that April evening, browse through *The New York Times* TV log, and consider.

On WABD, Channel 5, DuMont (remember DuMont?), the following was available:

6:05 P.M.	The Weather Report
6:15	Small Fry Club
6:45	News from Washington
7:00	*Doorway to Fame*
7:30	Camera Headlines
7:45	Film Shorts
8:15	*Magic Carpet*
8:30	*Swing into Sports*
9:00	*Sport Names to Remember*
9:05	Boxing, Jamaica Arena

Not exactly a stimulating lineup, but imposing when contrasted with what was offered on rival channels. Over on the mighty (pre-peacock) NBC black and white screen, you would be stimulated by the following somewhat limp feast for your eyes and ears:

Mr. Sarnoff's team switched their cameras on at

7:50	Newsreel Theatre
8:00	"Home on the Range." (This opened and closed on the same night. Preparing those crêpes on a fifteen-minute show presented complex logistic problems, and the NBC stagehands threatened to picket fu-

---

* Mel Tolkin, who, along with Lucille Kallen, was to become the mainstay of Max Liebman's *Show of Shows*, with Sid Caesar and Imogene Coca, remembers his own debut. "It was such an elementary period," he says, "nobody had television sets. I remember walking down streets with Max Liebman and we'd stop outside appliance store windows where they had sets turned on, and we'd watch them to get an idea of what *other* producers and performers were doing!"

ture gastronomic ventures. In years to come there would be successful TV cooks, Julia Child, et al., but their techniques would be more
sophisticated. We tried a retooled quarter hour the following week
with Hiram Sherman, guests, and no food. "That's Our Sherman,"
as it was called, also sank without a trace.)

8:15 Film. (The brief time allotted to it suggests a one-reeler, supplied to
NBC by some amenable PR man, seeking exposure for his client,
e.g., *The Right Way to Reshingle Your Roof.* Or a public service–
type short, *Nesting Habits of the Migratory Goose.*)

8:30 Americana Quiz, with Ben Grauer

9:00 Television Newsreel

9:10 Sports Film

In case what NBC and DuMont were transmitting bored you (and caused
you to wonder why you'd invested so much money in that damn TV set,
instead of watching the one in the corner bar and grill for free), it was back
to your evening newspaper. For there was no light burning in the window at
485 Madison; believe it or not, on that particular evening Mr. Paley and his
CBS-TV team had no programming whatsoever scheduled. (Remember, this
was several years B.L.—*Before Lucy.*)

That spring of 1948 the schedules may have been sketchy, but soon enough
TV programming would sputter into life. It was to be a period of complete
confusion; everybody and anybody assumed that he knew what the viewing
public would want to watch—and who could prove that the guy was wrong?
Television was the new show biz land rush—an electronic Cherokee Strip.
No money . . . yet, but packed with potential. Up and down Broadway, in
agents' offices, at the Lambs Club, at Sardi's and "21," anywhere two show-
business types sat down, they would instantly begin to blueprint an idea for a
potential TV show. Why not? The door to the ground floor was wide open;
the most stimulating nightly program concepts available in those Model T
television times ran the gamut from old Ken Maynard Westerns (circa 1932)
to wrestling matches and a jovial pianist named Bob Howard, who filled countless nights at CBS with his improvised jazz and talk.

If the horn of TV plenty hadn't yet been blown, soon, all too soon, it would
be. There would be such early ventures as *Celebrity Time*, starring Conrad
Nagel and Kyle MacDonnell, whose basset hound named Morgan, with soulful
eyes, turned him into television's first canine personality. There would be

★ 8 ★

hastily retooled old radio shows, *The Amateur Hour,* and *It Pays to Be Ignorant.* Soon we would encounter a new television mutant, the ex-film star turned lady "personality," the first wave led by Wendy Barrie and Faye Emerson. It would be the time of such curiosities as Kuda Bux, an Eastern fakir, who seemed to have the power of reading minds through a blindfold; he had quite a run on the home screen, and the time was not distant when an enterprising producer could present two equally enterprising personalities, Mr. and Mrs. Arthur Murray, in a series of endless dance parties. Another of those early ventures would serve to prove how cruel that TV camera eye could be, especially when it focused on Sherman Billingsley as he sat nervously at one of his Stork Club tables, awkwardly stuttering and struggling through "interviews" with his "guests," various cronies, newspapermen, and denizens of café society. Billingsley was proof positive to any of the prospectors who were out peddling program ideas. If *his* show can last on a TV screen, went the rationale, then my show *has* to be better . . . because it couldn't be worse!

In those early years, anyone who had the vaguest connection with a network or an advertising agency would be regularly approached by quondam TV entrepreneurs, each one of whom was convinced that in his briefcase he carried an absolutely unique program concept that needed only a bit of expertise from some director or writer to ensure its immediate acceptance by Messrs. Sarnoff and/or Paley.

Such dreamers would call and make a lunch date, usually accompanied by hints of vast riches to be made for a few hours of my time. Over the main course, I would be sworn to secrecy and presented with the proposition such as a large piece of the eventual profits in return for my preparation of a half-hour script. And then, over coffee, the pseudo-Mephistopheles would dangle the bait in front of his potential Dr. Faustus—the *concept.*

Sometimes the "concept" was a series of dramatizations of great works of literature: short stories by Bret Harte, or de Maupassant, one-act plays, or Victorian ghost tales. (Always in public domain, get it?—since that meant there would be no payment for literary rights to same.) One enterprising type once seriously proposed a unique quiz show; he suggested it be called *Go to Gideon* and employ a host who would be a minister quizzing small fry on their knowledge of the Bible. He was certain it would be perfect viewing for Sundays. Another promoter was more military-minded; his show would be staged out in the open and consist of re-creations of great battles from history. "Only on land," he said, very practically. "*Not* sea."

★ 9 ★

Sam Levene and Barry Nelson, *Light Up the Sky* (Courtesy CBS)

Should you be invited to the Lambs or the Friars, you could be certain that the graybeard you'd lunch with had conceived of some variation on a show that would be based on popular American songs. "Nobody knows the story *behind* the song!" went his refrain. "It's up to *us* to tell 'em!" Every old vaudevillian fancied himself a natural for TV; if Senator Ed Ford, Joe Laurie, Jr., and Harry Hershfeld could make it with *Can You Top This?*, why not he?

There were dozens of program formats proposed aimed at very special audiences. One luncheon host had a venture that would instantly corral for the sponsor a vast, ready-made audience: the stamp collectors of America. "It's got everything going for it," he burbled. "Greed, lust, avarice—each week we'll actually auction off stamps—and since we'll tell the story of where the stamp came from, and maybe do a little drama scene about its history, it's also *educational!*" Another lady had a half hour planned around sewing. By the end of the show, everyone at home would have been taught how to make a dress by following along with the hostess. But supposing there was no sewing machine in the home? "Well, certainly one could be *rented*," she snapped. Another lady proposed a gardening show, and the midtown streets were full of dreamers who were out peddling variations on animal friends and tropical-fish stars.

There was another self-confident type who confided to me what still remains the most surrealist blueprint for a game show that ever somehow slipped past Messrs. Goodson and Todman. This one would start with a card table in the middle of the studio. "Four players," he explained, "and we use very large cards. Now, the camera shoots over each player's shoulder, so we see the cards in his hand. We play an actual evening of bridge along with them—each one of these players is in the class of Ely Culbertson, or Goren, see—so the bridge lovers at home are actually playing bridge with the world's four greatest bridge players! I ask you—how can any bridge player bring himself to turn us off?"

When, dazed by this vision, I murmured something to the effect that it might be difficult to time out his all-star bridge game so that it would fit into a structured network time schedule, he shrugged that off as being of small consequence, and when I mentioned that his program might go a long way toward driving all non-bridge players to an opposing network, he refused to consider that as being of any importance. "Everybody likes to play bridge!" he insisted. "And if they don't—then they can goddamned well *learn!*"

In the fall of 1948 the Ford Motor Company put its corporate toe into the waters of commercial television and became the sponsor of an hour-long once-a-month dramatic program. Almost as inadvertently as I had found my original job at NBC, I found myself gainfully employed at CBS on *The Ford Television Theatre*; the pay was far from bountiful, but it was considerably more than taxi-fare and crêpes.

The producer-director who had been hired to do those shows was Marc Daniels; he remains one of the few pioneers who still function in that same capacity, a scarred but expert veteran, still able to smile after a quarter century's worth of rewrite sessions, all-night conferences, frenetic rehearsal schedules, and impossible deadlines. The concept for his first hour show, bold enough for those early days of 1948 and in retrospect even more so, was to trim available three-act Broadway plays (those works that were not legally tied to jealous motion-picture studios) down to fifty-odd minutes' playing time, and to stage them, with all-star casts, live, for the television cameras.

In the light of today's sophisticated production technology, in which 3M's videotape has made it simple to make a recording of any performance scene by scene, take by take, and then allows the director to go to the relative peace and quiet of a cutting room and splice together the show for eventual transmission on the tube; where sound technicians and engineers can record singers under optimum studio situations and replay the music and lyrics and voice back at any time they are needed, those early *Ford Theatre* productions of 1948–49–50 seem impossible. How could we near-amateurs in that new medium, struggling through uncharted waters fraught with possible disasters, ever have dared?

My first venture for Daniels was to help adapt a Broadway play called *Joy to the World*, by Allan Scott, which had just ended its theatrical run. While it was being edited down for time by me and another writer named Ellis Marcus, Daniels assembled a first-rate cast that included Eddie Albert, Janet Blair, Myron McCormick, and Philip Loeb. Not only did we carefully trim down Scott's play, but we had to supply connective lines for bridges from scene to scene, and rewrite the passages that couldn't be staged for Daniels' cameras.

So inexperienced were all of us that we had to learn everything as we went along—and that included the technicians, who were attempting to master their new electronic toys as fast as they arrived from the laboratory.

In our first "script" conference with Marc, I learned how the page format should look. "You put the dialogue on the left-hand side of the page," he instructed, "and leave the whole right-hand side blank, all the way down."

What would happen on that side?

"That's *my* area," he said. "And I'm going to need every square inch of it before I'm through."

Daniels was the right man for the job. He was a Carnegie Tech Drama School graduate who had gone through Infantry Officers' Candidate School during World War II. Out of such a meld of training was born an ideal TV director, one who could stage a play and retain the actors' confidence while simultaneously coping with dozens of split-second cues and the complex problems of timing and light and production, wrap the entire package up into an hour, and stage it for the cameras . . . *live*.

When those seventy-odd pages we'd prepared were duly typed up and de-

Marsha Hunt, Marc Daniels, Judy Holliday, Paul Stewart, and Richard Hart, *She Loves Me Not* (Courtesy CBS)

livered to him, he went into long, intensive sessions with his technical director, with his cameraman, and with his scenic designer, Sam Leve. We sat and watched with increasing awe as Marc and his technical crew proceeded to fill up the right-hand side of those manuscript pages with a minutely detailed plot of the movements of each camera. Blueprints, road maps, for four TV cameras (twenty-five years later, the camera techniques hadn't changed much: the majority of today's "sitcoms" are staged with the same three and four cameras), for hanging mikes, and for all the technical details that went into three acts of a play.

For seven or eight days thereafter, in a midtown rehearsal hall, he and the actors went through those movements, with us in attendance. Then, on the ninth day, the entire technical crew arrived, and with Daniels leading them here and there across the floor, they rehearsed each and every camera movement. On the tenth day we moved into a brand-new CBS television studio, one so newly built by the network that it hadn't been completed yet, and the carpenters and electricians worked around us, wiring and hammering in noisy counterpoint. Came the morning of the eleventh day, and we did a complete camera rehearsal with the cast working out there under the hot white lights. The next day we assembled in the morning for a full dress rehearsal.

Over in one corner of the studio, Cy Feuer, our seasoned musical arranger and conductor—later he was to depart this frenetic world for the more controlled structures of the Broadway musical, and to become the producer of *Guys and Dolls* et al.—rehearsed his small group of musicians through a series of music bridges and cues. In another area, jammed in behind scenery, a harassed crew from Kenyon & Eckhardt, the Ford advertising agency, rehearsed their automobile commercials—also live. (As yet, nobody had perfected that art form of the fifties and sixties, the film commercial.)

When all these components of the show had been rehearsed—never sufficiently, because of the press of time—the entire hour was run through from the top, and then again, in a full dress rehearsal, with commercials and music.

A brief rest period, in which our sturdy band of Equity members, their collective nerves by now as tightly strung as those of thoroughbreds headed for the Aqueduct starting gate, went off to their dressing rooms for last-minute meditation and prayer.

"Two minutes!" warned a stage manager, and everybody moved out onto the firing line. After all these days of preparation, it was zero hour.

Up in Daniels' control booth, the red lights were flashing. The technical crew was busily punching buttons, checking out all the screens on which the four cameras would be monitored. From a mike somewhere, a voice echoed through the studio. "Sixty seconds. Good luck, everybody." Down on the brightly lit studio floor, the actors, their deepened anxiety lines lacquered over with fresh coats of Max Factor's best, stood in their opening positions, muttering whatever it is that actors mutter to reassure themselves before curtain time.

Cy Feuer got the signal through his earphones; he cued his musicians. Nelson Case, the announcer, cleared his throat and let the waiting world outside know that *this* was *The Ford Television Theatre, live* from New York City. And off we went—over the top, embarked on a sixty-minute journey into space sans any sort of fail-safe or life preserver, a lunatic commitment to entertain based completely on the actions of a kamikaze squad of troupers out there beneath the lights, the sweating crew up in the booth, and those cameramen manning their king-sized monsters. An utter and final, go-for-broke roll of the dice.

The entire enterprise was imbued with a certain amount of *che serà, serà*. It had to be. For in that ensuing hour, should an actor miss a cue; should one of his props not work, or slip out of his hands and go clattering to the floor;

should our leading lady be unable to make a quick change from one costume to another because of a balky zipper; should one of the cameramen inadvertently dolly his camera backwards too far and by error catch the face of a CBS stagehand casually smoking a cigar behind the set; should one of those brand-new cameras blow a fuse in part of its complicated circuitry and leave us high and dry with no way to photograph the next scene—there would be no turning back, no recourse. Bite the bullet and keep going, that was the order of the day.

Remember, those were the years before an enterprising group of technicians had mercifully developed the TelePrompTer—that device which presents the script on a moving roll of paper to one side of the camera, for the desperate eyes of the actor out there. Later on, should the poor soul have trouble remembering his lines, TelePrompTer would save him from a complete wipe-out, as well as inflicting all those hours of glib political oratory from candidates upon us. But in the early 1950s no such machine existed, nor could anybody put an actor's lines on a series of "idiot cards" that could be held up off camera by a stagehand. So should one of our actors run dry in midscene, he would stand there, helpless, naked to the world, doomed, his eyes raised heavenward, as he waited for a nearby actor or one of the offstage technical crew to hiss his next line. And that was hardly a private hiss, not when it went soaring out into thousands of American corner bars and homes.

On went the actors, determined distance runners, slogging forward, their makeup running beneath the lights, smiling by reflex, playing intimate love scenes beneath banks of unwinking lenses, tossing off laugh lines into complete silence, staggering, a bit punch-drunk but game to the end, headed for the tape at the end of Act Three.

Then, blessedly, came Nelson Case's soothing closing commercial, with Cy Feuer's music over, the end credits, and a heaven-sent fade to black.

Finished. It was done, the entire venture. In the space of an hour we had transmitted a Broadway play with a live cast of actors performing it, and well, to an audience of a size vaster than ever dreamed of by the most avaricious producer since P. T. Barnum.

No applause, no waiting stagedoor visitors, no after-show party—all that was left was a weary group of technicians and actors, briefly thanking each other and shaking hands, and disappearing into the night. A review in the following week's Variety, perhaps, and that was that.

As we went along in that first season, we kept on encountering fresh possibilities for human error each time out. Those monthly ventures in front of the CBS cameras were leaky canoe trips through an uncharted Loch Ness, not only inhabited with monsters but with the waters mined in every direction. If Murphy's Law (i.e., that anything that can go wrong will) is valid, then its finest hour in the twentieth century has to be in those days of live television.

If one of our actors had been out the night before the show and suffered an attack of indigestion, he may have been *hors de combat*, but he had to get up from his bed of pain and play the show. Who had time to rehearse an understudy? Who *had* an understudy? With the help of paregoric, he went on.

Reflect on another problem, generic to those days—*timing*. No matter how carefully they'd been rehearsed and clocked, the actors could never play their scenes at precisely the same speed each time. They were, bless them, not computer-programmed devices out of IBM, but human, ergo fallible and subject to changes of tempo. Can anyone blame an actor who'd been on a steady treadmill of rehearsals for ten days or so for speeding up (or slowing down) in the home stretch? So our fifty-four-minute play, carefully cut and edited down, timed out to the second, might go on the air and then run out of control, speeding up in performance to a point where the play ended a minute or so short. Fifty- or sixty-odd seconds may not sound terribly long, but when it's very dead air, and there's nothing left to do but to run the closing credits at the lowest possible speed, it may seem like the longest segment of time you've ever experienced. *Stretch* is the proper word for such an endless wait. Many a night, our credits moved like glue upward on the screen.

And the following noontime at Sardi's, various of our actors might be met by waspish confreres, who would jovially inquire how much so-and-so had bribed the stagehands to keep his name on the screen for such a long time the night before . . . *mmm?*

Nothing was free from potential disaster, not even the commercials. If the agency people had been busy devising an artistic-type opening for one of the Ford minute sales pitches, one which, say, involved the camera shooting through a tank full of graceful tropical fish, could anyone have contemplated that said fish would, as soon as the ON THE AIR red light went on, develop a massive attack of stagefright? For the entire sixty seconds of the Ford commercial, the little finny friends huddled nervously together on the bottom of the fish tank, leaving the viewers at home with a beautiful, but empty, vista. One still wonders how that was explained the following morning at Dearborn.

The entire process was one long obstacle course. Why did anyone take on such a project? The tensions were grueling; since the audiences were small and the salaries ridiculously low, the reward was certainly not fame, nor was it money. Those of us who were involved in those pressure-cooker ventures have come to evolve a somewhat cynical theory about our pioneer days. Ask anyone who was there, and he'll agree. We were all simply too stupid to realize that it couldn't be done, so we went ahead and did it.

Daniels and his crew managed to get through an entire season of self-education, and in the spring of 1949 there came word from Ford. For some masochistic reason, the motor company wished to continue, but no longer on a once-a-month schedule. Mr. Ford was shifting us into second gear—one Broadway play every *two* weeks.

By that time all hands were sufficiently battle-scarred to accept the challenge, and in September the show settled into a well-organized, bimonthly production schedule. Plays of the stature of *Arsenic and Old Lace*, with Boris Karloff and Josephine Hull in their original roles; *The Man Who Came to Dinner*, with Edward Everett Horton as Sheridan Whiteside and Zero Mostel as Banjo; *Uncle Harry*, with Joseph Schildkraut; and *Night Must Fall* were successfully adapted to the hour-long format. But the home audience was still scanty. (The price of a TV set was as yet very high.) On such a night as November 4, 1949, when the late, great Judy Holliday ventured before the TV cameras for the first time to play the lead in the sturdy farce *She Loves Me Not*, the competition was very thin. Whatever viewers had access to a set could expect the following:

WCBS-TV

8–8:30	*Mama*, with Peggy Wood and others
8:30–9	*Man Against Crime*; Ralph Bellamy, Mildred Natwick, and others
9–10	*Ford Television Theatre. She Loves Me Not*, with Judy Holliday, Richard Hart, Marsha Hunt, and Chester Stratton
10–10:30	*Peoples' Platform*—"Who Should Pay the Pensions?"

WNBT

8–8:30	*One Man's Family*, with Bert Lytell, Marjorie Gateson, and others
8:30–9	*We the People*, with Roland Young and Elaine Carrington
9–9:30	*Versatile Varieties*, with Frank Cole, the Croydens, and others
10–11	Boxing, from Washington

★ 17 ★

WABD	(DuMont)
8–8:30	*Murder Market*: drama, with David Kerman
10–11:30	Boxing, from Chicago
WOR-TV	
8–9:00	*Old Knick Music Hall*
9–11:00	Wrestling, from Jamaica Arena
WPIX	
8:15–10:45	Football: Georgetown vs. Villanova
WATV	
8:35–11	Wrestling, from Laurel Garden, Newark
WJZ-TV	
10–11:15	Roller Derby, from 69th Regiment Armory

There was never a shortage of actors and actresses looking for ways to "break in" to the new medium. Even in those early days, when salaries and production costs were tiny, television was proving that it would be a profound influence in the creation of stars. Daniels' office door was always open to the hordes of hopefuls looking for work; in the course of that winter he gave many newcomers their first chance. One was an elegant young blonde who later retired from acting to take up more permanent residence in Monaco; her name was Grace Kelly. Another girl who cut her professional teeth in those *Ford Theatre* days is still very much visible; she is Cloris Leachman.

Daniels' production line soon functioned as smoothly as Dearborn's, but late in the spring, on one harrowing day, the roof caved in. All over the Kenyon & Eckhardt office the panic button was punched. A Broadway play that had been prepared and scheduled for the following week was abruptly canceled, the day before actual rehearsals were to begin. The play was *Edward, My Son*. Ford proposed to present the stage play, but MGM had filmed it, and at the very last moment, the movie company flatly refused to permit Ford, Kenyon & Eckhardt, and CBS to transmit over television a "live" production. Hidden behind a thicket of legal arguments over what rights MGM controlled was a solid commercial truth. The movie, starring Spencer Tracy, was opening at the Radio City Music Hall; why should MGM encourage competition? L. B. Mayer's feudal domain, accustomed to years of monopolistic block booking, would be the only company that never sold one of its films to television; in years to come, MGM would lease, yes, but that was all. And as far as *Edward, My Son*, was concerned, if CBS wished to risk a lawsuit . . .

★ 18 ★

Ralph Bellamy, *Man Against Crime* (Courtesy CBS)

CBS did not. Nor did Ford, nor Kenyon & Eckhardt.

Late Wednesday afternoon, Marc Daniels called from the K & E office. In the midst of such a day's panic, he was remarkably cool and controlled, especially so in the light of the fact that he was scheduled to begin rehearsals and produce an hour play for the following Monday night on CBS—and up till now he had no such play, nor a cast. But necessity had sired a remarkable invention; K & E had just minutes ago made a verbal deal with the author and producer of a current Broadway play to transfer the entire production, complete with its cast, directly onto the television screen for Monday! "It's Moss Hart's *Light Up the Sky*," Daniels announced, very casually, "and since

★ 19 ★

Subway Express, Ford Theatre (Courtesy Marc Daniels)

it's closing this Saturday night, all we have to do is to move the whole thing over to our studio. Should make an interesting hour show. How soon can you get over here to the office?"

It was nearly dinnertime; what did he need me there for?

"Oh, we'll need a script for tomorrow at eleven," he said, "and I figured you and Ellis Marcus could spend a few hours here at the office tonight putting one together . . . unless, of course, you have something more important to do," he added.

There's an old television joke. The writer is finishing his story conference with the producer, and as he gets up, notes in hand, to go home, he asks, "Do you want it tomorrow, or do you want it good?" "Tomorrow," says the producer, gulping down a double helping of Gelusil. . . .

It was that kind of a crisis. Ellis and I spent most of that night in the deserted K & E offices, with an occasional cleaning woman peering into the office to eye us suspiciously as we worked our way through Moss Hart's witty three-act comedy, paring it down, revising entrances and exits to fit our camera crew's capabilities, cutting and pasting actual playscript pages together and handing them over to a covey of loyal production secretaries who rushed them into the typewriter, cut stencils, and ran pages through the office mimeograph machine as fast as we finished gluing. Sometime after midnight a delivery boy from Lindy's staggered in with life-giving corned beef sandwiches and medicinal cheesecake, and then we went back to work.

Somewhere near dawn, we were finished with the playing script for an hour-long show. When Daniels' production staff began to arrive after 8 A.M., the first and second acts were being collated, and by nine the third act appeared from the mimeograph.

The first rehearsal was due to begin at 11 A.M., uptown in the ballroom of a West Side hotel. Scripts were being passed out to all hands, and as we piled into the taxi that was to take Ellis and me uptown to the first reading, I had a sudden thought. "By the way," I said, to my fellow editor, "do you realize we have no idea what we're being paid for this adaptation?"

"No, we don't." Ellis yawned. "Do you think writers are entitled to overtime?"

(Eventually we split the fee, which was $500.)

Promptly at eleven, the cast of *Light Up the Sky* appeared for the first rehearsal. The agency lawyers had to spend the next day or so negotiating their contracts, but verbal deals had all been agreed to, and the production proceeded on faith. Since the actors were still playing Moss Hart's comedy in the theater until the end of the week, they did not need to learn their parts. What they had to do was a strange reverse process: they had to adjust to our extensive cuts, to *unlearn*.

Thursday and Friday they rehearsed the cuts; Saturday they had to play their final two performances downtown at the Broadway theater. Sunday morning, blinking wearily, they were in the CBS studios for technical run-throughs in a set that had been miraculously designed and built by Sam Leve and his crew in forty-eight hours. Monday we went in for a day of full dress rehearsals, and that night, four short, intensive days after we'd begun this harebrained, impossible venture, *Light Up the Sky*, with Sam Levene, Audrey Christie, Barry Nelson, and Glenn Anders all re-creating their original roles, went out in an hour-long version over CBS.

And it was good. A production that had been mounted in less than a week —what in the words of some Broadway sage was a triumph of sheer dint— obviously pleased the viewers. "Television," said the hard-bitten *Variety* reviewer, later that week, "matured quite a few notches Monday night. *Light Up the Sky* came off as one of the TV treats of the season."

An hour-long show, prepared and produced in four days? Impossible. But those implacable MGM lawyers and their boss, Mr. Mayer, whose motive had been to throw a monkey wrench into the opposition's machinery, had unwittingly accomplished quite the opposite. They'd forced us all to prove that, in professional hands, TV was a resilient medium, and (as the future would prove) their nemesis. By taking away *Edward, My Son,* they'd hoped to scuttle us. Instead, we'd learned to swim.

The following fall, *The Ford Television Theatre* went on CBS on a once-weekly basis. Other sponsors had begun to underwrite shows, such as *Studio One* and *Philco Playhouse. Studio One* would concentrate on original drama, and *Philco* would begin with dramatizations of current novels. For good or bad, the medium was launched. And so was I.

WORTHINGTON MINER
AND *STUDIO ONE*

These days the mammoth CBS television network smoothly and efficiently operates its full schedule of daily programming out of a massive Eero Saarinen–styled skyscraper, an executive nerve center on West Fifty-second Street affectionately referred to as "Black Rock." Whatever production facilities the network utilizes in the East are mainly centered in the vast converted ex–Sheffield Farms dairy building on West Fifty-seventh Street that has come to be known as "the Cow Palace"; there are also some vestigial studios, used mostly for daytime soap operas, on East Fifty-ninth Street, in a building that was once Liederkranz Hall. (There is no connection between what is produced there and the cheese of the same name; it was once a recital hall, with superb acoustics, and was used by Columbia Records for much recording.)

Out in California, where most of CBS's production is done today, there is a huge complex of studios on Beverly Boulevard and Fairfax. There, at Television City, all has been structured, designed, and efficiently equipped at enormous cost so that television taping can take place under optimum circumstances. (Not without a few basic blunders, however. "When the place was first designed," chuckles one old CBS hand, "the architects laid out vast studios that were supposed to house musical variety shows, but they made no provision for where the musicians were supposed to set up and play in the studio —and the poor dancers were expected to do their tour jetés on floors of solid concrete.")

It was not always so—in spades.

Back in the primitive days, circa 1947–48, when the sleeping pygmy that was so quickly to mushroom into today's colossus first began to stir, Mr. Paley's television operation was far more primitive, frenetic, and convulsive. Television operations at CBS were berthed in an impromptu series of cubicle offices on one of the floors at 485 Madison Avenue, heretofore devoted to relatively simple radio operations. There newly hired nervous production hands struggled to bring some sort of TV show into life amid frantic conferences, endlessly ringing telephones, deadlines, and constant crises. Studio space was being improvised up in the lofty heights of Grand Central Station, on the Vanderbilt Avenue side, or in dingy abandoned legit and movie theaters that had been hastily leased by CBS all over Manhattan. (As for California, nothing much in TV was happening out there; movies were still better than ever and the executives who ran the studios were to a man secure in the theory that if you simply paid no attention to television, it would go away. "People," they pontificated, "have to get out of the house.") Everything was, for the time being, centered in New York.

It was all new and terrifyingly complex. Since until now no one had ever tried to do it before, nobody really knew how to do anything. An "old hand" was somebody who'd worked on the show last week. Scripts were often written overnight, and rewritten before breakfast; it was no business for anyone over thirty-five with even a vaguely nervous stomach. Improvisation, argument, tension: they were the daily diet, along with endless deliveries of delicatessen sandwiches, black coffee in containers, and hourly doses of what every CBS secretary kept handy in her desk drawer—aspirin in large bottles, referred to as "CBS candy."

Channel 2, which had been showing little more than its test pattern to the world outside 485 Madison, was gearing up to open its large CBS eye.

"Up till then," says Worthington Miner, who had begun his basic training in the medium many years previously, in the earliest pioneer pre–World War II days, "CBS had been concentrating on developing a color system for television. But the World Series of 1947, which attracted large audiences and showed they were hungry for more entertainment, forced CBS to abandon its insistence on starting with color, and to recognize that public demand for television was going to make it essential for the company to get into the picture—and fast. So when I was made manager of Program Development for CBS in the spring of 1948, plans were already drawn for going ahead full-

Worthington Miner, director of *Studio One* (Courtesy CBS)

steam. The specific assignments given to me were to prepare and produce, one, a major musical-and-variety show; two, a major dramatic show; three, a basic half-hour situation comedy; and four, a children's show."

An enormous order, even by today's more structured standards.

Over on NBC, a brash comic named Milton Berle would shortly begin to capture a steadily growing audience on Tuesday nights at eight for his Texaco sponsors. In September Uncle Miltie would explode like a noisy comedic atom bomb from his launch pad in Studio 6B in Rockefeller Center, and the fall-out would have such an impact that, short weeks later, Berle fever would infect the populace. Movie theaters would be empty on Tuesday nights, in restaurants one could contract snow blindness from the vast seas of white tablecloths at unused tables, and it is legendary that in Detroit, measurable water levels would take a drop in the reservoirs between 9 and 9:05 P.M., as devoted Berle fans patiently tightened their sphincters until after Milton's closing number, "Near You," before hurrying off to the nearest plumbing.

Faced with such potential competition, CBS would have to initiate some major entertainment-type show of its own—and soon. What would serve to lure mass audiences over to Channel 2?

"I determined that a weekly variety show depended upon talent," says Miner, "and also that a performing MC generally had spent from four to five years polishing his act. Then he often lived off that act for years at a time. In television, this act would be gobbled up in one television week, and no great performer was going to survive under those conditions. So I said, 'I'm going to conceive of a variety show where the master of ceremonies is a *discoverer* of talent,' and I selected Ed Sullivan."

Sullivan had been a Broadway columnist for many years and had actually had prior television exposure of a sort, when he had presided over a New York *Daily News* event known as the Harvest Moon Ball. After a certain amount of nervous backing and filling by the CBS brass, it was Paley himself who agreed to give Miner's concept a trial run. "In a matter of hours we'd made a deal with Ed, and then we began to face up to major problems," says Miner. "We had no place from which to do the show. So in four weeks we had to remake the old Maxine Elliott theater into a television studio—which meant tearing out the whole damn orchestra floor, putting in the control room, all the camera cables and power lines and lights, and installing all the sound equipment—from scratch.

"Meanwhile, I'd told Ed we wanted him to discover talent. He went away and tried to find out what bill he could get for the first show. He brought me back a very limp list of tired performers— stale acts that were second-string all the way down the line. Ed couldn't talk any of the top headliners around into coming on the show. They wouldn't go near it. So I said, 'Ed, you've missed the point. You're in there to discover talent. Nothing will sell this show as much as the fact that you are dealing with the stars of tomorrow— not yesterday. You find me two great bets for *tomorrow*—and we will have a great opening show.' And that's what he did."

In a matter of three weeks, Sullivan had gone hunting, and in Atlantic City, New Jersey, he bagged some potential comedy dynamite, in the shape of a young Italian-American singer who'd lately been teamed with a brash, noisy, and unsquelchable minor Borscht Circuit comic. On the night of June 20, 1948, Sullivan's first hour went out to the audience, with a peculiar mix of guests that included Eugene List, the concert pianist; dancing girls dubbed "The Toastettes"; a singing New York fireman, John Kokoman; the legendary musical-comedy creators Richard Rodgers and Oscar Hammerstein II; a dancer named Kathryn Lee; a fight referee named Ruby Goldstein; and, fresh from their recent triumph in Atlantic City, New Jersey, the comedy team of

Dean Martin and Jerry Lewis on the first Ed Sullivan show, *Toast of the Town* (Courtesy CBS)

Dean Martin and Jerry Lewis. "They came on," says Miner, "and they were dynamite."

After that first telecasting of *Toast of the Town* a thriving business grew up among gag writers, who were to use Sullivan as the butt of two decades' worth of flip cracks based on his stoneface, his malapropisms, and his decided lack of dynamic presence. Perhaps Fred Allen summed it all up when he said, "Ed Sullivan will be a success as long as other people have talent," and the tables down at Lindy's roared at Joe E. Lewis's quip: "Ed is the only man who can brighten up a room by leaving it." But certainly the award for the most unprescient assessment of that first show must go to *The New York Times*' own Jack Gould, who began his review of the previous night's display by remarking: "The choice of Ed Sullivan as master of ceremonies . . . seems ill-advised. In such a key spot, an experienced and versatile person must be in charge. Once [CBS] appreciates more fully the need for knowing hands to

Cast of the first Ed Sullivan show, *Toast of the Town*, June 20, 1948 (Courtesy CBS)

guide the proceedings, both on stage and off—it, too, should have an enjoyable hit. . . ."

Toast of the Town limped along with its first sponsor, Emerson Radio and TV, for thirteen weeks, and then found another underwriter, Lincoln-Mercury, who stayed with the enterprise for a much healthier and long-lived run.

That first show could hardly have been considered financially rewarding by anyone; the total production budget of $1,350 went to pay for all the talent, a technical crew of six, Sullivan, and an orchestra of fourteen directed by Ray Bloch, a veteran radio conductor. Two decades later, *The Ed Sullivan Show* would be costing $372,000 an hour and would, in the course of twenty television seasons, have sent to an early grave such long-gone competitive offerings as *Follow the Sun; Hey, Landlord!; Car 54, Where Are You?; Pete Kelley's Blues; Suspicion;* and an endless list of other concepts designed to dent the Sullivan charisma (or lack of same). Once CBS moved Sullivan, the noncompetitive MC, into the Sunday night spot, CBS was secure against onslaughts from such talents as Perry Como, Bob Hope, Jimmy Durante, Eddie Cantor, and even Ed's own first discoveries, Martin and Lewis, who'd gone over to the opposition on their own.

But it was Sullivan himself who was later to articulate the basic reason for his success, when he summed it up by saying, "I don't think you can ever get anybody but me content to introduce an act and get off. The most difficult thing in the world is to shut up."

And now Miner turned to the second most pressing assignment, the one-hour dramatic show. In the newly built studios up in Grand Central, where Marc Daniels and his Kenyon & Eckhardt crew were laboring to produce one hour of live television drama per month, Miner proposed to produce a new show called *Studio One*, in which he would telecast an original drama—*each week*—which would entail a back-breaking, mind-bending, stomach-twisting seven-day schedule.

"We couldn't get rights to great big Broadway hits or anything that had been sold to films during that period," he says. (Needless to say, the crowned heads of Hollywood were not prepared to lift a finger to assist television; the furthest that Mayer or Warner or Zanuck could possibly be persuaded to go would be to permit a contract player, preferably one on the skids, to make an appearance on a show for the sole purpose of plugging the studio's latest epic.) "So we went into public domain a great deal to find the classics, or we went into short stories, which weren't tremendously expensive. I devised a scheme that involved doing types of scripts in rotation—starting with a murder mystery. That would be sure-fire, and the easiest to do. After that, I could get into the heavier stuff."

Margaret Sullavan, *The Storm* (Courtesy CBS)

Betty Furness for Westinghouse, *Studio One* (Courtesy CBS)

The first play Miner produced for his new *Studio One* was a mystery called *The Storm*, and it starred the late Margaret Sullavan, a star who was cheerfully willing to rise to the challenge of this complex new medium—as opposed to so many of her Broadway and Hollywood peer group, who quietly backed away from any opportunity to expose themselves to that unwinking red-eyed CBS camera. "Our top salary in that first year was $500," says Miner, "far less than Miss Sullavan might have received for an hour's performance in any other job. But she was a remarkable lady who wanted to be in on the start of something. As a matter of fact, the cost of that show was minute—we had no more money."

Westinghouse was the sponsor. ("You can be sure—if it's *Westinghouse*," lovely Betty Furness was to chant for years to come, cheerfully opening countless refrigerator doors and assuring us of their built-in value—including one memorable evening when the refrigerator door came off in her lovely hand.) "They bought the show for $8,100 a week," he says. "It cost CBS, as I recall, between $12,000 or $12,500—so the network was losing."

Only money, for what Mr. Paley's organization was putting down in red ink it would certainly recoup far more in terms of production and technical know-how for future use in this most uncertain of mediums, this technological nightmare of cameras, booms, and bright lights. "On that first show I had no assistant; I had a secretary who sat beside me with the script. I had to learn every shot in the show during rehearsal, every camera setup. When I was on with one camera, I had to be telling the other two cameras where to go to get ready. Before the next show, I had an associate director assigned to that show, who preset the cameras," sighs Miner.

"We had in a very short time an elegant rapport. A great rapport and a great stimulus, and a challenge to the technicians on that show to meet the demands I made. Sometimes I pressed them too far, but they weren't outraged—they knew they were on the borderline of what was possible, and consequently, in those first four years, they worked very hard and very well."

Writers and adaptors? "Well, at first, there simply weren't too many of them around," he says. "And I couldn't afford those who were, so at the start I was writing most of the scripts myself. In the first two years of *Studio One* I wrote approximately thirty-nine of the forty-four scripts we needed." As well as producing, casting, and working long hours with the inexperienced directors who were handed the complex responsibilities of staging the scripts for the cameras on this implacable seven-day marathon?

Miner winces at the recollection. "I didn't normally get much more than four to six hours of sleep a night, and I lived on catnaps. I was able to lie down on the floor of my office for ten minutes, or in the aisle of a theater, or anywhere—just go out cold, and come back refreshed."

Gradually the *Studio One* operation began to take on talented associates. Most of the directors Miner was to train were from theatrical backgrounds, and the roster of his successful graduates is impressive. It includes such current heavyweights as Frank Schaffner (*Patton*), Sidney Lumet (*Murder on the Orient Express*), George Roy Hill (*The Sting*), Yul Brynner, Paul Nickell, and Robert Mulligan. "In my directors I was looking for a theatrical set of standards," says Miner. "A respect for the literate word and the provocative idea."

The drafting of writers for the show was far more haphazard. Miner shortly became aware that he was physically and mentally unable to supply a weekly script, "even if I'd wanted to, which I didn't."

Sumner Locke Elliott, the novelist, who was later to become one of television's most prolific dramatists, literally collided with *Studio One*. A chance acquaintance at a party mentioned that she was the next-door neighbor of Arthur Heinemann, the program's new story editor, and suggested that she arrange a meeting for Locke Elliott, a struggling tyro. "And just in time too," he says today; "I was practically broke." At the meeting at CBS, Heinemann, after a hasty cross-examination, brought Locke Elliott directly into Miner's office. "I arrived in the midst of a crisis. They had a script they'd commissioned for Maugham's *Of Human Bondage* and it was no good, and Miner said, 'We've got a script here, and it's no good, do you think you could get me a workable script by Friday?' This," comments Locke Elliott, "was Tuesday. Somehow that's how it always was to be—two days. Always two days."

All that was left in the budget for an author's fee was $200. "Only $200? It was more than I'd seen in weeks. 'But if it works,' Miner said to me, 'I'll guarantee you another assignment right now, because within four or five weeks, we're going to do *Jane Eyre*, and I can give you that one for $400—if you save *Of Human Bondage* for me.'

"I said, 'Mr. Miner, I could do *Of Human Bondage* AND *War and Peace* AND *Anna Karenina* by Friday,' that's *how* anxious I was! I'd never been in a studio in my life, nor seen a TV camera: I really knew nothing; but I took the book—Miner had marked with a slip of paper where the dramatization should start, two hundred pages into Maugham's story—and somehow or other I got that script written for him. It meant staying up all night and all day, with lots of black coffee, and improvising what I didn't know much about, but by Friday that script was in . . . and I'd become a television writer."

Constant crises and disasters, and yet it was an era ripe for an imaginative mind that could experiment with bold ideas and new concepts, unhampered by network nay-sayers and self-appointed critics. And since Miner's own background was theatrical, and he had spent several years before World War II and afterward learning the technology of the infant television, his know-how provided him with a certain amount of authority. To the credit of the network, he was permitted to go on his way with a minimum of interference. "During the four years we did *Studio One* I can't remember a single run-in in which my judgment was not backed. For a creative person, this is a rare and

Julius Caesar, Studio One (Courtesy CBS)

The Last Cruise, Studio One (Courtesy CBS)

marvelous thing. If you're struggling against the veto power of an advertising agency, as well as all the physical problems you've got to handle, it's very tough to put on a decent dramatic schedule."

Chances were certainly, and constantly, taken: Shakespeare's *Julius Caesar*, for example, done in modern dress (saving money on costumes, and with an as yet unknown Charlton Heston eagerly serving as a mere extra). The production may not seem all that startling in retrospect, but it moved the medium forward in its time. "And it did do one thing," says Miner. "People who'd seen it would come up and say 'Look, I *understand* this play now better than almost any Shakespearean production I've ever seen—every word was clear, and so were the intentions of the characters.'"

There were many other hour shows, long since relegated to dim memory, that had their impact as well. Henry James's *The Ambassadors* and his *The Wings of the Dove,* and an original script by Michael Dyne, *Pontius Pilate,* which presented Cyril Ritchard in the title role. "We did a show called *Waterfront Boss* that was very similar to Elia Kazan's *On the Waterfront*," says Miner, "and for that one we decided to try something completely new—to do a live show out there on the waterfront docks, where it all took place."

Gertrude Berg, *The Goldbergs* (Courtesy CBS)

The production of that show was to become complicated with much more than simple technological problems. Since the script was a factual discussion of current gangster influence on the New York docks, very little, if any, co-operation with the actual waterfront denizens could be achieved. Joseph Liss, who wrote the adaptation, came home one evening to discover his apartment had been broken into by unknown and certainly hostile persons, his furniture smashed, and his files strewn across the floor. Police protection for the CBS crew on location was difficult to obtain; for some mysterious reason, the precinct involved was loath to involve itself with the network people. "The minute the CBS trucks came down the ramp to the scene of the shooting," recalls Miner, "the police cars would silently steal away, and the crew would be out there, alone, in very hostile territory."

Frank Schaffner, who was directing the production, encountered sullen and apathetic resistance from local dock hands. The one pier, 69, on which he wished to stage his show, remained closed to him by the pier boss, and for the moment it seemed that the entire production would have to be scratched. It was at this low point that Miner came up with what is known in the business as a genius idea.

"I pulled a guy out of complete obscurity—he was Roy Hargrave, an actor who'd played the lead for me years back in a play called *Blind Alley*. I remembered he looked very much like the pictures we had of Cockeye Dunn, the boss of the docks down there—the very guy we were dramatizing in the show itself. I hired Roy, and we dressed him up for the part.

"Schaffner was supposed to have a meeting down on the pier with those waterfront characters who were blocking us. Frank walked halfway down the long pier to meet with the pier boss himself, to tell him what he wanted. He was getting absolutely nowhere, and suddenly one of the guys who was standing with the pier boss looked down behind Frank . . . and there was Hargrave. He'd walked quietly onto the pier, he was wearing a trenchcoat and a snapbrim hat, and his hands were jammed into his pockets, with his collar turned up. The pier guy took one look at Hargrave standing in the shadows—in the distance the resemblance was so absolutely extraordinary that it was as if we'd produced the ghost of Cockeye Dunn himself. And all of a sudden, the boss said, 'Anything you want, Mr. Schaffner—anything you want!'

"Absolutely eerie," recalls Miner. "The size, the combination of his features, even Hargrave's voice, which evidently sounded so much like Dunn himself that one of the longshoremen who stood by finally admitted he was getting cold shivers up his back. As long as he stood out there, in front of the cameras, there was absolutely no further interference. We got a terrific show out of it—but needless to say, we weren't anxious to do too many location shows after that one."

There was another *Studio One* production that teetered on the brink of major disaster. *The Last Cruise* was a published book that dealt with the story of two submarines, one of which was lost in a storm in the Arctic. Hardly the sort of material that would readily lend itself to a live television dramatization, and yet the challenge was accepted. In those prehistoric days of television so many impossibilities were tackled. In the words of another producer who was there, "We were all so new at the game that we didn't know you couldn't do those things—so we did them!"

It was Mrs. Miner, the actress Frances Fuller, who first unearthed *The Last Cruise*. "She read the review in the morning paper, handed it over to me, and said, 'This sounds like a really exciting book—if only you had film instead of television.' I read the review and got hooked. We bought it and decided to try and do it live."

Miner shudders at the memory. "There we were, up in that tiny studio above Grand Central Station, and we had to do the damnedest technical things. In order to get it to look as if we were on the deck of a submarine, we built a small door and shot through it with an 18 mm. lens. That made the deck look 165 feet long. Then we surrounded the set with tubs of water, with machinery to keep it making waves—a constant flow splashing over the bows, and all those actors working there on the deck. We almost had a disaster to begin with, because the water began seeping through the studio floor and almost flooded through it—which would have ruined that mural below in the main waiting room of Grand Central!"

This was merely the beginning of the CBS crew's problems. "Oh, it was just terrible," sighs Miner. "We put eleven guys in the hospital during that show—pneumonia, broken arms, broken legs—but the excitement around the production was terrific. I mean, all the guys who were on the production, even the ones that had been hurt, kept coming back the next day, bandaged, with splints on, and asking how it was going and could they watch. But the worst was to come during the actual show itself. By the middle of the performance we were running a bit long"—remember, in those days the speed of the actors' readings was a completely uncontrollable human factor—"and I had to go out and tell the captain of the actual submarine that had been involved, who was standing out there, waiting to go on at the end of the show, that he'd have to take some cuts in his speech. I suddenly stepped into water over my shoes, and I realized that we'd come within inches of water seeping out of the tank to reach our electrical connections—and that we could practically have electrocuted everybody on the whole damn set out there!

"But everyone was so excited to have been part of that show—to have helped make it happen. That," says Miner, "was what made working on *Studio One* such a rewarding experience."

And what of the other two projects that Miner had been assigned to prepare for CBS in that first period of the network's frantic productivity?

The situation comedy he produced in that year was *The Goldbergs*, starring Gertrude Berg as Molly and Philip Loeb as her husband, Jake. The show soon found a receptive audience and lasted for a good run. "I never wanted a live audience for that show because I thought then that it would be very difficult for the people in a studio to concentrate on the actors and get the comedy without becoming interested in the cameras. And I felt that canned applause or laughter was a pretty terrible device. In retrospect," Miner concedes, "I can see that I was probably quite wrong. I think that if we could have encompassed and used the facilities, the way they do now in Hollywood, with multiple cameras and a live audience (à la the *Mary Tyler Moore Show, The Bob Newhart Show, Rhoda, Barney Miller*, et al.), we could have made *The Goldbergs* into a much-longer-lasting show. But as it was, for the two seasons that it was on CBS, it was considered a success."

And what of the children's show, which Miner, busy as he was, would also find time to produce? That would be *Mr. I. Magination*, which would star Paul Tripp as the engineer of a miniature train, capable of traveling in any direction in time and to any place, to bring the juvenile audience along with it into different adventures, bounded only by the limits of imagination.

(*Mr. I. Magination* may not have had a long run, as opposed to such other first-rate kid shows as the venerable *Captain Kangaroo, Magic Cottage,* and today's *Sesame Street*, but its impact on its audience was obviously lasting. Twenty years later, Paul Tripp, the engineer, was strolling down a midtown Manhattan street at noontime and passed a group of hard-hats on a construction site as they took their lunchtime break. "Hey . . . look!" said one of the workers, staring at Tripp. "I know who he is! That's my boyhood idol—Mr. I. Magination!" He jumped up and confronted Tripp. "Tell the truth, wasn't you Mr. I. when I was a kid?"

Paul Tripp, *Mr. I. Magination* (Courtesy CBS)

"Yes, that's me," conceded Tripp.

"See, fellas, I was right!" chortled the hard-hat, as he vigorously pumped Tripp's hand. "I gotta tell ya, Mr. I., I'll never forget you and your fucking little train!"

"Oh, no, don't say that about our train," said Tripp. "That was a *nice* little train."

"Yeah," said his fan, abashed. "You're right. It *was* a nice little train."

"You're fucking well right I'm right!" said Tripp, and walked on.)

This half-hour show, all these years later, is remembered by its adult audience as a gentle yet stimulating experience, a rewarding half hour of fantasy considerably more pleasant than those endless hours of canned Saturday morning cheapjack animated huckster cartoons that short-change the kids by masquerading as entertainment.

Four trail-breaking television concepts produced within the space of one year. A considerable achievement, measured by today's rigidly structured network programming struggle, where massive infusions of talent, money, and effort can end in abrupt disaster with the first scanning of the Nielsen overnight rating figures.

"It was a very rewarding experience," Miner says, more than a quarter century later. "There was great excitement, you could see something grow and mature, and you did have competition that was stimulating and fresh. You see, I started in the theater, and I had only a brief and unhappy spell with motion pictures. Going into television was nothing to me but an opportunity to do all the things that I couldn't have done in the theater, and also to reach an audience so much more vast than any audience we'd ever reached."

Was it truly a golden age of television? He smiles. "Its legacy is a memory. It's a memory of something that is, for its advocates, hurt by the fact that it's been so extravagantly praised and lauded. The end of this era is clearly based on one fact: our total audience was then about 20 percent of *today's* audience. Perhaps 20 million, then 30 or 40; they were the ones we had to please, and since *Studio One* went along for four years with roughly 35 percent of that audience, that was enough of an audience for the types of shows we were doing. There's a law of diminishing return when you increase an audience. That 20 percent is now the expendable part of the audience—and this is why almost everybody who was an ardent viewer in the early days no longer looks at television. They may see the news, or a baseball game, or a football game, but as far as dramatic fare is concerned, they just haven't looked at it for years."

Miner is certainly not referring to films, old or relatively new, nor to the dramatic efforts produced on public television channels, where the lately found success of such shows as the London Weekend-produced *Upstairs, Downstairs* (it was at this moment being developed by CBS in a tape version relocated in Boston, *Beacon Hill*) and full-length videotapes of theater productions done in tributary theaters around the country can and do draw respectable audiences.

"No, they're fine," Miner agrees, "but those shows are the result of the development of videotape, where you can take and retake an actor's performance until you get the scene shot exactly the way you want it. Years later,

★ 40 ★

Twelve Angry Men, Studio One (Courtesy CBS)

when I produced *Play of the Week* on PBS, we developed a technique where we could tape whole acts, using live camera techniques, but recording it all on tape, and that was the best of both worlds. We could go into the cutting room and put together the best tapes of the live performance—and the results were terrific.

"But the thing that bothers me the most now is to look back and see the enormous wastage on the part of the networks of their own home-grown resources," he remarks, ruefully. "Think of the number of directors that were brought up, educated and eager to remain in television, that were eventually forced out of television, by the conditions, or by the distinct will of the networks not wanting them anymore. George Roy Hill, Sidney Lumet, Ralph Nelson, Arthur Penn, John Frankenheimer—all of them have gone on to pictures. But all of them, even after they'd had success in movies, would have been eager to go back to television and do dramatic shows. And as far as writers are concerned, it's exactly the same waste. Television nurtured and brought to maturity such talents as Reggie Rose (*Twelve Angry Men*) and Paddy Chayefsky (*Marty*), J. P. Miller (*Days of Wine and Roses*), Tad Mosel (*The Out-of-Towners*), Bob Aurthur, Sumner Locke Elliott, and a raft of others. And when was the last time you saw an original play by any of them on your screen? All of them have long since gone off to work for the movies, which may be fine for your neighborhood theater-owner, but is terrible for television."

That's quite an impressive list of alumni to which he can point. Not all of them matriculated at Worthington Miner's early CBS academy, but enough to make his case—and to make it safe to say those *were* productive days.

For a few days back there in the early 1950s, you could be sure—if it was Westinghouse. Sure of at least one hour a week of an interesting live hour drama, sometimes flawed, often awkward, but certainly never as slick and predictable as tonight's bill of fare. Nowadays the networks, in their infinite wisdom, have long since turned away from weekly "anthologies." Program executives insist that a dramatic show be held together by a continuing leading character, and that he or she function in three acceptable areas of drama—crime, medicine, and the law. Ergo, we have *Hawaii Five-O/Kojak/Columbo*, and the rest, and their police cars careening up and down the streets; Dr. Marcus Welby and a phalanx of other white-coated medicos; and Petrocelli and all his legal associates.

Perhaps *Studio One* outlived its time, but it was a dramatic hour whose impact could never be dismissed as readily as the the latest exploit of the Six Million Dollar Man.

And it cost a hell of a lot less.

REMEMBERING
MAMA

. . . Because Papa is reluctant to go to the special school to study for his citizenship examination, Mama goes to the school, and later teaches Papa, so that he can finally become an American citizen.

That is the simple plot line of a new half-hour live show that was telecast on Channel 2 on the night of July 1, 1949. The name of the program was *Mama*; it was adapted from a best seller called *Mama's Bank Account,* by Kathryn Forbes, which was then produced as a Broadway play written by John Van Druten, *I Remember Mama,* and eventually made into a film in 1948 by RKO.

In the part of the television Mama was the Broadway star Peggy Wood; and as Papa, Judson Laire. Although the previous stage and film dramatizations of the Hansen family, those pleasant Norwegian-Americans who lived in San Francisco at the turn of the century, whose story had been remembered by daughter Katrin, had proved audience-pleasers, the viewers in the homes who promptly took the Hansens into their living rooms as regular weekly visitors would prove to be a larger and more faithful audience than in any producer's most avaricious daydream.

Something in that simple, honest story must have made immediate contact with the television audience, because by the end of the summer of 1949 the closely knit Hansen family was firmly established on the shaky CBS program schedule, in what was certainly not one of the most auspicious of time slots,

The Hansen Family, *Mama* (Courtesy CBS)

8 P.M. of a Friday evening. (Most people in those pre-inflationary days still took the family out to the movies.) It was there, on Friday nights, that the Hansens, in their modest living room, dining room, and kitchen (with its ever-present coffeepot), were to remain, for what now must seem to harried network bosses, engaged in their programming war games, an incredibly long run. Eight years.

Eight years in which countless situation comedies and comedy families and cartoon-strip misadventures (Dad calls up at 5 P.M. and tells Ma he's bringing the boss home for dinner in an hour/Ma gets sick and goes to bed and Dad has to run the house sans prior experience/Willie, the family dog, goes next door and rips up the crusty rich old neighbor's prize peonies/Sis's first date,/ etc. etc.) came and went like migratory birds, flashing briefly past the cathode

★ 44 ★

tube. Over those years, there were other perhaps more glamorous stars than the Hansen family (the Days of *Life With Father*, for instance; the Rileys of *The Life Of* . . .; the Aldriches of *Hennnreeee*)—hardly a week passed in those years that some hopeful producer did not take his turn at Situation Comedy Roulette, Family Style, usually to be wiped out within weeks, to fold the latest family tent, and send it off into whatever limbo is reserved as the Port of Missing Ma's and Pa's. . . .

But on and on went the Hansens. It is not that their family saga was so radically different; consider another story, this one aired on the night of August 19, 1949:

> *Nels [played by Dickie Van Patten] takes dancing lessons from a little girl friend of Dagmar's [Robin Morgan; in later years, Ms. Morgan was to give up her acting career to concentrate on becoming one of the leaders of Women's Lib], so that he can dance with a visiting southern belle at a party. He discovers too late that he was taught to dance backwards—like a girl.*

Perhaps not the most original plot ever worked up by an author, but when the episode reached the home screen, somehow it "played," and again the Hansens satisfied their growing audience.

"We had good scripts—such good scripts," says Peggy Wood, the Broadway star who turned to live TV and soon became an American folk heroine. "Frank Gabrielson, the writer, set a pattern for them so that they were beautifully written, and we looked forward each week to his scripts. We had a feeling of security in them because they were so right. Never maudlin, never sticky. They were really solid, honest things, and part of that, of course, was Ralph Nelson's ability to direct."

Nelson was a fortunate choice; he had been an actor, written plays that had been produced on Broadway, and come to television very early on. Later he would go into films (*Lilies of the Field, Charly, Requiem for a Heavyweight*), with even more impressive results.

Both Gabrielson and Nelson were of Scandinavian extraction; their origins gave them a strong empathy with the family they were dramatizing each week. "Sometimes things were sent in, and I've heard Ralph say, 'But we don't do things like that in this family,'" remembers Miss Wood. "It would be something a writer might think could be a sure-fire formula plot—and perhaps it would have been, for some other show . . . but Ralph would always repeat, 'No . . . we couldn't do something like that *here*.'

"We all of us grew along with the show, you see," explains Miss Wood, a charming and alert lady who has lost none of her authority and magnetism with the passage of years. How old is she? You may derive a hint from the fact that it was she who first introduced Noel Coward's exquisite song "I'll Follow My Secret Heart" in the original production of his *Bitter Sweet*, back in the mists of the late twenties. "And we always wanted it to be absolutely right. I remember when Carol Irwin, our producer, first suggested to me that I might play Mama, I decided first I'd better find out exactly how that lady would have sounded. I went to the Norwegian Information Bureau and I said, 'Tell me about this accent—I don't want to sound like a Swede, or a Finn, or a stage German. How must I do it?'

"And the head of the bureau there said, 'There is a sound to this accent— you go *up* at the end, you see?' English is a falling cadence, but Norwegian goes up; that's why you don't often hear what an American actor says, because our actors just drop their voices down at the end—and you lose it. Norwegian is a very sweet accent . . . lilting. Once I had the song of it, I was fine."

She makes it sound so simple. But anyone who was ever within shouting distance of the preparation of one weekly television show knows how much hard work it entailed. And for the Hansens there were long years of learning an original half-hour script each week—and bringing it to performance.

Miss Wood shrugs. "Not so hard," she says, briskly. "All of us were theater people—and we enjoyed what we were doing."

Was being in a successful show responsible for developing a certain esprit de corps?

"That was probably part of it," she admits and suddenly smiles mischievously. "You know, nobody at CBS ever really expected the show to be a success. One of the network bosses said at the beginning, 'I give it a fast eight weeks.' We outlasted *him* by a good seven years."

Mama was also a very well protected operation; the sponsor, General Foods, was from the start well satisfied with the massive identification its Maxwell House Coffee derived from the show. And since, in those early days of television, sponsors called the tune, Carol Irwin, the producer; Gabrielson; Nelson; and Doris Quinlan, the casting director, were relatively immune to any network interference from program executives who might have brilliant notions on how to "give the show a little goose" over the years.

Just a few short years after we thought we'd ended war, over in a place called Korea, there was another one going, and somehow we were involved. But here at home, even though the unions were striking, and the younger generation was beginning to answer back, and antihistamines (which were supposed to be the ultimate panacea for the common cold) were turning out to have side effects, your Friday nights offered a weekly infusion of sanity. You could turn on your set and lose yourself in the peaceful, moral world of the Hansens, chuckling and empathizing with them as they encountered their weekly problems—and with laughter and good old-fashioned sense, managed, within the space of each half hour, to work it all out.

Dagmar's playmate, David, stutters, and is shunned by boys his own age. Mama discovers David's mother is pushing him to be as brilliant as his late father, which might be the cause of the difficulty. Mama persuades David's mother to go easy on the pressure, thus enabling David to recite flawlessly the Twenty-third Psalm at Visitors' Day exercises at the school.

Not precisely the sort of story line one would expect to be played out by the so-called Father-is-a-boob situation comedies that abounded on the networks then, and for the ensuing twenty years, all the way from Gale Storm and Charles Farrell (*Oh, Susannah!*), *Ethel and Albert*, and *Blondie* up to this year's model.

"It was never a pat formula," says Miss Wood. "It wasn't always 'Mama's right—and that's that.' Never that elementary. We tried to find more complications—more characterization—to keep ourselves real, and honest."

And there was one other built-in advantage to the *Mama* format. Difficult as it may be to explain in 1976, to an audience that reels away from its television set, eyes bleary and head spinning from an average hour show in which it has been bombarded with as many as ten or eleven commercials, *Mama* was a continuous half hour—with *no* middle break. Maxwell House Coffee was extolled at the beginning, and at the end of the show. "That gave us a chance to build the story from beginning to end, without stopping it halfway through. Once we had the audience involved, we didn't lose them. *Ever.*"

An opera singer of whom Papa was fond in Norway, before he married Mama, comes to San Francisco. She invites the Hansen family to the opera, and then backstage after the opera. Mama is jealous. . . . But when

Papa discovers the singer is not a good mother to her own child, he explains to Mama that he is disappointed that the singer has changed from the sweet girl he once knew in Norway.

Inevitably, after several seasons, Frank Gabrielson began to need assistance with his scripts, and eventually a few—a very few—outside writers were brought in by Miss Irwin to spell him on that constant weekly deadline.

Eventually, since I had worked with her on a far less successful comedy series called *Our Hearts Were Young and Gay*, Miss Irwin suggested that I might try to write a script for the Hansens. She added, "I have to warn you—it isn't an easy show to write." It was 1952, and the tight little cadre that produced *Mama* each week had already had nearly four years of close harmony. "We never go in for quick plots, with contrived twists and turns, and easy solutions. What happens here is that we're dealing with honest characters, and our audience knows them and identifies with them. We keep playing off their actual experiences—and that's why, I think, we're keeping our audience."

Years later, one must be struck by the parallel between the Hansens, and their hold on television audiences, and the cast of the current 1970s British television series *Upstairs, Downstairs*. Over many weeks, when confronted with honesty, the viewer slowly but surely becomes more than a friend of the family. The secret word is *involvement*.

After several false starts and a good deal of rejection, I was able to find the key that would unlock the first successful thirty-five-page draft, but it was a long time in coming. Most television writing in those days fell into the category of get-it-on-get-it-off-get-your-check-go-home. Not *Mama*. Trying to write that show meant slowing down and thinking, and digging for character, and one's homework was to study and find out just what Mama, Papa, Nels, Katrin, and little Dagmar were all about. There were no quick and easy answers; there were long hours spent in discussion and pleasant argument with Miss Irwin up in her office-apartment at 230 Park. In her living room I encountered the iron editorial fist in the velvet glove that held the show together for such a long run. Quite a few story ideas withered away, until finally we hit on one that seemed to work, based on Dagmar's childish greed and impulsive behavior.

I would write the story of the adventures incurred by Dagmar when she answered an advertisement that offered quick profits for the deft puzzle-solver, and then found herself burdened with unwanted cheap cologne that she would be forced to peddle throughout the neighborhood. It was an experience remembered from my own childhood, one that I could chuckle over in retrospect but that was part of every child's growing-up. "Dagmar's Haunting Fragrance," we called it, and when it was finally written, to the satisfaction of all concerned, the script then went to mimeograph, and to rehearsals.

That period was even more of an education, as Ralph Nelson quietly and deftly brought the script to life. His crew of actors were so immersed in their characters that they brought a wealth of characterization to each new script. No temperament, no argument; they were all truly a family. "Again, that was our theater training," says Miss Wood. "We were always prepared. We went into rehearsal at 10 A.M., and we finished by one, Mondays, Tuesdays, and Wednesdays. By that time we knew the thing by heart, we knew where we were, we had seen our scenery Lord knows how many times so that we just went ahead and did it. When we came to Friday night, we were always ready. And when we brought in other actors to play guest parts, we could help them along. We had quite a few of those, you know. Patty McCormick, Mark Rydell, Jack Lemmon, Ed Fitzgerald, who had a running part as a pal of Papa's we called Kelso.

"I remember once, we had a nice young man on the show for the first time, he was quite nervous, and in the middle of the actual show he went up in his lines, higher than the studio ceiling. He stood there absolutely mute—in agony. Well, I was able to give him his cue and cover for him because I knew his part as well as my own—but any one of us could have done it, because we worked as a family."

"Dagmar's Haunting Fragrance" was well received, and the proof of it was that I was asked back to write more scripts. Over the next year and a half I became a regular contributor. The pay was far from lavish, but it was decent, and (as Miss Irwin often reminded me and my agent, when we argued about a possible raise in the fee), the experience I was amassing was very valuable. And she did have a point when she also pointed out (quite often) that writing *Mama* gave me far more status in the television world than did supplying sketches for shaky half-hour musical revue shows and/or shoveling jokes into the maw of voracious ex-Borscht Circuit comics.

She was right about that; whenever my name appeared at the end of a weekly *Mama* episode, the next day I would be stopped on the street in the Connecticut town where we lived, and lavishly praised by all sorts of near-strangers who had heretofore paid no attention to my various TV efforts—

especially middle-aged ladies who never missed the Hansen family on Fridays. In tones of wonder, one said to me once, "You never *told* me you wrote *Mama*."

I did scripts about Katrin falling in love with a young radical poet who was under the influence of Jack London, and one about the night that Nels was first invited to a fancy-dress ball up on Nob Hill, and the crisis attendant on his getting a dress suit. There was an episode dealing with maiden aunt Jenny's romance with a local fireman who wanted to have her accompany him to the Firemen's Ball, and another that dealt quite subtly with the problems of capital versus labor, when the young man who'd taken over the operation of the carpentry shop where Papa worked brought in an efficiency expert to uncover ways to speed up production, causing Papa to put down his tools and walk off the job in protest.

Gentle stories, somewhat old-fashioned in their morality, certainly not related in any way, except in their half-hour length, to the high-pressure standards of "sitcoms" of today, all those three-camera taped shows performed in front of a live audience where, as a somewhat cynical California producer recently remarked, "the secret of a good rating on these cartoon strips is to have your cast planted in that single set, standing there yelling insults at each other for twenty-three minutes. If that's what the audience wants, brother, that's what they're going to get—until we run out of tape . . . or actors."

They weren't insulting each other on *Mama*, and very rarely did anyone yell, and yet the show went on, week after week, in its simple, affectionate way reaching some—far from all—the parents of the audience that today fancies the bigotries of Archie Bunker, the noisy arguments between Chico and the Man in their garage, the lunacies of *M*A*S*H*'s pressure-cooked crew, and the predictable battles of *The Odd Couple*.

San Francisco at the turn of the century, a simple American home, inhabited by an interesting Norwegian-American family that grew up gently, inexorably, before the viewers' eyes, and in the process perhaps taught us something about honesty and some of the other virtues . . . and ended each week by everybody gathering in Mama's immaculate kitchen for a good cup of fine, flavorful, freshly made, good-to-the-last-drop Maxwell House. (Who could ask for a better way to sell a product?) That was the sturdy spine of eight years' worth of *Mama* and her steady rating success. When you wrote for that family, you had to give them the best you could. But in return, they gave you back dividends—the best sort of subtle ensemble performance that any writer could ever expect, in that complicated, nervous world of live TV.

Papa is offered a job as a foreman at a construction company, but declines because he does not like to boss the men. At home, the children are bemoaning the fact that Papa does not get promotions—and so Katrin cannot buy new wallpaper. Papa decides to take the job so that they will have the benefit of the extra money. When he comes home the next day and says he's no longer foreman, the children think he failed. It comes out that night that he lost the foreman position because he could not fire a man, and the family tells him they are proud of him.

There are times when impact comes in less obvious forms, and you don't always have to make your points with a sledgehammer. Maybe that story won't play tonight, but as anyone who saw it on Friday night at eight back in the early 1950s, it played. And well.

"It wasn't that Mama was always right," remarks Miss Wood, thinking back to that time, two decades back, when she was as powerful a cult figure to her public as are Mary Tyler Moore, Rhoda, Florida, or Maude. "Matter of fact, Mama was quite fallible. She made mistakes, and her family behaved just like everyone else. But there was a sort of integrity to it all. Even though Mama was a schemer, she always had a good sense of ethics."

She smiles. "It would be very interesting to see the audience reaction if we were able to run one of our old kinescopes tonight, wouldn't it? Assuming, of course, we could find one. I'm afraid they were all destroyed a long time back," she says, ruefully.

Eight years' worth of the Hansens' adventures gone? Vanished? One can only hope Miss Wood is wrong. . . .

"But the most interesting thing for me is," she says, a bit defiantly, "that even after all these years—and I've done quite a few movies and plays in my time, remember—to most of the people I meet, there's an instant reaction when they see me. I'm always Mama."

Which, for a tall, erect blond lady to whom age is as irrelevant a statistic as a Nielsen rating, is perhaps the best sort of sponsor identification.

SUMMERTIME
FOLLIES

"In a sense," *Variety* noted, ten years later, "it all goes back to Berle."

The bible of show biz was referring to comedy variety, that staple commodity of television which has stayed with us all the seasons since the noisy arrival of Milton Berle and his *Texaco Star Theater*, those Tuesday nights at eight, the first season of 1948–49.

Spouting one-liners, leering, clowning, mugging, bursting into everyone's act, camping it up (Aw'll-kiwl-you-amiwion-times!), Uncle Miltie single-handedly transformed *vaudeo* (another *Variety* word) into a highly marketable TV commodity.

Heretofore it had been an art form fraught with slender budgets and uncharted disaster areas. But now that the Thief of Bad Gags had broken trail and amassed an ever-growing audience that was passionate for his burlesque bits, juggling acts, dance numbers, and celebrity guest stars, all his show-business confrères began to cast jealous eyes on the seven-inch screen.

The gold rush was on. Since imitation is not only the sincerest form of flattery but also a guaranteed way to make a buck, the success of Berle's weekly burlesque spawned a tidal wave of carbon-copiers. In the next few years new "personalities" would explode all over the home screen. It was something like the Alaskan gold rush of 1898 as every comic—male or female, high or low, stand-up or fall-down, monologist, quick-change artist, top or second banana, talking woman or straight man, dialect specialist or pantomimist—who'd ever induced the vaguest snicker from an audience was rushed by his eager agent to attend a top-level meeting with equally eager advertising men, sponsors, and network executives.

Should you spy a table of more than five lunching at the Lambs Club, or the Friars, or at either Lindy's Restaurant or Toots Shor's, it was a safe bet that it was a conference that concerned the birth of a new variety show to star Buddy/ Jackie/Benny/et al.—a funny, funny man guaranteed to convulse Mr. and Mrs. America out there (and hopefully to topple Milton, the King, off his precarious perch).

Milton Berle, *The Texaco Star Theater* (Courtesy NBC)

The late Allan Sherman once remembered that the biggest joke of that era was for the comic to say, "Since I've been on television, they've sold a lot of sets. My uncle sold his, my father sold his . . ." Even Berle used it. Often.

There was, as always, a lot of truth behind that flip crack.

The death rate of comics and future comedy variety shows would be high, as most of the greats and near-greats were to discover. It wasn't as easy as Berle made it look. Double and triple helpings of ego—the comic's basic equipment —wouldn't be sufficient. Perhaps Buddy/Jackie/Benny had been a headliner since the earliest days of vaudeville and had top-lined the bill at the Palace umpteen times. Maybe he had starred on Broadway, or convulsed them on radio, been under contract to MGM and Fox, or killed the people out at the Chez Paree. Those credentials might get him a show of his own—but whatever his track record, he would soon discover those implacable TV cameras a tougher audience than any Monday afternoon opening show in the coldest town.

Video was a whole new ball game. Hire a covey of good gag writers, rummage in the trunk for your best "bits," gather together a good production staff, and go out there and give them your best—and you'd still find out that those X-ray lenses that focused on Buddy/Jackie/Benny had a dreadful habit of cutting the funniest man down to size, stripping him bare and revealing him, warts and all, naked to the world, the perspiration streaming down through his pancake No. 7, his funny clothes merely ludicrous, and his putty nose melting in the heat of the whitehot lights.

Perhaps he did manage a good kickoff show. Every decent comic had at least that much good material. But as the cued applause ended, and the cameras were turned off, and the comic collapsed, exhausted, on his dressing-room couch, there was no time to sip champagne and exult in his success at the aftershow party. There was a meeting scheduled for 9 A.M. tomorrow. Subject: *next* week's show.

That was how the nightmare began. Most comics are not known for being secure types. To discover themselves perched on this once-a-week treadmill was harrowing. (Six days from now, it's zero hour again, none of that reliable old stuff I've used for years, but pages of jokes and *shtick* those writers will bring me, all new and untried that I've got to memorize, and then, there I'll be, out under those damn white lights, with the cameramen shooting me from all the wrong angles so that I look like a fugitive from Forest Lawn—I won't have time to rehearse anything properly, to try out my material and polish it, get the timing right—and if I bomb out, who the hell will care? They'll go find a new boy, and I'll go back to the Home for Busted Comics.)

Fred Allen, one of the few true great wits who'd achieved major stardom in radio, but who suffered through his share of sour experiences at the start of comedy variety, was to comment, "They claim a comedy show on TV is no good unless it has a lot of singers and dancers. I haven't been able to relax on a television stage with all those technicians wandering back and forth in front of me while I'm trying to tell a joke. They've been listening to me and the joke in rehearsals for two days, and by the time the performance rolls around, they're leaning on their cameras and staring at me with all the enthusiasm of a dead trout."

And genial old Ed Wynn, the Perfect Fool, after four decades of success with audiences, found the complicated technology of TV a roadblock. On the vast stage of the Center Theater (which NBC fitted out to be the home of *The Colgate Comedy Hour*) Ed struggled to make contact with the audience so many feet away, and finally gave up the effort, moaning, "You just can't get laughs out of cameramen's asses."

But the treadmill accelerated. Even though the cost of Berle's early shows was a mere $5,750—$10,000 for a lavish opening-show budget, with stars—the stakes mounted dramatically. In the summer of 1948 there were only 175,000 TV receivers in use, but by the end of the year entertainment-hungry home viewers would have installed 750,000 sets in their living rooms. As rapidly as TV antennae went up, so did advertising budgets and performers' salaries.

If sponsors were willing to pony up more money, the networks were equally anxious to shore up their nighttime schedules, and in the months after Berle became Number One in the ratings, the makeshift TV studios, be they remodeled Broadway theaters or radio studios adapted for video cameras, would echo with the sounds of misfired gags, sketches that didn't play . . . and accusatory silence. Unskilled production hands wrestled with technical problems; nervous comics hired and fired their weary staffs like so many fieldhands; and tyro Pygmalions in button-down shirts up in the executive offices continued to search for profitable and popular Buddy/Jackie/Benny Galateas.

For every comic who committed televised hara-kiri, and went reeling from loss of blood (and face) back to the Lambs, or to Lindy's, muttering bitterly that it was okay with him if Milton wanted to kill himself with that lousy once-a-week schedule, but as for him, he'd had it—there would be a ready supply of new Old Boys, waiting to walk the plank.

Orson Bean, Polly Bergen, Jonathan Winters, and Norman Paris, *The Blue Angel* (Courtesy CBS)

In the years that followed, some succeeded. Ken Murray, a relaxed and cheerful *conférencier*-type from California, would be able to produce and star in his own hour show on CBS for three seasons, before he returned to sunshine and home movies. Martha Raye, Eddie Cantor, Jack Haley, even Ed Wynn, were able to score with hour-long shows, but only by avoiding that back-breaking weekly schedule on *The Colgate Comedy Hour*, where they rotated on a monthly basis and proved that less is more. In Chicago a deft show emerged called *Garroway at Large*. No seasoned veteran of any previous success, Dave Garroway, a radio disc jockey, supported by his crew, proved to have audience appeal by keeping everything charming, witty, and unassuming.

Others were far less fortunate. Summon up the shades of Georgie Jessel, the Ritz Brothers, Joe E. Brown, Al Pearce, diminutive Joey Faye, Henny Youngman, Jean Carroll, Doodles Weaver, Red Buttons—all respectable talents, most of whom were soon to be brought down to earth by the demands of a weekly schedule.

Eventually there would be production techniques devised that would remove the crushing weight of doing a live comedy show from the backs of wearied comedy stars. There would be situation comedies, filmed on a California sound stage, with three cameras recording the antics of Joan Davis (*I Married Joan*) and Lucille Ball and Desi Arnaz (do you really need the name of that show?). And by the mid-fifties there would be the miracle of electronic videotape, the real breakthrough. With that merciful device, performers could play out their scenes and be recorded—and then, if something went wrong—a mistimed gag, a lost laugh, or a malfunctioning prop—they could redo the whole sketch from the top.

"Film and tape were the inventions that took the performer out of jeopardy," says Carl Reiner, a seasoned veteran of many live ninety-minute Saturday night shows, where Sid Caesar and Imogene Coca established themselves as the stars of *Your Show of Shows.* "You really can't blame any of us for wanting the security that they provided, although," he adds, somewhat wistfully, "those early live days had a vitality that's completely gone. I mean, if you were out there in front of the audience and you goofed, or something misfired, well, you just stood there and improvised, and sometimes what emerged was funnier than anything you could have thought of in a month of rehearsals."

(Remembering back to those days, Caesar himself told an interviewer from *Esquire*: "One Saturday night I finished my monologue and hurried off to get ready for the next sketch. I had a sixty-second commercial break in which to get out of a business suit and into a strong man's outfit. We were going to do some circus sketch. Well, my dresser and I ripped off the suit, and as I got into a leopard loincloth, the dresser laced up a pair of high-strapped Roman sandals. In seconds, I was in the wings ready to go on. I could see Carl and Howie Morris beginning the opening of the sketch. My mouth dropped open. Max Liebman—the producer—it turned out, forgot to tell me that he had reversed the order of the two sketches. Carl and Howie were wearing dark suits and talking to each other in a corporate office. I began muttering '. . . shirt . . . tie . . . jacket . . . Shirt . . . tie . . . jacket . . . shoes.' But I had no time to get a shirt, a tie or shoes. Frantically I put a sport coat over my leopard loincloth. There was no time to even begin removing the gold lamé sandals. Without hesitation, I ran out, as though nothing was wrong. There I stood, shirtless, a leopard-skin loincloth showing under a sport jacket, complete with Roman sandals. In short, your typical business executive. The audience roared. Carl, not knowing what to do, asked me why I was wearing the funny shoes. All I could manage was

★ 57 ★

Monty Woolley and Fred Allen, *Colgate Comedy Hour* (Courtesy NBC)

'Well, you know how sometimes you get a present and feel obligated to wear it at least once? And besides, it looked like rain this morning!' ") *

An inspired piece of ad lib. But most of the time, disaster dogged live comedy shows and compounded itself. For all those hands who signed on to work on any of those early abortive thirty- and sixty-minute weekly obstacle courses, the experience was unique; it was a sort of lunatic basic training made up of constant crisis and under-the-gun scribbling, raw-nerved argument, ego battles, all-night rewrite sessions and endless improvisation. The casualty rate was high, the pay was low, and all too often the end result was early hypertension, or an ulcer.

The summertime has always been a show business refuge—a relaxed straw-

* From "The Things That Were Caesar's," *Esquire*, May, 1972.

hat season when performers and creative types can try things out, experiment, and tour. So it was only logical for some harassed network thinkers to consider, back then, that the months of June, July, and August, before Labor Day, when audiences are fewer and far less critical, would also be ideal for television try-out time. And for a long time the summer would remain the time when networks could experiment (until costs had risen so steeply that reruns of filmed winter shows proved too profitable).

It was in the late spring of 1949 when somebody up at the Kudner advertising agency (which handled the Buick account for General Motors) conceived of trying out a big weekly television hour that would bring to the viewers, and car buyers, the reliable comedy talents of Ole Olsen and Chic Johnson, in a program titled *Fireball Fun-For-All*.

Olsen and Johnson had been stars for many years. Their elaborate slam-bang low comedy, replete with breakaway scenery, elaborate visual gags, women wandering through the audience holding ever-growing palm trees in pots and calling for lost husbands, embarrassed spectators finding a melting block of ice dumped into their laps, their stooges in gorilla suits chasing up and down the aisles, their parades of midgets (always referred to as "little people") had convulsed people all over the land. Their legendary *Hellzapoppin* had been a Broadway hit and made them rich, and when they came to the promised land of television, they came fully equipped with a vast coterie of stooges, an armory of blank cartridges for their prop guns, a warehouse stuffed with urns that exploded, cars that collapsed, scenery that flew apart, dead ducks that dropped down from the flies, crazy costumes, and a library of joke books.

There were nine writers who were press-ganged into the O. & J. staff for their television debut, and a yellowing set of scripts reveals that among my confrères on that long-forgotten debacle were Arnold Horwitt, a successful Broadway sketch-writer and lyricist; Ezra Stone, who also proposed to produce and direct this hour-long exhibit; a young chap named Mike Stewart, who later fled television to write a show called *Hello, Dolly!*; and a legendary character named Lew Lipton, who'd spent years out in Hollywood as a successful "weenie man," i.e., the guy who conceives of the gimmick by which a film could get into, or out of, trouble.

The whole project began most optimistically. After all, Chic and Ole obviously knew what they were doing. They'd been doing it successfully for years, hadn't they? From the start, everything sounded terrific. An hour of O. & J. patented bedlam, with all sorts of wild, imaginative nonsense. In a matter of weeks, three completed scripts were prepared, typed up, mimeographed, and distributed, by Stone and his staff. All of the gags and bits and comedy material would then be staged. Audience bedlam outside the theater, processions down the aisles, flash jokes, sketches with explosions for a finish, midgets leaping out of breakaway cars and running in every direction, comedy commercials, crazy musical numbers, and such guaranteed antique-corn bits as Chic, in a mad-house hotel room, calling up Room Service:

Chic

Hello, Room Service—give me scotch and soda!
> (Through the phone liquid is squirted at him.)

You forgot the soda!
> (Seltzer squirts through phone.)

How about some milk?
> (Milk is squirted through; then hand comes through phone and wipes Chic's face.)

Good thing I didn't order Planter's Punch!
> (Hand with boxing glove comes through and hits him.)

The windup of this high-corn effort, every kernel of which had knocked 'em dead from coast to coast, involved Chic's firing a pistol at the framed picture of a sailboat on the hotel-room wall. The boat fired back. Ole and Chic then let loose a salvo of shots at the boat. The boat sank. After which a sailor carrying a large dead fish entered the hotel room and waved the fish at the two inmates.

Ole

Hey, what are you so mad about?

Skipper

I was *on* that ship!

Ole

And the captain always goes down with his ship!
> (Ole fires gun; Skipper disappears through trapdoor on stage!)

BLACKOUT

★ 60 ★

Abbott and Costello, *Colgate Comedy Hour* (Courtesy NBC)

Neil Simon it wasn't. Noel Coward, Kaufman and Hart, and Billy Wilder certainly wouldn't find it competitive. None of *us* were in any position to find fault with such ancient wheezery. Ole and Chic obviously knew what they were doing. Why not assume that what had convulsed their audiences for all these years would work on NBC—and keep on writing it down for them?

So on we went, slogging away at program no. 4. "The only way to get a production as complex as this one onto the tube is to be prepared in advance," vowed our fearless leader, and (in theory, at least) he was dead right. In practice . . . merely dead. In our midtown Manhattan offices we stayed on the job, concocting more lunatic scenes and frenetic sketches. Sample *crazy O. & J. entrance*:

BEDLAM SPOT #3:

(Ensemble is singing onstage. No sign of O. & J. anywhere. As they sing, smoke or fog develops. Curtain begins to buckle and sway. CUT TO woman in audience in a prop seat that shakes. CUT BACK TO stage, as singers scream. Curtain goes up, it catches the dress of a girl singer, and she goes up with it! A BRICK WALL is revealed. Brick wall breaks away and CHIC and OLE step through, throwing prop bricks at the audience!)

Chic
(To audience)
All right—*who locked the front door?*

I was, if I recall correctly, assigned to concoct a piece of comedy writing (assemblage is a more precise word) to be called "Ole and Chic's Supermarket," and one of the other writers, an ex-cartoonist with a terrific memory and a fine lunatic gift for visual comedy, daily supplied me with long lists of possible gags that would satisfy the visual comedy needs of our two stars. "They're suckers for this kind of stuff," he vowed.

Viz.: Clerk with clothespin on nose selling limburger cheese/Man with kangaroo on leash, he puts purchases into kangaroo's pouch/Dame enters, asks for Swiss cheese; clerk holds up ordinary cheese and shoots holes in it/Chic and Ole throw fake tomatoes at audience/Motorcycle cop with sidecar attached to motorcycle drives through, filling sidecar with goods/"Service with a Smile" sign. Two clerks are smiling—the third one, who is frowning, is still on his lunch hour/Man enters with an animal on a leash. Manager: "Sorry, no dogs

★ 62 ★

allowed in the store." Man: "Yeah, but he's a wolf." Manager: "Oh, pardon me."

After a few days, we'd all become converts. If it was corn they wanted, then we'd supply it by the bushel.

Somehow, that first *Fireball Fun-For-All* telecast got itself staged and telecast within the proper space of an hour, within the vast reaches of the Center Theater. Ole and Chic labored mightily across a mountain of madhouse comedy.

But when the din had died down, and the closing credits rolled across the screen, there was nothing but a deafening silence. Somehow or other, nothing had worked.

Within hours after that first telecast, the panic button was being pressed all over NBC, at the agency, in the O. & J. offices, even out at the Buick factory in Dearborn—a real panic button, not one of Ole and Chic's props. This one, when pressed, produced, not a corps of their midgets or a swarm of their dead prop ducks, but one dead duck—the show.

All that cornball comedy, which had wowed 'em for so many years in tank towns and fairs, in nightclubs and at the Winter Garden on Broadway—somehow, nobody in command had ever stopped to consider that most home screens were usually a mere ten inches wide, and that all those hordes of O. & J. comics and midgets and stooges careening on- and offstage, up and down the aisles and here and there, appeared on the home TV to resemble nothing more than some very busy drunken ants.

And ants, no matter how busy they are, have never been known to get laughs —even at a picnic.

Ave atque vale, Ole and Chic. (Once again, if you don't remember, Ole was the tall one, and Chic the short, noisy one.) Long before July Fourth, we'd all been replaced, and so had most of our neatly mimeographed scripts, nos. 2, 3, and 4. "We've got to go back to the old, guaranteed stuff," they vowed. "None of this sophisticated Broadway junk for us."

They struggled on through their summer schedule, their energy level sinking lower with each successive show, but by Labor Day they retired from the cluttered Center Theater stage. Packing up all their props, their costumes, their flash pots and pistols, their faithful troupe of stooges and gorilla-suited aides, their midgets, and their vast library of jokes (ninety or so bound volumes of gags, all neatly indexed and categorized for instant switching), Ole and Chic withdrew from television, muttering to themselves that at their age, with their bank accounts, they didn't need the aggravation, thanks a lot. What no critic had been able to do to them in thirty-odd years, that ice-cold TV eye had accomplished in a few short weeks.

By the time somebody got around to notifying me that my writing services (such as they had been) were no longer required by O. & J., I had no time to mourn. I was already busy on another show. (That was how it went in those early, noncontractual days. You moved from show to show with all the job security of a lettuce picker . . . and precious little lettuce went with each transitory assignment.)

Along with a very talented group of eager young people—somehow in those days, we all seemed younger—I'd been hired to work on a weekly hour-long summer replacement show at the opposition network, CBS.

For no coherent reason that anyone could fathom, this show was called *The 54th Street Revue*, perhaps because it emanated from a legitimate theater CBS had leased that had a lobby on Fifty-fourth Street. The fact that the lobby ran through to Fifty-third Street didn't matter.

The name of the CBS executive who conceived this project is long forgotten. In those days, new show concepts were usually arrived at in helter-skelter conferences in elevators, or in after-work sessions at Louis and Armand's Fifty-second Street restaurant, or over a breakfast consisting of a container of coffee and a danish, and the results often proved less nourishing. There was one CBS executive who said "Go" at the very beginning; his name was Charlie Underhill, and in those early, unstructured days, you could usually get to confer with him by meeting him as he hurried down the hallway, as he hurried off to a crisis session somewhere else in 485 Madison, or as he hurried back to his unassuming office, and as he hurried, you could usually get a decision from him before he vanished. Underhill had committed CBS to a low-budget production of an original hour-long show, with sketches, comedy acts, new songs, dances, and a resident stock company of performers, headed by a permanent master of ceremonies.

The theory—which was sound—was that whatever the show cost would be justified by the discovery of talent for the future. And so we all went to work to achieve the end result, not knowing what a massive job it would be.

In years to come, many stars managed to live through the nightmare, and even to thrive on the hour-long revue format. Jackie Gleason and his crew, Danny Kaye, Garry Moore, Carol Burnett, Steve Allen, and others shouldered

Dean Martin and Jerry Lewis, *Colgate Comedy Hour* (Courtesy NBC)

such a burden, and survived. But—and this is a large but—they were supplied with considerable insurance. They had large staffs of creative people, sufficient rehearsal, adequate preparation, a corps of singers and dancers, and a steady procession of guest stars.

Not that summer. On *The 54th Street Revue* the young staff fearlessly flew solo. None of us had trunks in which to rummage for tried-and-true material; we wrote everything instanter, to order. The music and lyrics, and the ballet and dance numbers as well, were all custom-made, and what resulted from our labor was a wholly original weekly show, from the top—fifty-nine minutes of revue, ground out by a meager staff of cheerful pioneers.

The roster of our alumni is an interesting one. Our executive producer, certainly the oldest of the crew—he was in his mid-thirties—was a cheerful, unflappable fellow named Barry Wood. As a singer on the old radio *Hit Parade*, Barry had been famous. As a producer, he was as nervous as anyone else on Fifty-fourth Street, but he soon developed a fine kamikaze-pilot attitude, one that went what-have-we-got-to-lose/let's-try-it. As Barry's director, CBS had assigned Ralph Levy, a knowledgeable young man who liked musical comedy and who'd spent some months learning about the workings of cameras, lenses, and other such exotic technology. Could Ralph really get an hour-long variety show together in four days, rehearse it, get it up on the stage, and then televise it, live, with all those complex musical cues, bridges, comedy scenes, dance numbers, and . . . ? "You guys bring me the pages—I'll get it on the screen," he promised.

We were "the guys"—a mammoth writing staff of two, George Axelrod and myself. The previous winter we'd achieved some success on Broadway with a revue called *Small Wonder*, and such credentials were enough to convince everybody on the show that we were a two-man Old Faithful that could spout playable scenes on demand. Being young and arrogant, we agreed with them, and we signed on forthwith. It certainly wasn't for the money. We were paid $250 a week for the team, which, minus agent's commission and withholding, netted each of us around $80 for seven straight days of hard labor.

When we complained that the money was less than that earned by any good carpenter, or even one of the show's stagehands, the answer was "Yes, but it's not just the money—you're getting in on the *ground floor!*"

"So is the CBS doorman—and he's making more!" snapped Axelrod.

"Save the jokes for the script," urged the man from Business Affairs, amiably.

The original music and lyrics for the show were originally supplied by a young team, composer Al Selden and lyricist Bill Scudder. Selden was eventually to give up songwriting for more stable employment as a Broadway producer. *Man of La Mancha* and the recent Broadway success *Irene* were his, but in those days he was willing and not averse to sitting down at the rehearsal piano and churning out lively and serviceable tunes with the speed of a short-order cook. Later we were to supplement his work with songs by Ted Fetter and Dick Lewine.

Our dance director was a lanky young southerner with an ability to adapt his own choreographic talent to the most aggravating crisis. In spite of what he was being paid, he was also required to dance. During rehearsal coffee breaks, he confided that someday he'd abandon this rat race and subsidize himself as a serious ballet choreographer. "I'm sure the pay won't be as lavish," he said, "but maybe I'll *finally* get to do something that runs longer than two minutes and forty-six seconds—and has to be cut for time at the dress rehearsal." He was right. Within a few years John Butler would become one of our most original ballet choreographers, with his own dance troupe.

The CBS casting department sent over a cheerful and talented young pair of hoofers. They could do waltz-clog, tap, and ballroom. Their billing was Fosse and Niles. Later the male half, Bob Fosse, would go out on his own, and abandon waltz-clog, tap, and ballroom in favor of directing *Sweet Charity*, *Pippin*, *Cabaret* and *Chicago*.

Down in the orchestra pit, serene and unflappable in the face of missed musical cues, constant musical revisions, a sound system that often broke down, and other attendant disasters, was our conductor. Harry Sosnik performed miracles by the hour. Consider—he had to supply music for an hour in which there might be a round dozen musical numbers, bridges, and dance numbers, all original, all untried. That's as much music as there is in a full act of a Broadway show, and in the space of four days all of it had to be orchestrated, timed out, rehearsed, and then played out, on the fifth day at the dress rehearsals, and on the sixth day at the show itself. In the theater Sosnik presided over his musicians, earphones on his head, trying to give musical cues to performers up on stage through a screen of technicians, struggling with timings that often went awry, with songs that mysteriously speeded up or went dragging, and then finally trying to get the closing music played off before the network cut us and went to Master Control. Once he broke down in mid-crisis and asked, rhetorically, "Can *anyone* tell me why I left radio?"

As for the performers, the only adjective that applies to that bewildered crew of hopefuls is staunch. Their hours were endless, and if they got half a day off for rest and rehabilitation they were lucky. Most of the week they rehearsed in drafty old halls, learning sketches that had been delivered to them hot from our typewriters, or songs that had been put down on lead sheets within the previous hour. Then—rewrites. Changes, cuts, additions, all instant and frenetic. And endless accommodations for a nervous stand-up comic MC.

Since the purpose of *The 54th Street Revue* was to provide a showcase for future talents, in those first weeks the top banana was a potential "comer" named Al Bernie. Al was a young man with a machine-gun type of delivery who'd convulsed them in "the mountains." Years later, Allan Sherman was to remember "Al was a one-line comedian of the Bob Hope school. He was an open canyon down which a writer had to throw jokes, and you could never hope to fill that yawning canyon."

Bernie was the type of comic who could reel off gags like "Went to a wedding—the bride was bow-legged, the groom was knock-kneed, when they stood up together they spelled OX! . . . and speaking of traffic [next joke]." Since we were not one-line-joke writers blessed with IBM memory cores full of snappers, we struggled with Al to persuade him to try playing sketches and comic scenes. Having read our latest effort, a scene in which we proposed that Al would play Hollywood's oldest child star, a noisy nuisance aged thirty-four in a Buster Brown outfit, smoking a cigar, Al would gloomily complain, "None of that sophisticated stuff for me—where are the snappers?"

Came the night of Al's first show. The studio audience filed in, headed upstairs to the mezzanine. (Had they sat below in the orchestra, they couldn't have seen the vaguest glimpse of the show through the barriers of cameras and crew.) Mysteriously enough, the first two rows of the mezzanine had been roped off, and shortly thereafter were filled with a collection of ladies, most of them middle-aged, who were herded in by a very bossy matron.

When Bernie made his first appearance in front of the cameras, he was greeted with tumultuous applause, cheers, and shrill whistles from those first two rows. Each and every one of his rat-ta-tat one-liners about wives, cars, traffic, the cost of living, and so on, met with the same reception, and so did his comedy scenes.

Could the material truly be that good? Certainly not. That bossy lady up there was Mrs. Bernie, Al's mother, and that collection of her gin-rummy club pals in the mezzanine was an organized and loyal claque, dedicated to pushing Al into the winners' circle.

Doodles Weaver (Courtesy NBC)

Laugh and clap as they did through the next two or three shows, up there in the mezzanine, they failed. It had soon become obvious that Al was as unhappy with learning new sketches each week as we were with supplying them to him, and by mutual agreement he departed, headed back for "the mountains," with his one-liners, his mother, and the claque obviously in tow.

By now we had assembled a stock company of regular performers, reliables equipped with the magic ingredient—energy. There was a jovial girl named Wynn Murray who had a spectacularly loud voice (she'd introduced "Johnny One-Note" in Rodgers and Hart's *Babes in Arms*), an elfish young comedian named Mort Marshall, and another young man who'd recently made a splash on Broadway in revue—Carl Reiner.

The executive offices at CBS supplied another hopeful top banana, a pleasant chap who'd had success in radio, named Jack Sterling.

In years that followed, Jack would find himself a very profitable long-run CBS niche on his early-morning talk show; under those white-hot TV lights, in the storm center of our strenuous hour-long original revue format, he struggled hard, but it was a losing contest.

"I can vividly remember walking into a rehearsal," says Reiner, "and seeing Jack doing a sketch in which he played a scoutmaster with a troop of scouts. He was making an exit, followed by a drum-and-bugle corps—four extras, blaring and banging away—and I thought to myself, 'Oh boy, the writers have gone dry. There's no such thing as a funny Boy Scout sketch—you could bring in the U.S. Cavalry for a finish and it won't help!'"

It was an acute diagnosis of the situation. Axelrod and I had struggled so hard to concoct the necessary three new comedy sketches per week that we had finally persuaded Barry Wood to bring in a fresh pair of hands to spell us down at the machine shop. That was how Allan Sherman was discovered. In those days, writers weren't hired through agents or on any other such structured basis. They strolled into rehearsals and hung around backstage, or wandered into offices, proffering samples of their wit. There were times when we were so dry of ideas that we'd take a joke from the delivery boy who brought the corned beef from the Gaiety Delicatessen, even if his quip was a bit fatty. It didn't matter what the hopeful writer had done before—*nobody* had done that much before—it only mattered if he could come up with a funny line, or a gag, or a bit for *now*—five minutes from now, when the actors were due to rehearse it. Sherman mysteriously manifested himself in the middle of a crisis, and overheard us complaining that we needed help with sketches for Jack Sterling. "I can write funny stuff for Jack Sterling!" he promised, eagerly. "Are you sure?" we demanded. "I," said Sherman, "can write funny stuff for *anybody!*" "Stick with Sterling," we said, and had him at work within minutes.

By the third or fourth show *The 54th Street Revue* began to take on a certain shape. As our weekly zero hour approached, we were all beginning to get ourselves organized, so that we could meet that live-show deadline with more preparation and less panic. Barry Wood was learning how to produce, Ralph Levy was learning how to direct, the cast was learning how to get out in front of those cameras and do their best, under every possible roadblock—and George and I were both learning how to write comedy.

Not without a weekly quota of disaster, such as the night we televised a sketch that involved a couple buying china in a shop, along with their child in a baby carriage. The joke (if you can call it that) was that the china had to suit Baby. He was handed each piece of crockery. His hand emerged from the carriage and tossed the china to the floor. By the end of two minutes or so, the floor was littered with broken crockery. Blackout (mercifully).

On the opposite side of our stage, lights came up on Hayes Gordon and a girl named Margot Moser, who were cued by Harry Sosnik into a delicate love-song duet. As they sang, two CBS stagehands came out to sweep away the broken crockery—beneath an open boom mike. Crunch, crunch, crunch! Above the deafening sound of crockery, nobody ever heard the duet.

Another lesson. Beware of props. Especially broken ones.

It wasn't always disaster. Reiner remembers fondly a scene in the Grand Central Oyster Bar, in which he played a desperate out-of-towner who arrived at 11:57 P.M. on the night of April 30, hungry for a dozen fresh oysters. Three minutes from now it would be May, and oysters would be out of season, and for the next few minutes, as he grew increasingly manic, the gabby waitress behind the counter couldn't be dissuaded from an endless dissertation on seafood—and delaying delivery. The dozen bivalves were placed before him at 11:59—and as Reiner reached over to eat them, the clock struck midnight, and the oysters all shut up! The season was over.

How can Reiner remember material he did in the summer of 1949, twenty-six years ago?

"Easily," he says. "You forget all the bad sketches. But the good scenes—*those* a comedian remembers."

Somehow or other, on that weekly pressure-cooker schedule, we all survived, and *The 54th Street Revue* played out the summer schedule. After the tenth week of struggle, in that hotbox of an un-air-conditioned theater studio, we'd all had enough. Sosnik gave the cue for the closing music, the cast came out to take bows, the closing credits were supered in over the scene, and that was that. We all went out and got drunk somewhere, and moved on to other jobs.

Ralph Levy left for California, to commence a long and successful career on the West Coast as a producer-director. Within short weeks he would preside over the first CBS L.A.-based comedy show, starring Ed Wynn. Ed was willing to put himself in Ralph's care, and so was Jack Benny, a year later, when he would entrust his entire future TV career to the young man from New York. In those frantic early years, a summer of *The 54th Street Revue* had made Levy a respected sachem. He would also produce and direct the George Burns and

Gracie Allen show; and later on he would produce a film pilot with another husband and wife comedy team nobody'd ever paid any attention to: a half-hour comedy that would change the entire face of TV. It was called *I Love Lucy*.

Barry Wood produced many more shows at the networks thereafter. John Butler and Bob Fosse have rarely since been unemployed; Ted Fetter, who'd served as our floor manager, doffed his earphones and became a producer, as did Lewine, his piano-playing partner. George Axelrod and I were delighted to move our smoking typewriters out of that dingy converted backstage dressing room we'd used as our office, and to go on to less strenuous TV assignments, where the hours would be shorter and we could occasionally get home to visit with our wives. As for pay—well, our agent assured us that we'd have to get more . . . *anywhere* else.

"It was terrific training for me," says Reiner, after a quarter century of accomplishment as an actor, writer, and director. "Not to forget that it was a hell of a showcase for me, as well. Max Liebman was tuned in one night, and he happened to catch me in a bit you guys had written for me—some wild comedy hunk in which I played a gypsy fiddler serenading Mort Marshall and Wynn Murray in a Hungarian restaurant, doing a dialect rave to them after they asked me, if I was a real gypsy fiddler, how come I didn't know 'Melancholy Baby.' Next morning, Liebman called up to ask if I'd come join him in a new project over at NBC, which was to start early in the fall. It was called *The Admiral Revue* and the two stars would be Sid Caesar and Imogene Coca."

And as for our chubby apprentice gagman, Jack Sterling's shadow, Allan Sherman? He'd always been a closet entertainer, but none of us, not even Allan, it's safe to say, ever expected that with one recording of his comedy parodies, *My Son, the Folk Singer*, he would achieve instant stardom . . . and retain it, until his untimely early death.

Not a bad track record, from one brief summer season on live television, in those days long ago when anyone who had a television set could expect his living room to be crowded with uninvited audiences every night, people who wanted to drop in and see what this new invention was all about before they went out to Macy's and invested $199.95 in their own Hallicrafters seven-inch.

Nowadays TV is long since grown up, a medium with a potential audience of a couple hundred million each night. Program costs are huge, the nightly stakes enormous, and network profits run into yearly millions. And in the field of comedy variety, which has thrived for so long, there's a strange new phenomenon. The networks are running out of talent.

Listen to Perry Lafferty, who's the head of programming for CBS, out in Television City, in Hollywood. Lafferty, himself a veteran of those early live-TV days, from whom we'll hear more later, is candid about the problem.

"We don't know where to look for the new talent," he admits. "Right now the audiences love Cher, she's the biggest hit of anybody in the variety field since I don't know who—perhaps Flip Wilson, five years ago. But you look for these people, where are they? You can't find them. It's frightful when I look out my window and think, 'All right, tell me who's ready out there that you're going to put up as a star, to build a comedy-variety show around?' Remember, to do one today means a commitment of probably sixteen or seventeen weeks, at somewhere around $190,000 per show—that's for the cost of the show *alone*, not the hour's worth of network time. By the time you're through, there's millions of dollars involved. Whom are you going to hire, whom are you going to dare to gamble all that money on?"

And that same high-stakes gamble applies to trying out an hour revue on the summer schedule. Costs don't go down merely because the weather is hot.

So there's not much sense in suggesting that some affluent network try to go back to the days when summer-replacement shows resembled nothing so much as an MGM musical—those Mickey Rooney–Judy Garland fairy stories where I've-got-an-old-theater/you-know-where-to-locate-some-costumes-and-scenery / gee-great!-let's-put-on-a-musical-show-and-knock-the-people-dead was the order of the day.

We're all, alas, too old for summertime follies anymore.

MR. PEEPERS

"Some people say it was a light show," says Jim Fritzell, who wrote it, and ought to know, "but we got an awful lot of laughs for a light show."

He wandered into our lives one warm summer night in 1952, on tiptoe, almost apologetically, a shy, diffident little chap named Mr. Peepers, the science teacher in a mythical but most recognizable American high school. Behind the glasses, the hesitant smile, and the soft voice, there was a highly original comedian named Wally Cox. He had worked around in small New York clubs, doing an offbeat and charming monologue about his school friend Dufo—Dufo, who always convulsed his pals with his playground recess insanities, and who'd eventually climaxed his career by falling off a high roof, just for laughs. ("That Dufo," Cox would conclude, with genuine affection for a lost hero. "What a crazy guy.")

Somebody upstairs at NBC was certain that the soft-spoken young comic had a chance to become a television star—but at portraying exactly what, nobody up there was too sure. But mercifully for Cox, and for us, this was long before the era of committee decisions. There were sympathetic and creative hands and heads around, and eventually they all came together to work on his behalf. He made a few guest shot appearances, and then played one or two roles for producer Fred Coe on *Philco Playhouse*. When NBC decided to have a comedy show created for Cox, Coe, a talented young southerner who was to become one of the most gifted producer-directors in TV, was the logical person to tackle the problem, and so was David Swift, who'd written the scripts for Cox's *Philco* shows.

Nothing broad, no big boffolas, no pratfalls or slapstick—but a show lovingly designed and created to make the optimum use of a delicate talent. Swift eventually came up with Mr. Peepers, a modest little chap, and his daily life amid fellow teachers and students at Jefferson High. The Ford Motor Company agreed to sponsor it for a summer run, and Swift and his new collaborator, Fritzell, were given the go-ahead to polish up the script. "Dave had said to me 'No jokes—just a nice, soft, easy show,' " says Fritzell, but things changed along the way . . . as they usually do in television.

Mr. Peepers was to be produced in NBC's vast Center Theater, and performed live, before an audience of some twenty-five hundred people. "Fred Coe said, 'Ah think we better hear that theater rock at the end of the first act'— and it did. We just kept punching up and punching up, until we got that first good solid half hour out of it," says Fritzell.

NBC had scheduled *Mr. Peepers* for eight weeks. Again, it was subject to change. Cox and his supporting cast—which was to include Tony Randall as Harvey Weskit, his brash, aggressive friend; Marion Lorne, a somewhat befuddled middle-aged lady with a marvelous gift for extended double takes; and a lovely young ingenue, Pat Benoit, who would be Miss Remington, the high school nurse (and Peepers' eventual lady)—seemed to strike an instantaneous responsive chord in that huge Center Theater audience and all the people at home.

Critics applauded, mass-impact magazines such as *Time* and *Look* heralded Cox as a comedy find, and before the eight original episodes had been played out, NBC gave the green light for another five.

"For me, being on the show was an accident," says Tony Randall. "I was originally on for just a one-shot. At the time, I was much more interested in directing, and when they called me back, I was very busy directing something, and I tried desperately to get out of doing *Peepers* again. But Fred Coe wouldn't let me out of it, and that was the turning point in my career. If he *had* let me out—I might still be walking around, looking for work!"

The pressures of doing an original half-hour situation comedy, live, each week, from that cavernous Center Theater (it is long gone, replaced a few years later by the landlord Rockefellers with eight floors of office space) were enormous. By the end of that first summer, Swift had retired and left Fritzell to write the show by himself. There were plans to sell the show to another sponsor for the fall, but NBC decided against the extension. "On the last night," says Fritzell, "NBC had almost two thousand phone calls complaining about *Peepers* going off—but there was nothing anybody could do about it. The fall schedule was already locked up."

Once again there would be changes.

A gaping hole shortly opened up in that prime-time schedule. Something called *Old Doc Corkle* (its stars' names should be mercifully omitted on the theory that anyone can make a mistake) went on and, to put it just as mercifully, bombed. "It was murdered by the critics, stayed on perhaps two, three weeks," remembers Randall, "and NBC said we've got to get rid of it, doesn't matter if we have to pay everyone off—now, what'll we put on? Well, *Peepers* did well this summer, we got all those phone calls, remember? And overnight, they threw *Peepers* together again. They didn't have a single script, nothing except the rights to the show and Wally under contract, but within a few days they'd brought us all together again. By the fourth week of what had been *Corkle* time, we were back, and this time, we stayed."

Told that way, it all sounds rather simple and efficient. But for all those who participated in getting it together, and keeping it running, the memory of the intense amount of work that was entailed is still fresh. Feeding the boilers of a weekly live situation comedy was too much for any one man; Fritzell was soon badly in need of help. The producers located for him a hopeful young actor-writer named Everett Greenbaum, who was knocking around New York, hoping to break into television. "I'd just lost my job selling toy frogs at Macy's, in the toy department," says Greenbaum. "Had a big fight, got out and walked. I didn't know where I was going. Finally ended up at Talent Associates, where I'd been once or twice before, hoping to get a job. They said, 'Oh, we finally got you—we've been looking for you all day!' "

Fritzell and Greenbaum have remained a team, on and off, ever since. (Their credits include the film *Good Neighbor*Sam and dozens of scripts for shows such as *The Real McCoys*, and they are currently employed by *M*A*S*H*.) "From then on, we seem always to have been working," says Greenbaum, a jovial chap who clears his head most afternoons by flying his private plane up above the San Fernando Valley smog. "God, how we worked on *Peepers*. We once went eight months without a day off. Saturdays, Sundays, anything. In those days, nobody ever thought that you might have several teams writing one situation comedy series. They might have been doing that out in Hollywood, but in New York they hadn't heard about anything so efficient."

Wally Cox and Pat Benoit, *Mr. Peepers* (Courtesy NBC)

What Greenbaum alludes to is the common practice in California-based television of "staffing" various situation comedies, a system that continues season after season. The original pilot script for such a new show is usually constructed in steps, by a writer or a team of writers with solid comedy credits from the past. From the day that the original idea, or premise, is brought in, usually on a couple of pages, triple-spaced and with wide margins, stated in the simplest of terms, the process begins. First there are conferences and rewrites, dictated by the producer, at the behest of networks, potential stars, and anyone else who's concerned. If and when the original script is finally produced, and if and when the filmed or taped pilot is slotted by one of the three networks on one of the seven possible evenings—and the odds of such an event taking place are staggeringly against all concerned—then the process becomes even more complex.

The producer must now find a minimum of thirteen playable scripts to appear on the television tube. On some shows, producers have hired literally dozens of writers, or teams, to provide the ensuing episodes, under the watchful eye of a "script consultant." When the scripts are suitably rewritten, they will undoubtedly be *re*written by a staff "script editor" and even by the show's producer. After the script goes into production, you can be sure that the director will have his changes, and the show's star and/or the supporting cast will certainly induce further work.

To the outsider, such a writing treadmill may sound chaotic, which it certainly is, but when one considers the huge amounts involved—literally hundreds of thousands of dollars weekly invested by network, sponsor, and producer—plus the hourly pressure-cooker strain to keep the show going, the fierce survival battle becomes understandable. "There's an old show business rule that says that a good script isn't written, it's rewritten," sighs one anonymous veteran of the battle, "but what goes on here is ridiculous."

"I was reading a thing in the trade papers the other day," grumbles Fritzell. "Some lady saying how her husband, a young guy who's a writer out here, just lately wrote a script for *The Partridge Family*, and he did it overnight, and she was bragging how nobody had ever heard of such a miraculous feat before. And I got so mad. What the hell—we had to do that all the time!"

But the marriage of Fritzell and Greenbaum's slightly offbeat and antic wit with the soft-spoken Cox would be enormously successful.

"Well, you see, Wally *was* Mr. Peepers," says Fritzell. "He spent all of his spare time studying insects: it wasn't just part of his TV character. He read

Scientific American. That was Wally. And as far as the nervousness—well, that was genuine, too. See, Wally was never too sure of himself; all through rehearsals he'd be uncertain and hesitant. Then he'd go out there in front of an audience and get his first big laugh from the audience, and then he'd say to himself, 'It's going to work!'—and then he'd be off and running."

"I loved him," says Randall, today. "Saintly fellow. Marvelous man. I guess he was the funniest fellow to be around that I've ever known. Everything he said was brilliant. Not that I can quote it—but you just sat there and howled. And he didn't care if you heard it or not. He would never speak up and repeat it, he didn't care if what he said went right by. Unless you tuned in and listened to him, you'd miss it all."

Not that producing *Mr. Peepers* was a constant source of joy to its hardworking production crew. Fred Coe, its producer, who was simultaneously preparing and producing the weekly drama hour *Philco-Goodyear Playhouse* throughout those years, is quick to point out that the frenzied weekly schedule often allowed for instant flops. "You'd do a show and it would fail," he sighs. "Monday, it would be dreadful around those network offices. It wasn't the ratings that bothered us. It was the fact that we all *knew* we'd failed. And yet, when you did something that was good, it was exactly the opposite. We'd get a high that was as if we'd had a marvelous Broadway opening."

"In those days," Greenbaum confesses, "I was still a brash young kid, and I was afraid of Fred because he'd yell and scream when something was wrong. Once he banned me from the theater. But I'll never forget when I acted on the show."

In the midst of that backbreaking schedule, he found time to perform, as well as to write?

"It was at Fred's insistence," says Fritzell. "Ev had stepped in one week to do a little hunk as a department store clerk with Wally. See Ev had visions of himself as a comedy star—"

"Still do," says Greenbaum promptly.

"—so we went ahead and wrote Ev another scene. We worked our fannies off to make great jokes for him—"

"Naturally!" chortles Greenbaum. "Then over on the third floor at NBC, where all the unemployed actors sat around waiting for calls, a bunch of them grabbed me and accused me of taking the food out of their kids' mouths. Very dramatic. So I really began to get nervous, and by the time we actually went on the air, I just came out in front of the cameras and drew a blank. Went up cold—blew all those glorious gags we'd written. I figured Fred was going to kill me. After the show, I saw him coming down the hall, and I started to hide, and he just grabbed me and hugged me, and he said, 'It's going to be all right, everything's all right!' He knew what I'd gone through. Marvelous man."

"As well as being one of the best editors any writer could want," says Fritzell. "We'd bring in the first draft of a new script for Wally, and Fred would read it, and maybe we didn't know what was wrong, how could we? We were so close to it on that schedule. Anyway, Fred would look up, and in that southern accent of his, he almost sounds like a cracker, he'd say, in the simplest terms, 'Why don't you change this guy's attitude *here?*' And that would be the root of the whole problem. He'd put his finger right on it—and we couldn't wait to get back to the office at eight or nine at night and start to redo the whole damn script!"

"Coe was marvelous for the actors, too," says Randall. "He'd come to a rehearsal, and the way he would *laugh!* You thought you were the funniest person who'd ever walked. And he meant it. Anything broke Fred up. After his reaction, you were spoiled."

"And all that time, remember, he'd have three, maybe four shows in preparation for *Philco-Goodyear*," marvels Greenbaum. "All of them originals—rehearsing, being camera-blocked, and one actually being televised on the set. He'd go from show to show, wherever they all were being done, and digest everything simultaneously. Giving notes to the director, to the actors, telling the writer what needed to be fixed . . . and all on a regular schedule."

"I remember once," adds Fritzell, "we met him downstairs at Hurley's Bar—that's where everybody from NBC would go to have a drink between rehearsals. It was perfectly located, halfway between the Center Theater and 30 Rockefeller Plaza. There was one director that Fred had working for him, a guy we called Mr. Panic because he was always knee-deep in some crisis, and one of us said to Fred, 'Hey, where's *he?*' And Fred, who must have been real tired that day, blinked and said, 'Oh, he's upstairs, rehearsing his mistakes.' "

As the *Peepers* saga continued, and the TV audience became more and more involved with the gentle science teacher's adventures at Jefferson High, and with his tongue-tied adoration for Miss Remington, the school nurse, the question for NBC and Talent Associates, the packagers, began to be more and more basic. Should the couple finally be married? Could the bashful character Cox portrayed become as lucky in affairs of the heart as he had been with his beloved microbes and chromosomes? And how would the people at home react?

Eventually, after much discussion, it was decided that the audience would be happy if Mr. Peepers took himself a bride. Urged on by his friend Weskit, Peepers summoned up enough courage to ask Miss Remington for her hand, and on one memorable night in 1954, long before Rhoda married her boyfriend on CBS, twenty years later, the Center Theater became the scene of their marriage.

The televised nuptials were a national event. "I heard a story that Milton Berle was at a big party that night, and he made everybody in the place be quiet because he'd turned on the set and didn't want to miss the wedding scene," says Fritzell.

"I still think it was a rotten idea," insists Greenbaum. "Changed the whole emphasis of the show. Turned it into a husband and wife comedy series, the same as dozens of other shows."

"You're wrong, Everett," sighs Fritzell, with the tolerance acquired from twenty seasons of amiable creative hassles with his partner. "Their marriage kept the show going for the entire next season."

"But it was never the same after that," broods Greenbaum, who remains unconvinced. "Killed us."

"That wasn't what killed us!" says Fritzell. "We were destroyed by technology."

He is referring to the motion picture camera.

By 1954, out in the California studios, technicians were gearing up to produce what would be a steady avalanche of filmed situation comedies. Now that Lucille Ball, Jackie Cooper, Joan Davis, Blondie and Dagwood, et al., were thriving on the perfection afforded by assembly-line film techniques, a pattern had been set that was to last for many years. The days of a back-breaking "live" schedule, with all its incessant panic-session nights that plagued production crews and actors, were numbered.

"You see, we didn't have the coaxial cable between the East and the West Coast yet," says Fritzell, "and in order for our show to be seen around the country, they'd ship out kinescopes. Lord, you look at a kinescope of a 1954 show, and you simply can't believe how terrible it looks. The scenery was flimsy—it was all made of plasterboard—and the lighting was crude—it was all done in one day, remember. How the actors ever did it was always a mystery to me—running from set to set, changing their clothes behind the scenery, hoping to make it to their next scene, and praying that nothing would go wrong as they went."

It was indeed fraught with terror for the performers. "You'd be doing your dress rehearsal almost up to the time of the live show," marvels Randall, who thrives these days on the relatively relaxed schedule for his costarring role with Jack Klugman, in the long-run hit *The Odd Couple*. "That gave you less than half an hour before you actually went on the air—and since our show audience never came in before the actual program, you never knew how long a comedy script could play, *with* laughs. Laughs stretched the show, so we were almost always long, and just before we went on the air, they'd always give us cuts."

He shakes his head and sighs in wonder at the pressures of those early, primitive circumstances. "They couldn't give the cuts to Wally because he never knew his lines that well anyway. And they couldn't give them to dear old Marion Lorne, because her whole approach to comedy was that gasping, panting uh-uh-uh thing, and it would have ruined her timing. So the only person they could give cuts to was me. And the cuts would never be in one place, mind you. Throughout the show, one in one scene, take out a half a page here— that sort of thing. They'd show them all to me ten minutes before we went on the air! I could remember them . . . so I got them."

Despite all that last-minute panic and pressure, the fact remained that when the show went on the air, the cast delivered. Perhaps the scenery was shaky. No matter. The show was solid.

"The difference between live television and today's shows," comments Randall, "is not solely technical. It's the spirit of the thing. Remember, it was all new then, and everybody involved in it was marvelously excited by it. Even though we actors and the writers and all the other people were doing the same sort of work we'd all done before, TV suddenly gave us a whole new life. People like Martha Raye, or Phil Silvers, for instance, who'd had careers before, suddenly found a whole new dimension. They just zoomed. Sid Caesar had been around, he wasn't a baby, Imogene Coca had worked for years, Max Liebman was already in his late fifties, he'd been doing shows too . . . but when they came together and did *Your Show of Shows*, they really took off. It was like the early days of the silent movies. Remember how marvelous Chaplin was? He was doing the same thing he'd been doing in music halls, but the camera turned him into a comic genius. He *used* the medium, made it his. And that was true of *Mr. Peepers* too. We all came together, working with Fred Coe, and television brought out all sorts of talent from each of us that nobody had demonstrated before."

By 1955 *Mr. Peepers* had completed its run—three years of last-minute cuts, pressure-cooker writing—and what remained was its loyal coterie of fans, the echoes of Bernie Green's delightful theme music, and some blurred kinescopes that were stored away in a vault.

The Jefferson High staff graduated to other pursuits.

Wally Cox, now under long-term contract to NBC, spent the next decade or so in the fruitless pursuit of another such starring vehicle. Neither he nor the network ever came up with a show that would equal the success of *Mr. Peepers*. He tried it again with a show called *The Adventures of Hiram Halliday*, but with little success. "After that," says Fritzell sadly, "Wally was just a guy saying his lines so that he could get it over with and go home."

"He told us once that he didn't realize all he'd had in those *Peepers* days," adds Greenbaum. "He apologized to me for years for not realizing how marvelous that character was for him. You see, under that hesitant exterior, we always had him playing a *strong* little guy, and that must have communicated to the audience. Right up till the time he died, Wally told us he was proud to have created that part."

"It was a terrific cast," says Fritzell. And for the record, let them take another bow. Cox; Randall; Pat Benoit; Marion Lorne; Jack Warden; Ernest Truex and his wife, Sylvia Field; Reta Shaw; Gage Clark; and another talented young lady who recently passed away, Norma Crane.

"We've done a lot of other shows since then," muses Greenbaum, "but it's remarkable the impact that just those three seasons have had on our careers."

"Yeah," says Fritzell, with a touch of wry. "In a way, it's a little depressing. It was as if we'd flown the Atlantic in 1927, and that's the only thing people will ever remember us for."

Cox is gone, and with him the ghost of his crazy friend Dufo . . . the shade of Mr. Peepers, the gentle, understated chap who was so much his own alter ego. We live now in a louder, more frenzied era, and 1976 television situation comedy would allow little if any prime-viewing time for the daily adventures of an endearing schoolteacher whose idea of drama was the irrational mating habits of the bee, as compared to his own. Which is certainly our loss.

"He was so completely without aggression," says Randall. "If he had any hostility, I never saw it. Perhaps if he'd had more drive, he might have been a much more successful comedian."

"So he sat out all the rest of those years, on that long-term contract, enjoying his hobbies and writing an occasional children's book with Everett," muses Fritzell, "but Wally always felt that those seasons he played Mr. Peepers were his golden years."

And so, in retrospect, they were. For us all.

HAL KANTER,
ED WYNN
AND OTHERS

Hal Kanter remembers:

The very first TV comedy show I worked on was the half-hour show that starred Ed Wynn, produced out here in California. That was the fall of 1949, and CBS decided to throw behind Wynn's show the entire weight of their mighty resources out here . . . which consisted of three cameras, one radio studio at Sunset and Vine, and Ralph Levy, whom they imported from New York and whose job was to get the show on the air.

The show was done live out here, and then sent east via kinescope. You know what kinescopes looked like? We did a black and white show, but it came out gray and white. Watching a kinescope was like looking at a bowl of gray pea soup. Here and there you could barely make out the croutons.

I was working for Bing Crosby on his radio show at the time, but I took a cut in salary to work with Ed Wynn. Firstly I wanted to get in on the ground floor of this new medium, and secondly it was an opportunity to work with a great comedian. Ed *was* the Perfect Fool; I sensed I could learn a great deal about comedy from him. And I did. I also learned a lot about the complicated kind of machinery that's inside comedians.

That first night we premiered the show, it was a big, gala affair. After the actual show went off the air, Ed stood on stage and he did an after-curtain

Buster Keaton and Ed Wynn (Courtesy Ralph Levy and CBS)

speech that lasted longer than the half-hour show itself. He brought a raft of his friends up on stage to take bows with him.

Now, we were all standing around backstage; it was a big night for us, too. Ralph Levy, Harlan Thompson, who was the producer of those early shows, my co-writers Leo Solomon and Seaman Jacobs—all of us keyed up and excited, waiting for Ed to get offstage so we could talk about the show with him.

Ed finally came offstage, glowing with excitement, perspiration, and some bourbon he'd had earlier and which was beginning to leak out—and now it's a big festive thing, and the phone rang in his dressing room, and he got on, and he listened, and then he said, "Oh, yes? *Thank you!* . . . *Really?* . . . Thank you! . . . Oh, my, *thank you!*"

He went on like that for fifteen minutes, and we're all sitting there, listening, and finally Ed hung up and said, "Well, gentlemen, that's it. We are a smash, that's the definitive word. Do you know who that was on the telephone? That was Fanny Brice *herself*."

Fanny was living out here, she'd seen the show, and she'd kept on calling and calling afterward, trying to get through to Ed, but he'd been out there on-stage all that time. Fanny raved about the show, and Ed was ecstatic. He said, "Fanny Brice is the greatest comedienne who ever set foot on the stage. I don't care what they say about Helen Hayes or Ethel Barrymore—Fanny is truly the first woman of the theater!"

Now, the second week the show went on, and after the show, Ed did a shorter speech, then he rushed back. Fanny called again. Ed waited for her to give him her critique of the show, things she didn't like, things she did like—but all in all, A plus. A clean bill of health. Again, Ed's ecstatic.

This went on for several weeks. It got to the point where Ed waited for that nightly call from Fanny. Her praise was just marvelous for him. She was his Brooks Atkinson, or his Clive Barnes.

Now it was the fifth week. All of us were standing around after the show, outside one of the CBS offices. We were having a problem. By now we were beginning to run out of guests who were willing to go on the show. Remember, this was the first season there'd been any network television in Hollywood, and most of the stars out here were deathly afraid of exposing themselves to this medium. On a live show, they were too vulnerable. We could get vaude-ville headliners like Leon Errol, or Victor Moore, or actors like Jack Holt, or Howard Duff, Ella Raines, or singers like Gertrude Niesen, or Dinah Shore, but we were running out of headliners.

We couldn't suggest other comedians. After all, it was Ed's show, and he wanted to get all the laughs. Later on, he loosened up and used Buster Keaton, and Lucille Ball and Desi Arnaz, but right now he wanted jugglers, acrobats, the kind of performer whose act he would work with.

Anyway, we're standing around, making suggestions, trying like mad to think of somebody, when, as regular as clockwork, Fanny Brice's phone call comes in. Ed talks to her, and she tells him again how great his show was; he hangs up the phone and goes into his usual weekly rave about Fanny Brice. The funniest lady in the world, the great American theatrical star who loved his show, et cetera.

And Seaman Jacobs said, "Hey—what are we all standing around here talking about a star for? There's your star right there!"

Ed turned to Seaman and said, "Who?"

Seaman said, "Why, Fanny Brice!"

Ed stared at him. And then he asked, "Fanny Brice? What the hell can *she* do?"

★ 87 ★

Ed Wynn poking fun at TV (Courtesy CBS)

I remember another time, Ed was moaning about the future. He was worried about what would happen to show business; things were changing so rapidly now, with the advent of television. He said, "What are they going to do with old people like me, and Jolson, and Eddie Cantor, and Jack Benny? Build an institution for us?"

Seaman was standing there, listening to Ed ramble on, and he said, "They've already done that for you, Ed. It's called the Bank of America."

I must say, Ed had the good grace to laugh.

A couple of weeks later, Ed had booked as his guest star James Barton. We were very fortunate to have him; Barton was one of the greatest vaudevillians who'd ever played the Palace Theater, he was a song-and-dance man, and he'd also gone on to be a great dramatic star. He'd played Jeeter Lester in *Tobacco Road* and gone on to play one of the leads in Eugene O'Neill's *The Iceman Cometh*. I'd seen him in that, and later on I was lucky enough to catch him at Loew's State, and I knew that Barton was probably one of the best singers that ever sang and danced on a stage. He had a classic drunk-and-mad-dog routine, he'd end up by singing "Miss Annabelle Lee" (which Dick Shawn was performing in New York in 1975 in *A Musical Jubilee*), and it was a thrill to watch him.

We rehearsed with him all afternoon—the orchestra was led by our concertmaster and then, for the dress rehearsal, our musical director came in. He was a man named Lud Gluskin. Lud was once described to me as a bald-headed man who walked as if he were trying to catch a chicken.

Lud came in for the dress. Ralph Levy was in the control booth, and I was down in the audience, and Barton came onstage. When Jim wasn't dressed for his performance, he wore a rumpled suit, and I must say he really looked like a bum, a kind of a cheerful panhandler. There he stood, while Lud is running through the music for the show, and Lud saw Barton's arrangement, which is for a song called "You Made Me Love You." Lud asked, "Have we got *Jolson* on this show?"

Ralph, over the talk-back, said, "No, Lud, Mr. Barton is going to sing the song on the show." Lud said, "Mr. Barton? Who the hell is Barton?"

I was sitting right behind him down in the orchestra, and I walked over and whispered in Lud's ear, "*James* Barton, and he's standing right there, by the camera." That didn't bother Lud. He asked, "Who the hell is James Barton? Who *is* he?"

Ralph heard us over the mikes—everybody in the whole rehearsal could hear us—and he said, "Lud, just play the number, will you please?"

Barton had been standing there all this time, saying not one word. Lud gave his orchestra the cue, and they started to play, and Barton began to sing "You Made Me Love You," and he sang the whole song directly to Lud. He never once took his eyes off Lud—he just stood there and sang; and after he'd gotten into the third or fourth line of the lyric, those of us sitting behind Lud could see the color rising up the back of Lud's neck, past the gray fringe of hair and onto his bald pate, which turned purple with embarrassment . . . because nobody ever sang "You Made Me Love You" the way Jimmy Barton did at that rehearsal. Goosebumps on all of us, as we listened. When the final note died out, everybody in that theater just sat there. It was what they tell us about the end of Lincoln's Gettysburg Address. Nobody stirred.

And Barton, who'd never taken his eyes off Gluskin, stood there, still staring at him, and then he said, "*That's* who James Barton is, you bald-headed son of a bitch," and walked offstage.

In our desperate search to try and get other stars to appear with us, we went after everybody. Ed came in one day and said he'd been to dinner with Al Jolson, and spoken to him about being on the show, and he suggested that I go out to Encino and speak to Al, who'd sounded receptive.

I went out to Al's house, and Mrs. Jolson ushered me out to the pool where Al, who was an inveterate sunbather, was lying there nude. He said, "Take off your clothes and join me, kid," but I explained that I couldn't stay long, I'd come to talk to him about being on the Wynn show. He said, "Oh, for God's sake, I'm not going on his show." I asked him why he'd suggested to Ed that he might, and he said, "Oh, what are you going to say to a friend when you're sitting at dinner? He asks you to come on his show, you say, 'Sure, sure'—but you don't."

Then he explained his grand design to me. He said, "I am saving myself. When I go on TV, it's going to be an event. I'm not going on somebody else's show, no-sir. It's going to be *my* show—it's going to be Jolson—and there won't be any commercials. It'll be something like General Motors or Mobil which comes on the air—and they say, 'Ladies and gentlemen, General Motors is proud to present—*Mr. Al Jolson!*' Then I'll come out on the stage, I'll tell a few stories, I'll sing a few songs, I'll sit on the footlights and I'll chat the way I used to do at the Winter Garden Theater, I'll talk to the people, I'll sing a few more songs, and then the hour will be over, and a voice will come on and say 'General Motors has presented, with pride, Mr. Al Jolson.' And *that's* the show *I'm* going to do," said Al.

Well, television wasn't ready for any concept as broad as that one—although a quarter century later, Frank Sinatra was to come very close to Al's mammoth ego projection, when he did his solo live hour from Madison Square Garden.

A couple of years later, I went out to see Jolson again. I was writing for Bing Crosby then, and Jolie was supposed to be a guest—this was still radio. Al had just come back from entertaining the troops in Korea, and when I got out to his house, this time he was sitting in his den, watching TV. He had one of those remote-control devices that had just come out: a long cord which was attached to the set, and which you could use to turn off the sound during commercials.

Al was sitting there watching Arthur Godfrey, and he turned off the sound and said, "Look at that—*look*—there's Arthur Godfrey, he's playing the ukelele and singing a song. Can you believe that?" Al asked me. "That son of a bitch proves one thing about show business today—in order to be a success, all you have to do is to show up!

"Let me ask you," Al went on, "have you ever seen a TV show with Morton Downey?" I told him I hadn't. He said, "Morton Downey is on TV, and he's a big hit on TV. A big hit!" said Jolie. "He has got the nerve to go on tele-

Carmen Miranda on *The Ed Wynn Show* (Courtesy Ralph Levy and CBS)

vision to sing to people. Morton Downey! I can fart better than he can sing—and *I'm* not on television!"

That was lovable Al. He never did get to do any TV appearances, because he died shortly after. Which was a shame, because despite everything, he was a brilliant entertainer, probably the greatest of all time.

Ironically, in those early days out here in Hollywood, there was a great deal of discussion about the potentials of television: how we could use the cameras to do this and that, and widen the horizons of entertainment. All sorts of vivid imaginations were brought into play, designers and directors, people who were supposed to make the most of the sight values in comedy, and to dramatize comedy scenes.

But it was Groucho Marx who first proved the philosophy, which at the time was very unfashionable, that if people were laughing at you in radio, they'd continue to laugh at you in TV, without any embellishments. Groucho merely took his radio show, *You Bet Your Life*, and transferred it to TV intact. And he proved his point—that the only thing you had on TV that you hadn't had on radio was the sight of Groucho sitting on a plain stool, puffing his cigar and waggling his eyebrows as he leered at pretty girls. That's all he added, and the show was a big hit.

Subsequently, on TV shows, especially variety shows, everybody took to sitting on stools and singing and talking to the people. Maybe doing a few sight gags, but with no real use of the visual aspects of TV.

The pioneer was Groucho. And does anybody need to remind you that all those old episodes of *You Bet Your Life* are running on your home screen tonight—while all the other wildly "inventive" TV concepts of the fifties and sixties have long since been forgotten?

For every comedian such as a Groucho, who did make the transition into TV successfully, there were dozens of other established stars who never accomplished the move. Take Fred Allen, who for years had been a major radio star. The first few shows he tried to do in New York, mammoth hour-long productions from the huge Center Theater, on NBC, were heavily overproduced. All sorts of clutter onstage; his shows collapsed beneath the weight of the so-called visual aspects. Poor Fred was never able to project any of his brilliant verbal humor amid all those surroundings.

(In one of Allen's letters, written in 1952, he remarked: "Television is a triumph of equipment over people and the minds that control it are so small that you could put them in the navel of a flea and still have enough room beside them for a vice-president's heart.")

Happily, Fred did enjoy some success on the tube later, on such panel shows as *What's My Line?* where he could merely sit there and be himself, and get off his marvelous ad-lib lines. But those shows came after all the so-called mavens of TV comedy had advised Fred to try out their doomed formats.

The simple thing would have been to put Fred into an intimate talk situation, the sort of thing Groucho did, and let Fred match wits with various guests on a simple one-to-one basis. But in those early days (and today, for that matter) what venturesome network and/or sponsor would ever dare to underwrite a show that's so basic, in which all that matters is, not the production or fancy camera angles, but merely talent?

Gloria Swanson and Ed Wynn (Courtesy Ralph Levy and CBS)

Later on I did work on a show where we evolved a special technique for TV comedy, but that only came about when we found the comedian who could make the best use of the format.

He was a short, charming monologist named George Gobel. I'd seen him do his act down at the old Coconut Grove, at the Biltmore Hotel in Los Angeles, and I'd been absolutely delighted by George. He was refreshing and genuinely droll, and he combined a rustic sense of humor with an urbanity that appealed to me. I've always loved country-style humor, and George, with that sly delivery of his, elevated it to a very sophisticated level. ("Well, I'll be a dirty bird." "You know, you don't hardly get those no more," and so on.) The guy was absolutely unique.

Somebody had done one of those typical assembly-line TV comedy pilots with George, and it hadn't worked at all. It never captured an ounce of his particular style. When they showed it to me, I knew instinctively that it was all wrong for him. But I decided George was well worth the effort; somebody had to try and work out a format that would actually use the medium, and meld his talents into it. When I finally worked it out, the key to everything came from the late, great Thornton Wilder. In *Our Town* he had his stage manager stroll in and out, commenting on what was about to happen, and what had happened. I borrowed from Ed Wynn's technique, as well. I'd have George talking about our set. He'd say, "We're going to our little house now. Of course, this isn't really a house, it's a set that's behind the curtain here." We had a stagehand whose name was Fay, Fay Thomas. George would say, "Fay, pull the curtain." That's pure Ed Wynn.

It was all letting the audience in on the fact that we're making believe, we're all pretending. And if the right guy with the right personality says that sort of thing, and does it, and the audience takes a shine to him, they eat it up.

We even extended that technique to our commercials. They were integrated into the show; we gave the audience a reason to watch them. George would say things like "You know, commercials are the life's blood of television, and this anemic industry needs all the blood it can get," something like that; "so please watch this." It worked, not only for the client, Pet Milk, but also for the audience, because it made of the show a cohesive entity—not one that's all chopped up into little pieces.

Gobel was a marvelous example of audience acceptance. One of the great things television has taught us is that if there's a guy who can sit in your living room, over a drink, or at your dinner table, or merely talk to you, and you can enjoy his company in your own home, then you'll enjoy him on television, because there he is, in your home again, as a guest.

That's the secret of Johnny Carson's enormous success. If you were in his company, you'd love him. And you can almost always tell with people he's had on his show, his guests, which ones you really would like to spend more time with—and you can always spot the ones you never want to come back into your house again.

"GOOD EVENING. FROM WASHINGTON, THIS IS..."

Good news, bad news—it's always traveled fast, but through the medium of today's television it's instantaneous.

Lately, it's also omnipresent.

Starting this morning at 6:05 A.M., there's a news program on one or two of the major channels, and in one form or another you can keep up with what's happening until 9 A.M. By avoiding the various panel and talk shows, you can have a two-hour period of respite, but you can catch up on current events again at 11:55 A.M., and again at 12:55. When you've finished journeying through daily daytime serials and those various exercises in human greed called game shows, your tube will light up promptly at 5 P.M. with reports from all over this troubled planet; you can indulge yourself until 8 P.M. with news. And if that much firsthand reportage hasn't satisfied your needs, then you can flip over to a local channel at 10 P.M. for an early hour wrap-up of the day's events, and then at eleven the networks will supply you with yet another half hour. For you insomniacs, the various stations will run through it all again at 12:30 A.M., and again at 1.00 A.M., and at 2:35 A.M. And starting tomorrow, at 6:05 A.M. there's a news program on one or two...etc., etc., etc.

"You could call it news pollution," remarks one observer of the scene.

To the rest of us observers the influence of TV news programs has become immense. Certainly TV news has more impact than anything in print. Commentators—Cronkite, Sevareid, Reasoner, et al.—command a much vaster audience than do the most widely syndicated columnists. Mobile TV camera crews take us into busing riots, fires, murders, scenes of disaster, into Patty Hearst's court hearings, into emergency wards, onto fields where airliners have crashed. News reportage has become a form of living daily comic strip, one that enables us to sit back and let the miseries of the World Out There flash by, interrupted only by the rhythmic pulsebeat of all those thirty-second commercials.

The whole news scene has become a surrealistic visual sandwich—Cup-a-Soup flanked by a shoot-out in East Harlem; Eastern, the Wings of Man bounded by a rent strike; Alka-Seltzer edged with a Senate hearing on abortion laws; the new AMC Pacer followed by midwestern tornadoes; Dial Deodorant Soap followed by the latest bomb explosion in Belfast. Politicians answer leading questions by avoiding them, and baseball players sell Trac II razors; No Nonsense Panty Hose introduces the latest New York job cuts.

News *sells*.

Both the three major networks and their local affiliated stations have discovered that they can turn news programs into a highly profitable advertising medium. Local, national, international—it doesn't matter where the bulletins and the on-the-scene interviews come from; you can be certain that management has proved to itself that it's far more profitable to switch on the cameras and dolly in on those various newscasters than it might be to search for some elusive program concept that's based on a writer's fancy.

It also follows that if Hollywood has long since supplanted New York as the G.H.Q. of television production, then Washington, D.C., has also nosed out dear old Manhattan as the scene where most hard news is happening. Hollywood turns out our escapist dreams; Washington supplies us with our real nightmares.

It wasn't always so.

Short years back, Washington was a remote outpost, far removed from the Big Apple of New York, linked to the city by brief filmed reports flown up once a day.

"When I first came here, I think there were only four hundred television sets in the city," says Ray Scherer, who came to the nation's capital from Fort Wayne, Indiana, and became one of the pioneer television newscasters, one of the first of that corps that would eventually include Bob McCormick, David Brinkley, Larry Le Sueur, Marvin Kalb, John Chancellor, and the rest.

"On television, we were doing the most primitive sort of news reportage. I started in radio, and then I worked on a local TV show with Earl Godwin. He was a very well known radio commentator during the war, and the show we did on TV in 1948 or '49 was on this funny little set, a sort of a country store, where Earl acted as the proprietor. He'd stand behind the counter, wearing suspenders, the lights reflecting off his bald head, and I would come through. I was supposed to be the reporter for the local paper, and he'd say, 'Well, Ray, what's new?' And I would say, 'Well, Earl, today Harry Truman fired off an angry letter to the music critic of *The Washington Post* complaining about the nasty review he'd written about his daughter Margaret's singing.' And then Earl would launch into a rambling sort of commentary about that. Pretty elementary stuff.

"Remember, though," says Scherer, a tall, amiable gentleman who has become over the years a trusted confidant of politicians and Presidents, "our facilities weren't very elaborate. Our first news cameras held only 100 feet of film. We had one cameraman; he had a 16 mm. silent camera. I'd clip the morning *Washington Post*, and the *Times-Herald*—at that point there were two papers—I'd pick out news and feature stories, he'd go out and shoot some film. Fifty feet of that event, twenty feet on this story—he'd bring it back, we'd assemble it all into a newsreel and run it that night with a live commentary. Strictly a local show—and it looked it."

By 1948 there would be the first attempts to cover major political events. In June there was television coverage of the Republican National Convention. The broadcasts were transmitted from Philadelphia, where the delegates were in session, by means of a process called "stratovision," in which the signal was beamed up to a plane flying 25,000 feet above Pittsburgh; the pictures were then rebroadcast to a nine-state area below.

The following year NBC began to transmit its first nightly fifteen-minute newscast from New York. Called *The Camel News Caravan*, it would be hosted for some years to come by John Cameron Swayze, whose natty tailoring, spread collars, and "Glad we could get together" sign-off would shortly turn him into one of the very first star personality newscasters.

Down in Washington, things were slowly beginning to pick up for the newsmen who were working in television. "Pretty soon we went over to sound cameras," says Scherer, "and you could do interviews. Not long ones; we still didn't have much film in the cameras. Finally we went to 200-foot cameras, and that was a major technical advance. *The Camel News Caravan* would pick up a couple of inserts from Washington each night. We'd run out and shoot some film, run back to the studio, run our film through the 'soup'— that's the laboratory—and then do a voice commentary over it. Bob Mc-Cormick did those first inserts—and then, in 1952, David Brinkley became the voice you heard.

"But where I really got to see television develop was in the White House itself. When I first came to town, I was assigned to cover Harry Truman, and even though they were his closing days, they were damned interesting."

President Truman had been televised in 1947, delivering his State of the Union message to Congress, and in 1948 he had appeared during the campaign, but the new electronic medium was something of an unknown quantity to the man from Missouri; as yet, it had not proven itself to him. "He'd hold his news conferences once a week, on Wednesday morning, and for the first time we were permitted to tape them for radio. You'd get a little excerpt here, a little there—but you never got the whole news conference on the air, the way we do today. All you gave the voters was the flavor of a Truman news conference. Toward the end of his term, Truman began to make speeches on TV from the Oval Office, generally fifteen minutes long. Fairly pedestrian affairs; he would simply read from a notebook and look up into the camera.

"But when Eisenhower was elected, Jim Haggerty, his press secretary, sensed that if you could put television into the White House, you could add a much larger dimension to the office—put the President into many more living rooms. But he didn't quite know how to do it, because in 1952 TV was still in a fairly elementary mechanical stage."

Technical facilities were still unrefined, but live news reportage on the small home screen was beginning to take on vivid immediacy. In 1951 Senator Estes Kefauver, head of the Senate committee devoted to investigating organized crime, permitted network cameras for the first time to be set up in a Senate hearing room. The results were startling; the impact on the American public went far beyond anyone's wildest predictions. Overnight, fictional heroes and villains were dwarfed and supplanted by a procession of real-life characters. Homespun Senator Kefauver—alert, dogged little Rudolph Halley, the shrill-voiced prosecutor, riding forth each day, a rumpled Galahad, to do battle with such underworld *capos* as Frank Costello, the mythical "boss" of New York, who would refuse to permit his face to be shown on TV because "it constatutes a vilation of my poisonal rights, Mistuh Halley."

John Cameron Swayze (Courtesy NBC)

(The camera showed only his nervous, twitching hands, as he denied any possible connection to any sort of crime.) The hundreds of thousands who stayed home, or deserted their offices to watch the daily proceedings will never forget such other characters as Virginia Hill, a flamboyant lady with tangled mob connections and a cheerful you-go-to-hell attitude, or "Longie" Zwillman, New Jersey's patriarchal who-*me*? crime boss.

Later on, in another senatorial arena, an even more vivid real-life drama would play itself out before more of a television audience. Before the unwinking cameras of ABC, in 1954, the Army-McCarthy hearings would be televised in their entirety, with results that revealed higher dramatic tension than even the most gifted dramatist could have produced. Senator Joseph McCarthy, who had assumed that the attendant publicity to be derived by his permitting the proceedings to be televised, would be destroyed as a political force on the home screen. When Joseph Welch, the quiet legal counsel from Massachusetts, answered one of McCarthy's scurrilous personal attacks on a member of Welch's own staff by crying out, "Mr. Senator, have you no shame at all?" the impact of reality transcended the climax of any great Greek tragedy. The fall of McCarthy would be the first example of televised hara-kiri.

Eventually, at the behest of Eisenhower and Haggerty, the actor Robert Montgomery, a staunch Republican, was induced to come to Washington. Montgomery had considerable expertise around the cameras; he had become the successful producer of his own hour-long live NBC weekly show *Robert Montgomery Presents*.

"He was around the White House a good bit," remembers Scherer, "and I used to ask him about his role. He said, 'My job is to relax the President and to make him come across as comfortably as possible.' He never thought he could turn Ike into an actor, or to tinker with his 'image.'"

It was not an easy task. Eisenhower distrusted the TelePrompTer. "Ike wasn't comfortable with it, he'd had a bad experience in the '52 campaign, where the machine ran away from him, and he lost his place trying to read it. A few choice cuss words were heard over the air that day, and he never trusted it again, believe me."

Under Montgomery's professional coaching, Eisenhower was supplied with a professional makeup man; he was fitted with rimless glasses that would not reflect under the white lights; and Montgomery rehearsed the camera crews before air time so that the camera angles would show Eisenhower in the most flattering manner. "And it was all a big help," says Scherer. "It relaxed Ike and permitted him to be much more of a human being out there in front of the cameras. But that was all they tried to do. You have to be very careful what you do with the President, you know. You want him to be natural, and comfortable . . . but you can't make him something he isn't."

After Eisenhower had been in the White House for several years, he and his advisers decided that he was secure enough now to permit cameras to record his news conferences in their entirety. But the problem of the white-hot lights was still primary. No one, least of all the President, wished to be trapped beneath that blinding glare for any longer than was absolutely necessary. Luckily, Eastman Kodak had by now developed a new fast-speed film, Tri-X, which would do away with the need for such intense lighting. "At first a lot of the reporters, the pencil boys, resented us for filming the conferences," says Scherer. "They felt it would make actors out of reporters, and it would end up with a lot of them asking questions merely to be seen on TV that night. Well, it's possible some of the reporters did, but we television people predicted that if we all just ran true to form and didn't 'ham it up' for the cameras, this would be a useful innovation. And it was. For the first time, the people could see Eisenhower answering questions, a good thing for the voters, and for him a good political weapon. By 1956 Ike was secure enough with TV that he agreed to hold a *live* press conference in San Francisco, when he announced he would run again.

"By the time Kennedy arrived on the scene, he knew that TV was for him," says Scherer. "He ran the gauntlet with the 1960 Kennedy-Nixon debates, and came into the White House with Salinger as his press secretary. We immediately went to live TV coverage of his news conferences. Kennedy was completely comfortable with the medium—but not Lyndon Johnson. He tinkered with all sorts of formats, and I remember once he complained to me, 'You know, Ray, every time I go on TV, I lose money.'

"Nowadays," observes Scherer, who has been on the scene for a lot of history, "it's all very different down here in Washington. NBC has six or eight film crews employed every day, one assigned to the Senate, one to the House, one to the White House, one going over to Secretary Simon and the financial situation, another crew going around, maybe going to the Pentagon, or covering the CIA hearings, or following Vice-President Rockefeller. It's all become very competitive, with three networks covering the events that way, and then don't forget the independents, and the locals. Washington does seem to be

The Democratic Convention, 1948, Alben W. Barkley (Courtesy CBS)

where it's all happening. Why I remember one night recently, we had eight separate stories being picked up here from Washington by the network."

And yet it doesn't seem such a long time ago that Scherer and all the rest of those pioneer television correspondents were jogging around the landscape with their primitive early equipment, trying to capture a moment or two of our daily American history for televising to the home audience that would sit back that night, beercan in hand, casually taking in the brief, fifteen-minute précis of the day's happenings.

"Nobody will ever really know what we went through," says Scherer. "I can remember once, back in 1954. Mr. Eisenhower was on vacation in Colorado. Ike would leave Washington for as long as two months, an unheard-of thing these days, when President Ford has to scheme and plan to get away to Palm Springs for a day or so of golf. . . .

"We were covering Ike. I was there with a radio engineer, radio was my main responsibility, but we also had to do TV because that medium was coming along. We fed things in from wherever we were to John Cameron Swayze and *The Camel News Caravan* through the Denver affiliate, which was station KOA. We'd take the film down there, edit it, and we'd go on the air live when the program came through. 5:45 P.M. Denver time, 7:45 P.M. in the East.

"Well, Jim Haggerty told us one day that Herbert Hoover was coming out. He was a great fisherman, you know, and he and Ike were going to go fishing together. I called up New York and I said this would make a great picture— the only living Republican ex-President and the Republican President fishing together. They said splendid, we want that on the air. So it turned out that we were going to get our pictures by 2 P.M. Denver is at least two hours away from where we were, way up at a place in the mountains called Granby, near the Continental Divide. How were we going to get the film back from there in time? I called around and somebody told me there was a fellow up there with a plane, and if I'd pay him enough, he'd fly me down there. So I called the guy up and made a deal to meet him at a little postage-stamp airfield near Granby, and he'd fly me out of there at 2:30.

"They allowed us into the ranch at two, and we all went in and started making film. Hoover was dressed in a blue business suit, and Ike wore a western hat and Levi's; they'd caught some fish and they were frying them on some sort of a barbecue pit. There was a lot of smoke rising, and it wasn't much of a picture, but it was kind of symbolic, I guess, the top-level Republican reunion in the Rockies.

"My problem was to get the film and get it back and get it into the lab; there was only one film lab in Denver, and I was out to get there before CBS did, because I was afraid they could tie it up if they got there before I did, and then NBC would be scooped, so to speak. So my cameraman quickly shot 100 feet, and we edged over to the side of the crowd, very quietly, and he tore the magazine out of his camera and put it in a can and pressed it into my hand, and I raced out to my car and I went chugging off through the mountains.

"I finally found the airfield, and there was a guy waiting for me with a single-engine plane. I noticed that when we walked toward the plane he was swaying in a peculiar fashion, and I asked him was he all right, and he said, 'Oh, fine, I've got two artificial legs, you see!' Turned out he'd flown in World War II but then he'd cracked up. That didn't exactly fill me with assurance. . . . Anyway, we got into this little job and he warmed it up, and then we took off and headed up. To get to Denver you had to go over the Rockies. The prevailing winds were blowing like hell from east to west that day, and we were going west to east, and we got up to the Rockies, and the airplane couldn't get altitude, so we swung back and made another pass, and we still couldn't make it, and after the third try I yelled, 'Don't you think we ought to give up?' 'No, no!' he yelled. '*I'll get you over!*' The fourth time we finally got the altitude, and I was pretty undone, believe me, looking down and seeing all those sharp peaks with the snow so close below us. I don't know how we made it, but we finally did. We landed at a tiny airfield on the north side of Denver, and there was no way to get into Denver, no cars, no rentals, no nothing. Pretty primitive days, remember.

"Anyway, there was a guy there delivering milk in a truck. I told him I had some film I had to get into Denver, very high-priority stuff, would he take me into Denver? He seemed a little hesitant, but after I flashed some of NBC's green stuff under his nose, he agreed to take me in. So we roared into Denver in this milk truck. And when we got to the lab, the CBS guy was already there! They'd driven him in from Granby and gotten there five minutes ahead of me!

"Well, their film got out, and then the lab people pushed my film in, and by that time I think we were about twenty minutes away from air time for Swayze's show, so I jumped into a taxi and raced down to KOA, and handed them the film, and I said, 'Here it is—we've got to get this on!' We didn't have any time to look at the stuff, or edit it, we had no idea what the devil we had, so the guys just threaded it up for transmission, and in New York John Cameron Swayze was on the air, and he switched over to me—and just as he did so, the monitor in the studio, the one I'd be watching as I improvised my narration of the film, suddenly went crazy. Some technical fault, and all there was on it was venetian blinds! So there I was, doing an improvised narration to a piece of a film of Eisenhower and Herbert Hoover fishing —and I couldn't even *see* the film!

"Just as I finished—and I don't know how I did it—they flashed to me sitting in the Denver studio, and there I was. I was rather ragged-looking and frazzled at that point, I needed a shave, and I think I was wearing jeans and a red sport shirt . . . and back in New York Swayze made some crack about he was surprised at the informal getups reporters were wearing these days. He should have only known. . . .

"Well, the show was over, and I took a cab back to the airport and got into the plane, and we taxied out to the runway to fly up to the Rockies, back to where Ike was, and at the end of the runway, the engine sputtered and died. The pilot tried, and tried, and he couldn't get the damn thing to start again, and I said, 'Thank God!' And I went back to Denver, hired a car, and *drove* back. . . ."

All of that for a story that ran a scant forty-five seconds on the air that night and has been forgotten ever since.

"Sure." Scherer shrugs. "You'd do anything in those days to get your story on the air—and most of the time you had to do it all by yourself. Nowadays you travel around, you have a producer and you have a cameraman, you have a sound man, you have a light man, a crew, a truck—they call you up and say where you're supposed to go and pick up the story—you get there and everything's laid on. Quite a difference."

Scherer glances at his watch. He has spent the entire day downtown on his assignment, which is the coverage of the House of Representatives, he has come home, had his dinner, and then hurried back to NBC for a televised round-table news pickup following Speaker Carl Albert's statement on President Ford's tax message, then he has taped another three-minute segment on the same subject for the Late News, and now he is home . . . but it is only minutes away from 11 P.M. By reflex, he reaches out to snap on a small television set, one of three scattered throughout the house within easy reach. "Just want to see what's happening," he remarks.

Which, for a reporter who's been covering Washington for the past quarter century, is a very superfluous observation.

THE THREE
WEIRD SISTERS OF CBS

Frank Heller remembers:

At one time there were three live mystery shows running on CBS; they were referred to around the network as "The Weird Sisters." The first to go on was *Suspense,* which began in March, 1949, and it had a long and successful career with Bob Stevens as director-producer. The following year, CBS produced *Danger,* and before that one began, a third one was put on during the summer, called *The Web.*

The way that one came about was typical of those early days—convulsive and unplanned. I was directing *What's My Line?* for Mark Goodson and Bill Todman, who also had two other game shows on: *Winner Take All* and *Beat the Clock.* Mark and Bill wanted to get into the big time—to do drama, which in those days had much more status than their shows. I don't remember which one it was, Mark or Bill, who happened to be on the fourteenth floor at 485 Madison, where the CBS production department had executive offices, but it was one day when the sales department called up to inform the CBS production department that they'd have to deliver a summer replacement show for *Suspense.* Bob Stevens had insisted on taking an eight-week vacation, and in those days, since you didn't have reruns, you simply went off the air. The sales department went ahead and sold the eight weeks' worth of time to a sponsor, that's how they always did it, they'd tell a sponsor, "Sure,

Paul Newman and Grace Raynor, *The Web* (Courtesy NBC)

you can have a show there"—and then somebody would have to figure out how to deliver the show. That was the best thing about working in television in those days. You'd go in every morning and you never knew what was going to happen that day. Sometimes it was terrible, and sometimes it was marvelous.

Anyway, somebody up on the fourteenth floor looked out of his office and said to Mark or Bill, "Hey—do you want to do a dramatic show?"

Of course they wanted to. So they got together with Charlie Underhill, who was running the department, and he gave them the title *The Web*, and Goodson and Todman agreed on a budget—I think it was about $8,000 a week for everything—and that was that. A month from then, they had to be in production.

I came from the theater; I was one of the few people around them who hadn't gotten into television from radio—and they figured I must know something about scripts and production, so they called me in, and that's how I became the producer of *The Web*.

Four weeks to prepare, and a week to get the show cast and rehearsed and on the tube. In a few days I'd assembled a staff, with a story editor named Jack Turner, he and I would proceed to work around the clock, and we were ready for the air date, the Fourth of July.

I was staying in New York, not at home in Old Greenwich, three or four nights a week; I'd get home once in a while, but most of the time we were writing scripts and commissioning scripts and rewriting, and casting actors, and building scenery, and all the hundred and one things that had to take place, and nobody knew what the hell he or she was doing, but it was marvelous.

Well, we got to the opening show, it was called "The Twelfth Juror," from a story by Vincent Starett, and to show you how stupid a guy can be, I was producing *and* directing, and I proposed to do this every week for the summer, live—while still doing *What's My Line?* on Sunday nights as well!

We got through the first show, it came off pretty well; after we finished, I left the studio (we were upstairs in Grand Central in those new studios CBS had built) and I went down and got a local train to Old Greenwich. I finally got home, my wife was waiting up for me, we talked about the show, I had something to eat, then I came upstairs and took a shower. It was now about 1 A.M. I'd been going forty-eight hours straight, without going to bed, and I came back into our bedroom, and my wife was sitting up, reading. I went

Walter Hampden, James Dean, and Betsy Palmer, *Danger* (Courtesy NBC)

over to the bureau and took out clean underwear, put it on, then unbuttoned a clean shirt, put it on, then I went over to the closet, picked out a clean suit, and all the while, my wife was sitting there fascinated, watching me go through this, and when I put on the pants, she finally said, "Frank, what the hell are you doing?"

I suddenly realized that I'd been going day and night for so long that I had absolutely no sense of time—day and night didn't mean a thing to me! Next day I went in to see Charlie Underhill and I explained what had happened, and we agreed from then on I'd have an alternate director. After the show went on for a year, I gave up directing and stayed as the producer, but ever since, whenever I've met Charlie Underhill, he always asks, "Are you putting on your pajamas when you get to bed, Frank?"

Elinor Kilgallen, who was Dorothy's sister, was then an actors' agent at MCA. I thought and still think she is the absolute genius of casting. She'd read our scripts as they came out of the mimeo, and send us prospects for different parts. She called up one day and told me she had a young man she was sending over, he'd never had a job in television, but he'd had a few small parts around town, she'd caught him in some studio workshop production. I mustn't be bothered by the fact that he was a bit strange, he was perfect for a part in the script she'd just read.

The boy came over, and I thought he was just that: rude, and badly dressed, and something of a mess, and I didn't want to take him. Elinor said to me, "Frank, I'll never recommend a good person to you again if you don't take this boy, because he's going to be a big star!"

I gave him the job; he was very difficult to work with, but he did the show, and eventually we got to be friends. Later, when I produced another half-hour mystery called *Danger*, I used him again. But between jobs, the kid was poor, very poor, and he needed all the help he could get, so I got him a job on *Beat the Clock*—another Goodson-Todman show—as a sort of stand-in, a helper.

On that show, Bud Collyer would put the contestants through all sorts of strange stunts, racing against the clock. We had two writers, Frank Wayne and Bob Howard, who lived in Teaneck, New Jersey, where they'd spend their time thinking up stunts and practicing them out in the garage. Then they'd bring them to New York and they'd go down to the cellar of Lieder-kranz Hall, which was now CBS studios, and they'd bring in a bunch of actors, and they'd have boxes, balls, bats, and all sorts of props that they needed for the stunts, and then they'd try it all out on real people, to make sure the stunts would work on the show. Some worked, others would be impossible, or perhaps even too easy, and that's how they'd schedule the show.

Then, with the stunts for each week, we'd go to the theater studio, and we'd do three run-throughs of the stunts, on cameras, for the technicians. But we didn't use contestants, we used professional actors to substitute for the contestants—all members of the union, who were paid a fee, five dollars an hour. Actors who wouldn't show off, but would try to be exactly like ordinary contestants, trying to react as if we'd just brought them up from the audience to be on the show.

I knew that young kid needed money, so we had him on. But we simply couldn't keep him at that kind of work—he was the best-coordinated human being I have ever seen! There was no trick or stunt that we did on *Beat the Clock* that he couldn't accomplish with the greatest of ease; we had balancing stunts and all that jazz—nothing he couldn't do. He had absolute unerring control over his body.

Grace Kelly, *Suspense* (Courtesy NBC)

He certainly wasn't anything like a typical contestant. He was more like himself, James Dean. *Actor.* . . . Very soon after that, he was out of our orbit, and into his own, proving that Elinor Kilgallen really has the talent for discovering them.

It was terrific training for the actors, too. I was rummaging through my card files the other day; I kept a file on all the actors we used on *The Web* and *Danger,* and I turned up one on Jack Lemmon. He worked for me twice. I sent him his card; he got $200 the first time, and $250 the second.

But he was only one of the stars that were being spawned in those days. There was a young girl named Grace Kelly who worked for us, another young chap named Paul Newman, there was Charlton Heston, and a tall kid named Lee Marvin. And it wasn't only the fact that they could get jobs as actors—it was the *range* of parts they got to play. Take E. G. Marshall, for example. I had him playing Inspector Maigret, in Simenon's detective stories. He was a young character man who'd only had a very small opportunity to do anything on Broadway. But when television came along, everything opened up for him. I once made a list of all the different things he did back then. In one year it ranged all the way from an hour-long production of *Macbeth* to *Mama*, on which he had a regular character. *Thirty* different parts in one year, each one completely different.

And when you remember how difficult it was to do *one* show—rehearsals for three days, then we'd get into that little studio up at Grand Central, about eight in the morning, the crew had been working all night setting up our scenery; we'd start with full facilities about one in the afternoon, turn on the cameras, and then we had five hours to stage the whole show with the actors. Dinner break, then we'd go across to a restaurant, have a drink, and pray a little. Back to the studio, and at 9:30 we'd go on the air.

After a thirteen- or fourteen-hour day, you were called upon to give your best in the last half hour.

What training!

NBC SPECTACULARS

Henry Jaffe remembers:

Very few people get to be old in this business. I'll be seventy in a year and a half, and I am probably the oldest active person in any capacity around television—at least, the oldest I know about.

[At the time Mr. Jaffe interrupted his busy schedule to indulge himself in these reminiscences, he was the executive producer of Dinah Shore's highly successful five-times-a-week CBS show *Dinah!* In the past twenty years, he has also been involved in numerous other television ventures: Miss Shore's weekly hour for Chevrolet, *The Bell Telephone Hour,* and the prestigious *Producer's Showcase.*]

The whole idea of the "spectacular" was a very bold concept that originated with Sylvester ("Pat") Weaver. Pat was head of programming at NBC in the early 1950s, and in the years that he ran the network he was a terrific innovator. You only have to think back on the names of the shows Pat conceived—*The Today Show, The Tonight Show, Home,* and, on radio, *Monitor,* to understand how large his contribution was, and still is, in shaping television's structure.

My friend Leland Hayward, the theatrical producer, had put on the "Ford Fiftieth Anniversary Show" in 1953, which ran on both networks for two hours and was a terrific success. People still talk about it. Leland was fasci-

Mary Martin, Leland Hayward, and Ethel Merman, "Ford Fiftieth Anniversary Show,"
June 15, 1953 (Courtesy NBC)

nated with television's possibilities; there was a huge audience out there that
hadn't yet been reached, and he was full of bold ideas for getting entertainment to them. It was only natural that he and Weaver would get together
and discuss the problem; since I was Leland's lawyer, I became involved in
these very exciting discussions.

Weaver was not only a visionary, but a dynamic salesman, at times almost
evangelical in his fervor; he was capable of enrapturing even the most cynical
audience with broad verbal vistas of the future. When he spoke to the NBC
station affiliates, in Chicago, in 1953, he gave them a hint of what was to
come. "If we allow television to degenerate into a living-room toy," he
warned, "when it should be the shining center of the home, then we deserve
the worst from our fellow-citizens. For if we keep this great service vital, if we
make our programming serve all elements of our population, if we use entertainment to keep everyone watching, and use showmanship combined with
scholarship to make that viewing have a positive influence through the inclu-

sion of cultural and informational and enriching, enlightening material, then we, as much as any group of men in all the world, will affect the fate of the future. Television, by itself, can influence the world for good beyond all present thinking."

For once, these were not merely overblown paragraphs of jazzed-up hyperbole. Weaver was even then developing another one of his concepts that was to be as bold as his promise. *Wide, Wide World*—a show which roamed all over the United States and did live "pickups" everywhere. But you must remember that, at that time, NBC was hungry for programming ideas that would not only enlighten, educate, et cetera, but also sell some color television sets for its parent company, RCA.

So Pat proposed an idea for shows that would be special, completely different from regular network programming. I remember him saying to us, "We ought to do something which is now considered absolutely impossible—which is to interrupt the regular schedule. People see the same thing day in and day out. We've got to put some spark into the medium—it reminds me of a monolithic society." Then Pat tapped his forehead and said, "Nothing happens up *here*."

He outlined his plan, which was to get the greatest stars in show business to perform in shows done by name directors and producers. He talked about Bogart and Audrey Hepburn, Mary Martin, Alfred Lunt and Lynn Fontanne, and all sorts of other legendary names. I asked him what sort of a budget he had in mind, and he said, "I know General Sarnoff won't like this, but I'm telling you that I'm not going to let money stand in the way. We'll fix a budget, but we'll also do whatever is necessary to get these shows on with the best possible talent."

You can imagine what an exciting prospect that was. Remember, in those days, everyone was fond of looking down on television. Picture producers would say, "Television? That's a business for amateurs. It's nothing—it's like a public school presentation for graduation day." Pat figured that with a man like Leland running such a project, with his tremendous reputation, he'd bring into television all the talented people that they needed. Big names didn't want to risk themselves in such dubious ventures as television shows. A play could have a long run, movies would be shown all over, and in those mediums there was always the element of control. But in live television shows there wasn't much protection against possible disaster—actors were happy to avoid running that gauntlet.

Mary Martin spoofing dress designs on the "Ford Fiftieth Anniversary Show" (Courtesy NBC)

Eventually there was a meeting arranged with the Ford Motor Company, and it agreed to put up half the cost for these spectaculars—and the contract was a spectacular one, as well. The company would pay for thirteen shows, one each four weeks, right on through the summer. The other half of the cost came from RCA, which figured that since the shows would be in color, they would boost color sales.

Our first show was *Tonight at 8:30*, by Noel Coward, which starred Ginger Rogers. [The very first of Weaver's "spectaculars" was a widely promoted original musical comedy called *Satins and Spurs*, which starred Hollywood's Betty Hutton, and was given a lavish production in the NBC Brooklyn studios under the aegis of Max Liebman, then the successful producer of the

Mary Martin, *Peter Pan* (Courtesy NBC)

Sid Caesar–Imogene Coca *Your Show of Shows*. All the elements were there for success, but, like a balky soufflé, the show refused to rise to the occasion.] Leland was not only involved in the production of *Tonight at 8:30* for television, but he'd also gotten his film of *Mister Roberts* started out in the Pacific, with John Ford directing Henry Fonda and James Cagney and Jack Lemmon. (The film was eventually completed by Mervyn LeRoy.) Obviously, all the pressure involved in his various projects had gotten to Leland, because he developed very serious stomach trouble, and eventually he had to bow out of producing all the rest of the shows. Remember, we had that implacable schedule—one big spectacular each and every four weeks. A very large assignment.

Dinah Shore on her show (Courtesy NBC)

So it was up to me to fill in for him—somebody had to do it, and I'd been in on all the original planning. I knew I needed all the help I could get; I went and talked with Fred Coe, the producer, and Delbert Mann, the director, and they agreed to pitch in and prepare some shows, and I got in touch with Jerome Robbins and asked him if he'd do a show or two for us. Robbins said he didn't want to do television, but that if we'd do *Peter Pan* with Mary Martin re-creating her part as she'd done on the stage, he'd be involved.

We'd discussed doing *Peter Pan* before—in fact, we'd wanted it for our kick-off show, but there were tremendous costs involved, Mary Martin was still touring in it, there were royalties to pay to the Sir James M. Barrie estate in England. We finally solved all those problems, and *Peter Pan* went on, and I don't have to tell you what was the audience reaction. Probably the most fabulously successful television show that's ever been done; it got more news-paper attention than the invasion of Poland. The audience adored it. It's been televised since then a half-dozen times—but later on, it had to be produced all over again, because in those days, alas, we had no tape. Only kinescopes.

Which is sad, because we have no really decent records of all those marvelous shows we did on NBC—a lot of which were truly what Pat had wanted them to be: spectacular.

To give you a few examples: we brought in Humphrey Bogart and Lauren Bacall and Henry Fonda to play Robert Sherwood's *The Petrified Forest*. The Hollywood people were furious with Bogie for appearing on TV; they were afraid that if he was on the screen for free, people would stop paying to see his pictures. But Bogie was sentimental about that play, he'd made his first hit on Broadway playing Duke Mantee, the gangster, and it tickled him to be able to re-create the part all those years later on television. Also, very profitable for him; we paid him $50,000 for the show, which was in those days an unheard-of fee. Even now, it's damned good.

Then we did a lot of other very distinguished productions of plays—Sidney Kingsley's *Darkness at Noon*, with Lee J. Cobb and David Wayne. *State of the Union*, by Lindsay and Crouse, in which we starred Margaret Sullavan and Joe Cotten, *Dodsworth* by Sidney Howard, with Fredric March and Florence Eldridge, we did Shaw's *Caesar and Cleopatra*, with Claire Bloom, Jack Hawkins, Sir Cedric Hardwicke and Dame Judith Anderson. We were the first show that was ever able to lure the great Katharine Cornell into tele-

Jack Klugman, Richard Jaeckel, and Humphrey Bogart in *The Petrified Forest*, 1955; this was Bogart's only TV appearance (Courtesy NBC)

Fredric March and Claire Trevor, *Dodsworth* (Courtesy NBC)

Paul Newman, Eva Marie Saint, and Frank Sinatra rehearsing for *Our Town* (Courtesy NBC)

vision, when we got her to do *The Barretts of Wimpole Street*. And then we had the Lunts doing *The Great Sebastians*. Can you imagine what a treat it would be for the future if we had taped versions of all those great performances?

We also did musicals. One was a musical version of *Our Town*, with Frank Sinatra as the Stage Manager, singing a score by Sammy Cahn and Jimmy Van Heusen—one of their songs turned out to be a big hit: "Love and Marriage." Eva Marie Saint played the young girl, Emily, but we didn't

Sir Laurence Olivier, *The Moon and Sixpence* (Courtesy NBC)

have a young male lead. We must have interviewed a hundred possibles, and one of them was a young kid out of the Yale Drama School who came up and auditioned by playing the guitar and singing. We hired him, although I must say, Paul Newman turned out to be a better actor by far than he was a singer.

There wasn't a single day—or even an hour—that went by in producing those shows that didn't produce some sort of a crisis. You never knew where the next one would crop up. Don't forget, we weren't only doing plays, but we

Sir Laurence Olivier and Hume Cronyn, *The Moon and Sixpence* (Courtesy NBC)

were producing full-scale revivals of Broadway musicals, such complex projects as *One Touch of Venus, Bloomer Girl,* Sir Laurence Olivier in Somerset Maugham's *The Moon and Sixpence,* and even originals, such as *Heidi.*

All in all, *Producer's Showcase* was a hell of a series of shows, and if it does remain on the history books as a monument to the arts of that time, then the credit really belongs to Weaver. He had the guts to do it at the beginning, and then to keep it on.

But remember, those were very different days. A producer on that show had the ability to experiment, and there were no molds or forms—the world was your objective, you were tied by no tradition, you could explore. With a guy like Pat behind you who would say, "Go ahead—do whatever you want," you had terrific latitude. The only circumscription you had was "*Can* we get it on the tube?"

Nowadays, the question is only "If we get it on the tube, who'll watch it?"

"AND NOW, LIVE FROM NEW YORK..."
PHILCO PLAYHOUSE

It's not often that lawyers can be accused of creativity. But a whole generation of contemporary playwrights and directors owe certain attorneys a lot more than legal fees. One might even suggest that they owe them their existence.

Witness the early history of the *Philco Television Playhouse*, which debuted on NBC in October, 1948. In the seven years of its existence, that hour-long show was to become a spectacularly successful training school for playwrights, a nursery of talent. But had it not been for the phalanx of implacable lawyers for film companies who sought to kill off the show at birth, Philco might never have been forced to seek out original material. And as a result, who is to say that such authors as Paddy Chayefsky, Tad Mosel, Horton Foote, Robert Alan Aurthur, Arnold Shulman, Sumner Locke Elliott, Gore Vidal, and many others (yours truly included) would ever have been given a chance to try writing for the new medium?

Philco-Goodyear (the program acquired its second sponsor in 1951) was scheduled to debut in that fall of 1948, and in its first conceptual stages nothing but tried-and-true material was ever contemplated. In order to reach an audience, NBC and Philco planned to put on a weekly show that would specialize in hour-long versions of hit Broadway plays, adapted for TV.

But before the fledgling program ever got off the ground, its format was riddled with a barrage of legal flak, fired by high-priced legal representatives of major film companies with an intent to destroy. Messrs. Mayer, Warner,

Cohn, Zanuck, et al. had no intention of tolerating TV as competition—their hearts were in the box office, not on a home (and free) TV screen.

Their lethal weapon was the definition of the word *film*.

In those primitive days, before ATT developed its coaxial cable that would link TV stations from east to far-off west, the networks were forced to transmit their weekly programs to affiliated stations across the land by means of filmed kinescope: i.e., photos of the show, taken directly off the cathode tube.

Film is film! thundered the film company lawyers. Whether it be a 35 mm. theatrical print, or even a blurred 16 mm. kinescope! *Our* clients own the film rights to these plays you are planning to televise, they insisted, and ergo, you upstarts at NBC and CBS may not, repeat, not transmit them anywhere on film kinescope, on pain of injunction and/or lawsuit.

It was truly a scene out of some nineteenth-century melodrama, but the game was deadly serious. Instead of attempting to foreclose a mortgage, these lawyers were bent on foreclosing a medium, before it became a threat.

Luckily for us, that high-priced corporate legal talent managed to hold back the NBC and Philco concept, at least for a while. Later on, they were inundated. But in 1948 they prevailed. "We were all set up to go on the air," recalls Fred Coe, who was then, at twenty-nine, a youthful producer-director who had decided to seek his fame and fortune in television, "and then we found out that we couldn't get the properties that we were supposed to produce. Say we wanted to do *Dinner at Eight* by George Kaufman and Edna Ferber. The playwrights were happy to let us do it, but MGM wouldn't allow it. Oh, sure, they'd let it be shown as a live production here in the New York studio—but what good was that if it couldn't be sent out and shown on kinescope to the nine other NBC stations?"

Faced with such a formidable roadblock, fainter hearts might have thrown in the towel and gone on to find an easier way to earn a living—by developing, say, a game show or a family-type situation comedy. Not so Coe and the NBC pioneers. In those early, improvisational days, when network hierarchies were loose, if not nonexistent, experiment was the order of the day. Coe had come to TV via the Yale Drama School, where he had been exposed to a considerable amount of classic drama, and he was young enough to be unafraid. "We decided to go ahead and try to do the show anyway," he says.

Which was fortunate indeed. Over the years that followed, Coe and other producers would steer clear of established playwrights and develop their own.

Those motion picture lawyers would prove to be so many grains of sand, responsible for a multitude of future pearls, on Coe's seedbed.

"That first year we did a lot of shows that we *could* do," he says. "*Cyrano*, with José Ferrer, a few plays that were available because they hadn't been tied up by films—*The Story of Mary Surratt*, for instance—and a couple of Shakespearian dramas. By the end of that first year, I had directed thirty-nine shows. One a week. I was a basket-case, a vegetable; I figured that was enough. I went off on a holiday and came back and took a job in management at NBC, where it was more relaxed."

Meanwhile, two young agents, Al Levy and David Susskind, had formed a packaging firm called Talent Associates, and had sold Philco and NBC on a different concept—a sort of televised book club, whereby each week they proposed to produce a dramatized version of a current published novel.

"A disastrous idea," says Coe. "Nobody knew how to take a novel and cut it down to fit an hour format. The writers were struggling to do it, and things were a complete mess. So I came back—I found I didn't much care for working in management anyway—and I took over the *Philco* production. The first thing I got were the rights to F. Scott Fitzgerald's *The Rich Boy*, and I started off with an adaptation of that. I figured in an hour show we could handle short stories and novellas, and thank heaven, I was right. Then I started to look around for writers who could not only adapt other people's work, but who maybe might come in with some original ideas for plays of their own."

Not only was he on the hunt for authors, but young Coe would shortly bring together a cadre of directors who would later go on to make their reputations in television. Permanent staff members who alternated on the weekly show would include Gordon Duff, Delbert Mann, the late Vincent Donehue, and Arthur Penn.

"Gradually," says Coe, "we just moved away from the novels—even though, in all those years that the show was on the air, we always started the program with a book as the title background."

Away from published and produced works and into the uncharted waters of original hour-long plays.

To find promising authors, to sit with them and induce from their typewriters an original three-act drama, or mystery, or comedy, to assemble a good cast for the untried play and to manage to get it produced and on the air once each seven days—it was certainly an exhausting task, chancy and fraught with unknown peril. But those who worked with Coe out of his suite of offices at NBC and in the eighth-floor studios are agreed that the young southern gent more than rose to the occasion.

"I've never known an editor in the book world like Fred, I've never had another producer as good," says Sumner Locke Elliott, who was to become one of the *Philco-Goodyear* "regulars." "Not that we always had good shows; far from it. For every one that people still remember after all these years, we'd have three that were mediocre, and some could be quite bad. But you'd come into his office with a story idea, Fred would read it carefully, then nod and say, 'There's problems, pappy, but they're healthy problems.' And he'd proceed to give you a very clear idea of what was wrong; somehow he always managed to put his finger on exactly the things that needed to be done. Then, when you'd written it, he'd tell you where you'd gone wrong; sometimes it meant a complete rewrite, but you did it because you knew he was right."

On such a treadmill schedule, multiple production was necessary. Three such plays would be constantly overlapping: one in preparation, one show in rehearsal, and a third on the studio floor ready for the actual telecasting. Coe would shuttle among all three groups, listening, watching, and then offering suggestions. "Not that everything always went smoothly," says Locke Elliott. "We had our share of on-the-air disasters. I remember one show with Kim Hunter. It was all done in flashback, and the story began with an automobile accident in which she and the leading man were killed, we shot it in a mock-up of a car, and somebody up in the control booth gave the order to release the two actors so that they could get to their next scene too soon—the camera was still on them—and there, in front of the whole audience all over America the two 'dead' people got up and walked away from the accident! And another time on a show, somehow the tempo of the performance slowed down—that was another thing you could never control on a live show. This time I think it was Kim Stanley who was our star, and it was getting along to the climactic scene when a door was supposed to open and a nun was to enter. Fred was up in the booth, we could tell the show was going to run overtime, and so he ordered the floor manager to tell the actors we would eliminate a scene down toward the end and cut directly to the nun. Two minutes before the end, and somebody up there goofed and left the mike from the booth to the floor open, and Fred was heard all over America saying, 'Get the nun on—get the nun on ... *get the damn nun on!*' "

Throughout those early years, the authors who gravitated into Coe's orbit began to develop into full-fledged dramatists. "Part of the success of the show was the involvement of the writer," said the late Gordon Duff, who directed many of the productions. "Which was absent on other shows. There writers would turn in a script and that was that. Not on *Philco*. Once the script was in, we kept the writer around to help cast the show, he'd sit in with us on the meetings with the set designer, and we always wanted him around during rehearsals, so that he could make the necessary changes. There was a lot of give-and-take around the office—and it was healthy. Always creative."

"We all liked each other's work," adds Locke Elliott. "We learned from each other. We weren't competing: if Tad Mosel did a good script, we all felt good for the show; if Horton Foote had a show on next week, everyone watched it. And when Paddy Chayefsky starting writing his plays, he taught me a great deal about simplicity."

"I usually kept some material I liked tucked away on an office shelf," recalls Coe, "maybe a little story or something I'd read which I thought might make a good show, that I could hand to a writer and ask him if he'd try an adaptation. That's how it began with Paddy Chayefsky. He came into my office one day and said he wanted to do something on the show. I gave him a little story from the *Reader's Digest* and he took it away and turned it into his first show, which was called *Holiday Song*."

Holiday Song dealt with the character of a Jewish cantor who had temporarily lost his faith in God, and the effect of his loss of faith on his congregation. "They didn't want to let Fred do such a story," remembers Chayefsky. "That's all Fred needed to hear. If you ever told Fred you couldn't do something, you could be sure he'd go right ahead. Fred was the core character of that era, the linchpin. Oh, sure, there were other producers, but none of them came up to Fred. After he quit *Philco-Goodyear*, there was a big void; they were never able to replace him with anybody as good."

Chayefsky was then a struggling playwright, a young hopeful who was hoping to find an outlet for his talents somewhere in the theater. He had managed to pick up a few assignments on half-hour shows, such as *Manhunt* and *Danger*, but with little success. "On those shows you wrote a script and turned it in, they didn't even bother to let you know when it was televised," he remembers. "Once I got started with Coe, I found myself a home. One night I saw a show written by Horton Foote that was done on *Philco*: *A Trip to*

Joseph Buloff in *Holiday Song*, by Paddy Chayefsky, on *Philco Playhouse* (Courtesy NBC)

Bountiful, a lovely simple play laid in the South, and it hit me right away. I thought to myself, 'Boy, that's how to do television'—and after that first script for Coe, I started trying to do stories of my own."

The financial rewards were far from overwhelming. Chayefsky's first fee was $900, and nine original plays later he had moved up to an enormous $3,000. "It certainly wasn't the money," he says. "The rewards were much more satisfactory than that. You could get an idea and write it, and a couple of weeks later, you could see it being performed. Tremendous satisfaction. In those days, practically anything made a story—it was a kind of miniature work that was required, the equivalent of a short story. You could take any impulse and make a show of it. Original writing—with your own characters, your own motivations."

In the space of one year, Chayefsky turned out nine scripts, among which were such first-class works as *The Bachelor Party, Printers' Measure,* and *The Catered Affair.*

"I just became engrossed with the possibilities and the techniques of television," he explains. "At that time, television was a great medium for all of us who were working on those shows. Look at the breed of writers that era produced—Bob Aurthur, J. P. Miller, David Shaw, Reggie Rose. To this day, every one of them can sit down and deliver a worthwhile piece of original work on demand."

("It was the only medium I've ever encountered where you could earn a living by working on scripts and at the same time learn how to write," remarks Rose, another major playwright-author who emerged from those early live years [*Twelve Angry Men, Dino, The Remarkable Incident at Carson Corners, The Defenders,* et al.]. "I was being handed script-writing jobs over at CBS, on *Studio One,* while I still held on to a daytime job writing copy at an advertising agency. Eventually I had made enough of an impact to give up my day job and go into writing full-time—but in the meantime, I'd been gifted with a chance to learn my craft.")

Shortly afterward, Chayefsky produced a modest drama about a young unmarried butcher whose mother insisted that he should find a wife. *Marty,* which told of his meeting a simple, plain girl at a dance, and of their eventual romance, has long since been documented as perhaps the most outstanding example of the original dramas that Coe and *Philco-Goodyear* produced. Produced in 1953, it was subsequently filmed with Ernest Borgnine and Betsy Blair, and won for its author an Academy Award.

When the play was first produced on a Sunday night, with Rod Steiger and Nancy Marchand, however, no one around the NBC studios was aware that some sort of a minor masterpiece had been created and produced by Coe and his director, Delbert Mann, as part of a regular weekly schedule. "Ten minutes after the show was finished, the studio was empty, they were taking down the sets, and everybody had gone home," muses Chayefsky. "The big surprise was that Jack Gould gave it a full review in *The New York Times* the next day. Nothing terrific, but almost reluctant, it wasn't an earthshaking review, but he gave his entire column to it. *That* was earthshaking. You see, in those days, television plays didn't get that much attention. Maybe a paragraph or a line from some critic, that was all. But then we began to get terrific mail. I can't remember how many letters, but that doesn't matter. What matters is they *wrote.*"

What the stocky, cheerful playwright is referring to is the hypersensitivity of network executives to mail, any sort of written communication from the audience. Since viewers rarely bother to take the trouble to express a written opinion, letters from Out There carry extra weight. Good, bad, literate or not, attention is paid to the mail.

"I guess," Chayefsky concedes modestly, "that *Marty* hit a nerve."

Of his original teleplays, several others went on to be the basis for films: *The Bachelor Party* and *The Catered Affair*. Soon, the Hollywood factories would be picking up properties from television quite regularly. *The Rabbit Trap*, by J. P. Miller, and *Edge of the City*, by Robert Alan Aurthur, were filmed. Producers out west would begin to hire television playwrights to work on adaptations; why not? Each week the home screen was a convenient audition hall for new talent. Those same motion picture lawyers who had thrown up roadblocks against television drama were now busily engaged in drawing up contracts to hire its discoveries.

Chayefsky's teleplay *Middle of the Night* was produced on Broadway and launched his career as a playwright. Later, he and Coe teamed up to present *The Tenth Man*, with Coe as the director of Chayefsky's original script. Chayefsky has also written many successful screenplays since then, *The Goddess* and *The Americanization of Emily* among them, but he is staunch in his insistence that his *Philco-Goodyear* experience was a seminal one.

"Right at that time, it was a writer's medium," he says. "Think of all the shows that were being done in New York—*Philco, Studio One, Kraft Television Theater, Robert Montgomery Presents, The U.S. Steel Hour*—all those other weekly half-hour shows, perfect for writers. If you could come in at the right time and do something that caught on, it was the beginning of a career."

Discovery was not the exclusive province of *Philco-Goodyear*. On *Kraft* an unknown playwright named Rod Serling wrote *Patterns*, a very dramatic play that dealt with the shifting of power amid the corporate boardrooms and offices of a large American company. Shortly afterward, Serling's original became the basis for a film and started his career. On *U.S. Steel*, James Costigan wrote *A Wind from the South*, and later the memorable *Little Moon of Alban*, for *Hallmark Hall of Fame*. And Rose's *Twelve Angry Men*, done on *Studio One*, has become a classic film—all of which serves to document Chayefsky's insistence that those were better days for creative minds.

"Sure, we were stuck with every possible technical difficulty," he agrees. "None of the Hollywood efficiency. We were doing those shows out of old

Sidney Poitier and Delbert Mann rehearsing for *Philco Playhouse* (Courtesy NBC)

radio studios that had been rebuilt, with ceilings about nine feet high, no place to put the lights, nothing elaborate in the way of scenery. But when you were stuck with those restrictions, the writing *had* to be better. You had to accommodate the difficulties. Go out to Hollywood, and they hand you everything in the world—except the need to do any imaginative work.

"You see, in those days, it was so much more simple. Everything I did at *Philco* was on a handshake. A visit to Fred—Fred said, 'Sounds good to me, pappy, go ahead'—and I knew I had a deal. I never thought about a contract. Maybe they came in later, I guess they must have, but it wasn't so important.

I knew I'd be paid, and I was busy writing. Sometimes we had to work under terrific pressure. Once I did a script in *three days*—something else had dropped out, and I stayed up for three days and three nights, wrote and rewrote through rehearsals, and right up to the day we were shooting. Great experience. Any writer that doesn't go through that is missing something." He smiles. "But I wouldn't go through *that* one again.

"Today, what a difference. I wrote an original script for my film *The Hospital*. Took me eleven months to write it. When we set up the movie deal, the lawyers took *twelve* months to get all the contracts written!

"Oh, I realize how much money is involved today," Chayefsky sighs, "and how vast the audience shows are playing to has become. But back in those days, we had so much more latitude. If you had an idea for a story, it didn't have to be a blockbuster. The way it has become today, you can't deal in small stories about people. And I must say, I think that sort of portraiture is the best thing you can do for the TV screen. Movies need much broader scope—but as far as I'm concerned, on the home screen you work best on a small canvas. You create character, and that becomes your plot." Chayefsky shakes his head sadly. "Nowadays there's no opportunity for a writer to do small dramas and reach the audience with something intimate. Sometimes I think you can often get closer to reality on a network situation comedy, like *All in the Family*, where Archie Bunker and his family are actually dealing in truthful attitudes, than you can in what passes for television drama."

Chayefsky's gloomy assessment of the scene is unfortunately true. These days there is little drama available on the commercial networks. Not that the audience for it isn't there; public TV channels carry London Weekend Television's *Upstairs, Downstairs*, and it attracts large and faithful numbers of viewers. (R.I.P. *Beacon Hill.*) But on NBC and CBS and ABC, apart from the numerous daily half-hour "serials," and an occasional afternoon "playbreak," what passes for drama is churned out by the film foot in West Coast factories. There is absolutely no home for the so-called anthology show: unconnected, individual plays. If you want to write a drama, it will have to involve a family such as the Waltons; a melodrama or a mystery revolves around a detective or a cop, or a lawyer, Mannix, Kojak, or Petrocelli.

And two decades after the fact, it has become almost fashionable to deprecate those early, often awkward attempts at hour-long drama on *Philco-Goodyear*, and all the other contemporary shows of that long-gone period. Critics are willing, almost eager, to pounce on "live" and to maintain that its golden content glitters only in the fond memories of those who thrived in the era.

"Certainly we did our share of lemons," concedes Fred Coe today. "All the producers and writers of that period did. Hell, there was always that weekly schedule to meet, an original that had to be produced, sometimes out of a hat, and boy, did we all do some bad ones. But if you're not ready to make a big mistake once in a while—if you want to play it safe—then your show's never going to be really good."

Perhaps the major difference between that period of the 1950s and now lies in the measure of control. Sponsors were not telling producers what play to put on, and networks were not as yet so tightly structured. "Good or bad, it was *our* responsibility," says Coe. "Sure, they could tell you that you mustn't do a show about abortion, or something like that, but they couldn't control the show once the subject matter had been chosen, because we were running things . . . *we*, the producers, the directors and the writers."

"It was like having the ship steered for you," says Sumner Locke Elliott. "Fred kept everybody off the bridge. We were guarded from interference. If anybody came from the sponsor or the agency, they were allowed to go to a small viewing room and watch the rehearsal of the actual show, and then Fred would go in and speak to them for a minute or so, but if one of them set foot on his set, there would be an explosion. Fred had a sixth sense about intruders; he could see them through the back of his head, and he'd start yelling.

"And if something went wrong, he took the rap. If the show was bad, and believe me, when it was bad, you knew it, Fred would say, 'Well, next time we've got to come up with something better, that's all. Got any ideas, pappy?' "

Philco-Goodyear Playhouse was not only a remarkable showcase for the talents of the creative crew behind the camera—Arthur Penn went on to direct *Bonnie and Clyde,* Vincent Donehue to do the Broadway musical *The Sound of Music,* and Delbert Mann to direct such film hits as *Pillow Talk*— but it was also a marvelous academy for the actors. "For a while there, we were something like the theatrical stock companies of the early part of this century: a sort of place where actors could learn by playing all sorts of different parts. There was all sorts of marvelous talent around New York, and Bill Nichols, our casting director, would bring them in, we could start them in small parts and work them up to bigger ones. Steve McQueen was a young kid hanging around waiting for a break—we put him to work. Joanne Woodward had her first chance in a *Philco* show called *The Champ*. Rod Steiger, Eva Marie Saint, Grace Kelly, Kim Stanley, Jack Klugman—all of them worked for us. In those days, Walter Matthau was gambling a lot, and at that time he'd try to get on every *Philco*—just so he could pick up betting money," says Coe, chuckling.

"I don't agree with the critics of that period," says Chayefsky. "I've got kinescopes of my old plays, and I took them out lately and ran them. I think they held up pretty well. Sure—over the years they've begun to call it 'ashcan drama,' 'kitchen drama.' Not at all. What we did was to dramatize the lives of those people out there in the audience, and we contributed what any artist is supposed to contribute, some sort of understanding. It's the job of the artist to let his audience have some insight into its otherwise meaningless pattern of life. They say my stuff was sentimental. Not so. There's nothing sentimental about shows like *Marty* and *The Catered Affair*. They're relentlessly unsentimental.

"You take the works of all my contemporaries—Bob Aurthur, *A Man Is Ten Feet Tall*; Tad Mosel, *The Out-of-Towners*—all of us then were writing about our audience, and saying to the people, 'This is your life, this is what's going on, and this is one shred of understanding about that life.' That's why that drama was important and significant—and why it produced a crop of such first-rate writers."

A collection of talented authors, and a pride of directors, most, if not all, of whom were to abandon the medium that gave them their first opportunities. For the ultimate irony of those early television years is that today, all the gifted creators spawned in makeshift TV studios all over New York find little opportunity to produce anything for the now-huge audience.

Is it because they have departed the business—or has it evicted them?

"Me, I'd rather get back into television than anything I know," says Chayefsky today.

Then what is it that stands in the path of his return?

He shrugs. "They come to me, they come to all of us old-timers, but what they want from us is some sort of a huge blockbuster of an idea, or one of those prestigious adaptations of something—a show like *Long Day's Journey into Night*—on which they'll probably lose money and not get a high rating, but which will give them a lot of prestige in the public image, and do something for their own self-esteem. But if you try to do one of those things, the pressure on you is worse than on any opening night on Broadway. They do *not* come and say, 'Write us a show.' They don't want an original play for the medium, and that's what we were all doing back then. That was an era when writers could be writers."

And as for Coe himself, the cheerful young man who could set up and maintain that incredible weekly schedule twenty years back, who could produce a procession of hour-long originals for *Philco-Goodyear*, while at the same time supervising the production of *Mr. Peepers*, his has been a long and successful career since then. He went on to produce *Playwrights '56*, and numerous prestigious TV specials, and on Broadway he brought forth not only Chayefsky's *The Tenth Man* but Herb Gardner's *A Thousand Clowns*. The Broadway success *A Gift of Love*, with Rex Harrison and Julie Harris, was staged by him.

But as for television?

Coe shakes his head. "No, I'm afraid not," he says, with a slight trace of wistfulness. "You work on a TV special now and try to put it all together and you can work for a year and a half. Too long. I haven't the patience. And I can't adjust to the process. Today, my God, it's all committee time. Not only do you go and discuss in great detail some story outline, with some program manager or executive who's never set foot in a theater, but then you go on to other committees, full of people who've never produced anything, never failed or succeeded at it—and every step of the way you're dealing with them, until finally the whole thing is completely formularized and rigid. If you're doing a comedy, it's committee time all the way through, almost down to the individual jokes!

"It's not for me, I guess. Even after *Philco* went off, and I went on to do ninety-minute dramas, like J. P. Miller's *Days of Wine and Roses*, or the dramatization we did of Faulkner's *The Old Man*, we were still doing dramas that were created directly for the medium, but we never had that interference from committees.

"You see," adds Coe, "the minute everything in this business went onto videotape, or film, it became frozen. Everything you watch at night—frozen. That's why sports are so popular. Sports, and live news coverage like the Watergate hearings—they're the only areas left where you don't know how it's going to come out. You know it's *happening*—happening right there in front of you. But you *don't* know who's going to win—so you have to be interested.

"Turn on any show tonight, and you know it's going to wind up a certain way, because it has to. There isn't anything you don't know is going to happen between 8 P.M. and 11 P.M. Kojak has to find the villain by forty-two minutes in, and there has to be the shootout by forty-four minutes, and then it's time for the commercials, and on we go to the next. Now . . . knowing how predictable that is, night after night, wouldn't you think you could say to *somebody* at one of the networks, 'Hey, pappy, look—knowing how predictable all the other shows are, couldn't we put on *one* show that isn't cut to a pattern? One show where the audience is in suspense as to how it's all going to come out?' "

Coe shrugs sadly.

"And I'm sure—just as sure as I am that Kojak will turn up the killer— what the network answer will be."

According to the 1974 annual corporate report issued by Eastman Kodak: "During the 1974–75 season, 89 percent of all prime-time television viewing originated on film, up from 85 percent the previous year."

This statistic may be enormously satisfying to the Kodak stockholders, but for Mr. Coe, Mr. Chayefsky, Mr. Locke Elliott, Bob Aurthur, J. P. Miller, Reginald Rose, Tad Mosel, et al., who were once practitioners of a now-lost art known as live TV drama—and for those of us who sat at home and watched it, night after night—it is less of a statistic than an inscription on a tombstone.

But one thing is certain. In years to come, when courses are given in the history of television, *Philco-Goodyear* will be in the curriculum . . . if not all of it.

"HIYA...RALPHIE-BOY!"
Art Carney
and Jackie Gleason

Summon up—if you're old enough—the memory of something called *Cavalcade of Stars*. It was an hour-long variety show that was seen on Saturday nights, on DuMont's Channel 5, beginning in 1950, et seq.

Cavalcade was a noisy affair; the format was trite and true. An eager, on-the-way-up comedy hopeful as master of ceremonies, a troupe of hardworking girl dancers, some hokey sketches, and here and there an occasional "guest star." (Since the show was sponsored by Whelan's Drugstores, the rumor was that everybody got paid off in toothpaste.) The sets were shabby, the camerawork was nervous and under-rehearsed, and the band played loud, not good. By today's elegant nighttime variety show standards, *Cavalcade* was strictly El Cheapo. But then, even in its own time, the show was considered Poverty Row—with music.

However, as George Burns once remarked, "All comics need a place where they can be lousy."

That was truly the function of DuMont's Saturday night show. As it turned out, *Cavalcade* was an academy, a comedy trade school. In its first few weeks, it served as the launchpad for young Jack Carter and Larry Storch. Then came a cheerful lunatic comic named Jerry Lester, who was to go on from DuMont to become the first host of a network nighttime show, NBC's *Broadway Open House*.

Then, in July, 1950, there arrived a new MC. A rotund, aggressive character, a brash veteran of nightclubs, revues, of bit parts in long-forgotten movies, and a brief run as the original lead in *The Life of Riley*.

The name was Gleason, Jackie Gleason, and from that night on, it was strictly *Away ... we ... go!*

On his second show, Gleason bellowed his way through a rowdy comedy sketch in which he played a gent being photographed for a "Man of Distinction" liquor advertisement. The photographer, a rather inhibited, nervous-nelly character, played by a gawky, rubber-faced actor named Carney, displayed a highly disapproving attitude toward his noisy subject. By the end of the sketch both the photographer and his subject had become noisily drunk on their props—bottles of the sponsor's good booze.

Hardly Eugene O'Neill or Neil Simon. (They would came later.) Rather, a scene straight from the pages of Minsky's tattered sketchbook.

(For the benefit of those under fifty; Minsky's stands for burlesque, or—as *Variety* preferred to call it—burlecue. A modern-day exhibit of the traditional Italian commedia dell'arte, Minsky-type shows flourished in the twenties and thirties and featured choruses of gum-chewing cuties known as "ponies" who danced and sang, plus exhibits of statuesque ladies who removed their exotic clothing to the strains of "Sophisticated Lady" and "Creole Love Call." Easily the most famous of these strippers was the wonderful Gypsy Rose Lee.

Interspersed amid such cultural moments, a night [or a matinee] at the burlecue would include comedy scenes featuring comedians, various gents in baggy pants and funny hats, known in the trade as "top bananas," whose performances are forever remembered with love and affection by their audiences. Among the graduates of the Minsky Academy of Comedic Arts during this era were Rags Ragland, Bud Abbott and Lou Costello, Phil Silvers, Hank Henry, Bob Alda, Pinky Lee, and Joey Faye, and their standard comedy material included such immortal "scenes" [or "bits" or *shtick*] as "Slowly, I Turn," "Who's On First?," "Honey Moon Hotel," "The Rest Cure," "The Fart Doctor," and "The Gun Isn't Loaded."

If and when such material was performed in front of a TV camera in the early days, it goes without saying that it underwent a certain amount of revision for the home audience ... alas.)

But the scene worked. By the time it had ended, the audience was roaring with laughter at the antics of the two, and when the commercial flashed on, a new comedy partnership had been formed, one that would last for many years. Jackie Gleason and Art Carney.

Jackie Gleason, Art Carney, Audrey Meadows, and Joyce Randolph, *The Jackie Gleason Show* (Courtesy CBS)

"The funny thing is," says Carney today, "I was never a comic. Oh, sure, I started out as a kid in high school, in Yonkers, doing impersonations of people I saw in the newsreels or heard on the radio, but I never wanted to be a comedian. I was doing them strictly as a mimic."

No graduate of the Yale Drama School, or of the American Academy, Carney the actor is refreshingly candid about his lack of formal training. "I never took any acting lessons. Not even the dramatic society in high school, no way, they couldn't get me into that. I was scared of it. But doing those impersonations—that must have been the tip-off of what I was going to do, even though I didn't know it at the time. Doing imitations of *somebody else*—it must have meant all the time that I wanted to be an actor."

Jackie Gleason and Art Carney (Courtesy CBS)

Young Carney's imitations were worked into an act. In 1937 he was hired by bandleader Horace Heidt and toured with Heidt's organization. "Did a little vaudeville and some clubs after the war by myself, but my act was pretty lousy, you know?" he says, grinning. "I didn't get any real training until after the war, when I got into radio. Got some parts in soap operas, working with different people, doing a lot of character and dialect stuff.

"I'd go to the newsreels a lot, watch and listen to famous people. Al Smith, Harry Truman—I'd study their gestures and then come home and practice doing them. Eventually I got on a show called *Report to the Nation*, it was kind of a carbon-copy of the old *March of Time*," Carney says. "They'd have excerpts of President Roosevelt's speech, an announcement of what Wendell Willkie had said, or maybe Churchill. I could do them all, even political commentators like Elmer Davis. He sounded like Ned Sparks, the old movie comic, very nasal, like this." Quickly, he changes the timbre of his voice. "*Good evening, Americans,*" he says, and the effect is remarkable, a true echo of the long-gone Davis.

"Radio taught me a lot," he says. "Gave me confidence. Once in a while I'd get a few lines on some show, and I'd listen and watch the other actors. I began to realize this wasn't just a voice thing at all, these people were *actors*, with terrific technique. You'd see a girl pick up a script and read her part—even the first time, the tears would be coming down her face, she was already doing the character, and you knew she was acting. I developed a lot of respect for those radio people. They taught me how to get *into* the character."

In the mid-forties, radio drama was still thriving. "A very nice medium, too." Carney grins. "You could work all over the place, doing a little thing here, something there, and picking up loot along with the experience. Some days I did two, three shows. Come in, grab the script, mark your lines, read the pages, time it, go on the air and do the show, then hustle on over to the next one."

One of the shows on which Carney was to become a "regular" was a relaxed comedy and music affair starring the rotund rapid-fire comedian Morey Amsterdam, who was himself to become one of Dick Van Dyke's permanent cast on television. That show, *The Silver Swan Cafe*, was transferred to television in 1948, for a thirteen-week run on CBS.

"It all took place in a club. Very original idea. First I played the doorman, and then I got promoted to be the waiter. Irving Mansfield produced and directed, and his wife, Jackie Susann, made her TV debut. She played the cigarette girl." (Yes, the same lady who was soon to forego acting in favor of a literary career.)

"Morey's still got some of those kinescopes," Carney says, fondly. "He says they're a riot to look at now. The bad jokes, the mistakes we made. You have to remember Morey didn't rehearse much. He'd get out there with his cello and do a monologue, half the time he never knew what he was going to say next. We made up a lot of it as we went on. More terrific experience."

When Amsterdam's show was canceled by CBS, it was moved crosstown to DuMont, where it remained on the air for another year and a half. By that time Carney had acquired a considerable reputation around town as a reliable funny fellow. He made sporadic appearances on all the shows being produced in the studios, doing his "bits."

But his first real "break" came with Gleason, and from that first night the two men clowned around together they were to develop their own stock company of characters. Gleason originated a noisy character called Charlie Bratten, the Loud Mouth—Carney became his prissy foil, Clem Finch. When Reggie Van Gleason III emerged, complete with high silk hat, flowing cape,

Hitlerian mustache, and a bottomless thirst for *mmm . . . good booze!*—his disapproving gray-haired father had to be Carney. But the ultimate teaming of the two audience-pleasers came in a sketch that appeared very early on at DuMont, namely, "The Honeymooners."

In it Gleason portrayed Ralph Kramden, the noisy, opinionated bus driver, married to his long-suffering wife, Alice. (She would be portrayed for many years by Audrey Meadows.) "One of these days, Alice, *one of these days,*" Gleason would bellow, in an excess of fury, waving a fist, "*pow*—right in the kisser!" Downstairs was Kramden's good buddy, who worked in the sewers, Ed Norton. Carney, of course, and the perfect partner for Gleason. Easily as stupid as his bus-driving friend, he was cheerful and not too bright. "Norton!" Gleason would bellow. "*You . . . are a mental case!*"

To which Norton would cheerfully nod assent.

Their bumbling adventures, in which the pair and their wives challenged the world, were an immediate success. "Don't forget, we were on against tough opposition," says Carney today. "Friday night at ten, opposite the fights. One week we dropped in the Honeymooner sketch among all the other stuff we were doing—whammo! We started to build an audience."

Many affectionate observers have remarked on the parallel between the Gleason and Carney Honeymooners sketches and the two-reel comedies of the Laurel and Hardy team. "Sure, it's all absolutely there," says Carney. "We were the Brooklyn-type version, the same sort of fumblers. I'd always loved Laurel and Hardy, I could see their shorts over and over again, and people are always telling me they have the same feeling about the Honeymooners shows. You know the plots, you sit back, and even though you know exactly what's coming it doesn't matter, you still enjoy it. Even more *because* you know it."

In the fall of 1952 Gleason's show was so successful that it moved into the big time. The Great One signed a long-term contract with CBS and moved himself, Reggie Van Gleason, the Loud Mouth, Joe the Bartender, Rudy the Repairman, and Stanley R. Sogg (the television pitchman for Mother Fletcher) over to Channel 2, where he was to become one of television's biggest stars.

"Jackie said to me once, 'Art, we get along great together, we have to stick together—whatever network we go to, I'm going to get you started off at a thousand a week. That'll be it—I swear it will!' I told him, 'Jack, you know how I love to work with you—but that's a hell of a lot of money. . . .' Son of a gun, he followed through, and when I started at CBS, that's what I got," marvels

Art Carney in *The Incredible World of Horace Ford* (Courtesy CBS)

Carney. "A thousand a week . . . I still think it's a lot of money." (Or as Norton would have said, *"You're a good kid, Ralphie-boy!"*)

Even though he had now achieved such considerable status as a comedian, Carney persisted in pursuing his own career as an actor. In the original contract that was negotiated at CBS, his agent Bill McCaffrey secured his client three weeks' freedom in each thirteen-week cycle, in order that Carney might be free to accept outside acting jobs on other noncompetitive shows. "Anything that came along that gave me a chance to *act*—I grabbed at it," Carney confesses. "I didn't want to be tabbed as a second banana—a stooge, a comic— which I wasn't. With Gleason I was always a comic *actor*. But I also wanted the right to develop myself. That's how I got to play the lead in *Uncle Harry* on *Kraft Theater*, and I could do original scripts for *Danger* and *Suspense*. Anybody who offered me a good part, I ran. *Studio One* was great for me. I got to play the lead in a marvelous script by Reginald Rose called *The Incredible World of Horace Ford*. Wonderful idea—a guy on the edge of a nervous breakdown, works in a toy factory, keeps thinking how wonderful it would be to go back to his childhood, finally, at the end, he just disappears, vanishes from this scene. Fantasy. There were all sorts of opportunities like that around, gave an actor a chance to flex his muscles—and Gleason was great to me. He always figured out a way to let me do them."

★ 145 ★

In 1955, so successful were the weekly sketches featuring the Honeymooners (*"Alice, you're the greatest!"* was Gleason's standard affectionate curtain line) that Gleason & Co. spent a season devoted to producing thirty-nine separate half hours starring the four characters. The mishaps of Kramden, Norton, and their two fraus were filmed on a remarkable schedule: two complete half-hour shows a week, performed in a theater before a live audience. A system called Electronicam, which combined TV and film in one set of four cameras, was used. (Today's "sitcoms" are usually shot with cameras that record on tape, but the mechanics of production are very similar to Gleason's first series.) "We always worked to a live audience," says Carney. "Terrific training. People used to ask me, 'How do you do it? How can you stand the pace?' Such a schedule—not only all those half hours we did, but remember, all those years we did the hour-long live shows each week. Every week, an opening night."

He grimaces at the memory. "It *was* hard work. But Gleason and I developed a terrific sense of give-and-take with each other. See, I had confidence in myself, and I could take care of myself out there if anything went wrong—and I knew Jackie sure could, too. So, if he went up in a line, I was there to help him, and vice versa. A lot of people thought there was ad-libbing on the Gleason shows. There really wasn't. If we came to something that went wrong in a scene—maybe a prop didn't work, or a miscue—we always got out of it *in character*. Jackie would never stop being Kramden and ad-lib something about 'Well, I'll have to talk to the prop-man about that,' no-sir. We'd stay in the scene and work our way out of it as Kramden and Norton.

"Jackie used to say, and he was right in this respect, that in the final analysis, it's the actors—the performers—they're the ones who have to *deliver*. Sure, you've got to have the material—you can't go out and be funny without it. TV is such an ogre: it eats up material . . . those are the guys who have it tough, the writers. But sink or swim, *we* were the guys out there doing it."

It was not only on the CBS stage that there would be mishaps during variety shows. Carney winces at the recollection of other, more personal moments of crisis. Playwright George Axelrod once wrote an original hour script for *Studio One* called *Confessions of a Nervous Man*, in which Carney portrayed a lead role, that of a dramatist, fresh from his first success, sweating out the reviews of his second opening night. "Live show, remember. I'm the star, and I do all the narration over the scenes, too," Carney recalls. "So you could safely say I was pivotal, right? Okay. Opening scene. I'm at a cocktail party, sitting at a table by myself, all alone, drinking. The camera is supposed to pan all around the room, a complete circle, to show all the guests at the party. Okay, quiet, we're on the air, the camera starts to make the trip around the room, I'm supposed to be at the end of the trip, I'm sitting there waiting for them to come to me. Suddenly, I go blank. *What's my first line?*

"Nothing." He shudders. "The camera's slowly moving, all around the set, the little red light's on, it's coming around to me—I'm all alone out there. *My first sentence,* that's all I want! And nobody out there who can give it to me!"

He shakes his head. "I don't know where it comes from. Adrenalin, or somebody watching over you up there—but the line finally came. The camera hits me, and I'm off . . . sailing away. That's what live TV was all about."

Carney's range was expanding along with his stature. In the ensuing years he would appear in a *Playhouse 90* production of *Charley's Aunt,* do intimate revue material by Larry Gelbart and Burt Shevelove, and even play the only live character in a production of *Peter and the Wolf,* with the Bil Baird puppets. On another show for *Playhouse 90* he portrayed the life story of the Jewish mayor of Dublin. "I guess I must have done a pretty good job learning the *kaddish* and the prayers." He smiles. "Mr. Briscoe himself called my agent McCaffrey afterward and said, 'Say, I never knew Art Carney was Jewish!' "

It was that performance which was to bring Carney to Broadway. The playwright Morton Wishengrad had seen the show and suggested that Carney play the lead opposite Siobhan McKenna in his play *The Rope Dancers.* "My first show," says Carney, "but not my first audience. I couldn't be frightened, not after all those years with Gleason."

The Rope Dancers was a critical success and enjoyed a respectable run on Broadway. Later, Carney essayed a comedy when he played the lead in *Take Her, She's Mine.*

(What was sauce for Norton was equally attractive to Kramden. Gleason was expanding his horizons too. The Great One was to demonstrate his considerable acting talents in the film *The Hustler,* in which he played Minnesota Fats; to play in *Papa's Delicate Condition;* and then to star on Broadway in the hit show, adapted from Eugene O'Neill's *Ah! Wilderness, Take Me Along.*)

In the intervening years, Carney has appeared in *Lovers* by Brian Friel and taken long and profitable tours in Neil Simon's *The Prisoner of Second Avenue.* "Television is fine, I've been very grateful to it, and it kept me going for a long time," he says, "but the real challenge is to get out onto the stage and work in front of the live audience."

He journeyed to Hollywood numerous times to tackle varied parts in television filmed dramas, but it would be almost a quarter century after his first appearance as the genial doorman at the Silver Swan that Carney would be offered his first chance at a major motion-picture role.

"Everything in this whole business is timing," says Carney. "I don't just mean timing your performance—I mean your life's timing. That script came along—I read it, I liked it. I knew Paul Mazursky, he'd worked with me on the old Danny Kaye show. My wife read it, my friend McCaffrey read it, both of them said, 'Do it.' I didn't say no—I just hesitated. I mean, I was thinking to myself, who wants to see a picture about a crusty old man whose only real friend in the world is his cat?"

He shakes his head in wonder. "Amazing. We started. Not one scene in the picture was made in a studio. We shot everything out of doors, or on locations. After the second or third day, I began to get that wonderful feeling that I'd made the right decision. All of us, Mazursky, the cameraman, the crew, the grips—I don't know how you explain it, but at the end of each day's work we felt so good. We *knew* it was good, and we all loved what we were doing. And that's a pretty rare experience. Must have communicated itself to the audience."

Must have, indeed.

On a rainy night in April, 1975, twenty-five years since Art Carney pranced through his first comedy sketch with Jackie Gleason at DuMont, the Academy Awards were announced in Los Angeles. While there may have been all sorts of controversy over the rest of the winners that night, there was unanimous agreement about Best Male Performance in a Starring Role. It went to Art Carney, for his performance in *Harry and Tonto*, that story of the crusty old man and his feline pal.

Carney's speech of acceptance was a witty and wry summation of the event. "McCaffrey said to me, 'Don't be afraid of playing an old man—you *are* one!'" he told the audience.

The Oscar winner crosses to the hall closet of his New York apartment, opens the door, and rummages up on the shelf, to emerge with a battered old felt hat. "My first," he says. "Bought it back in high school days, in Yonkers. Used it all those years when I played Norton, on *The Honeymooners*. See?"

He carefully adjusts the hat on his head, pushes the brim back, tucks his thumbs under his armpits, his shoulders go back, and a smile covers his amiable face.

"Hiya, Ralphie!" he says, in Norton's familiar voice.

Magically, he has re-created the character, with one hat.

"But that's easy to do—if you're an *actor*," he says.

SEEMS LIKE OLD TIMES:
Julius La Rosa and Arthur Godfrey

American show-biz success story (TV version).

It's also the stock musical-comedy plot, Fox or MGM, circa 1943. The callow kid from Brooklyn who dreams of becoming a famous singer. He's in the Navy, see, Manny, the Korean War has broken out, and he's in Pensacola, Florida, assigned to an aircraft carrier that's headed for foreign waters—but before he leaves, a famous TV star, one of the biggest, shows up in Florida, down in Pensacola to get his naval wings. The TV star is doing his practice landings on the aircraft carrier, and the hopeful kid from Brooklyn is up on the flight deck, on the crew that's involved in those same landings!

Now the kid's best friend is a cook, who sneaks into the Bachelor Officers' Quarters to confide in the big TV star: "Excuse me, sir, but my pal has talent, sings like Sinatra, you ought to hear him and maybe give him a shot on your *Talent Scouts* show up in New York." "Okay," says the TV star, "let's give your buddy a try and see if he's any good, why not?"

(Sounds pretty familiar so far, doesn't it? The only missing element is a possible romance between the singer-seaman and the crusty old rear-admiral's daughter. . . .)

But in this case, reality stays pretty close to script formula.

The young kid sings for the TV star, who's got a camera crew down there in Pensacola, the TV star likes what he sees and hears and ships the films up to New York, to the network.

Julius La Rosa and Arthur Godfrey (Courtesy CBS)

Crisis—complications! The films are ruined in the New York lab. *Plot*: the TV star calls up the Navy authorities in Pensacola and explains his problem. He'd like to bring the young kid from Brooklyn up to New York and put him on his show live, in person. The kid has some leave coming to him, it's arranged.

Up from Florida comes the young singer, bright-eyed and on the ready, convinced that fame and fortune are his, once he gets on the air. Crisis time again. On the Wednesday night he is scheduled to make his debut, the famous TV star, who is noted for his relaxed, casual style, runs overtime, and there's no time left in which to bring on the kid from Brooklyn. (What do we do now, Manny? He's got to get back to his ship, right—but he's got to have his Big Chance!)

Relax, it's easy. The TV star arranges with the Navy to get the kid an extension of his leave—and finally, the kid goes on. In front of the cameras, with the whole world watching—and he sings. He finishes, and the audience gives him a big hand, and the star-maker says, "Kid, when you get out of the Navy, you've got yourself a job with me. Don't call us—we'll call *you*."

Which is exactly how it happened, this Act One of the story of Arthur Godfrey and his most famous singing discovery, pleasant young Julius La Rosa from Brooklyn.

"Nobody can really understand how powerful a force television is, until it's turned on you," says La Rosa, twenty-odd years after the fact. "In the years before TV, you could work for weeks, months, years, pay your dues in night-clubs and up on the bandstand, go up to the Borscht Circuit and work— *learn*. That's where all the old stars came from. Television wiped all that out overnight. The only place where it would matter would be the TV studio, smack in the public eye. We moved into the era of the instant star. Kids like me who were discovered, shoved out in front of the camera, and were turned into public heroes overnight. Pretty heady stuff, if you don't know how to handle it . . . which I guess I didn't."

A year after his debut, civilian Julius arrived at the CBS studios, where Godfrey promptly put him to work, in the fall of 1951. Godfrey's instincts were correct; La Rosa was an audience-pleaser on the five-days-a-week radio show. "Oh, how I needed to learn," Julius says. "I had never been on a stage before—I'd never even had voice lessons, until after I got on his show."

Six months later, Godfrey introduced his "find" to the Wednesday night TV audience of *Arthur Godfrey and His Friends*, and for the next year and a half, La Rosa shuttled back and forth between the radio and the nighttime TV show. His popularity grew with amazing speed. La Rosa was possessed of a refreshingly modest personality, a naïveté that communicated itself to the audience. "I guess the only way you could explain me is that everybody's mother got mad with her own son for not being like Julius," he says today. "I used to get letters, 'Dear Julius, my son was killed on Guadalcanal, please send me your picture, you remind me of him.' I was everybody's kid brother. Phenomenal. By the end of my second year with Godfrey, here's this twenty-three-year-old kid who'd never really dared to believe it would happen, getting five, six thousand fan letters a *week.* . . ."

Soon the Brooklyn kid was to become a recording star. Together with musical director Archie Bleyer, he formed Cadence Records, and their first release was Frank Loesser's lovely song "Anywhere I Wander." "It had been done before, by other singers, but such was the power of my being on Godfrey's show as a regular that the record sold 750,000 copies. All of it due to the exposure I had working for him. It's amazing, the attraction he had for his audience. Nobody else in the business had it, then or now," he marvels. "I was his discovery, and he gave me room to grow. I didn't realize it at the time, but he'd also become a surrogate father figure in my life."

Given such a classic situation, it would be inevitable that the young stag would eventually lock horns with his older mentor. "He found out that I was spending $600 a week to answer all those fan letters. I was only making about $900, and he said to me, 'You know, Julie, that's ridiculous, spending all that money.' And I said—and again, this wasn't arrogance, just my own naïveté—'Listen, I don't mean this in the wrong way, everybody's very nice to me now, and you're taking care of me, you and your lawyer, and your producer, but God forbid you go up in your plane and it comes down the wrong way. Unless I'm nice to the people *now*, they ain't gonna like me after that.' That's what I told him, and I don't think he was offended by that, because it was a fairly realistic appraisal of our relationship."

Surrogate father, and surrogate son. The original story line, not only for a musical film, but also for Arthur Miller, Shakespeare, and for real-life people on a weekly television schedule. Godfrey had created a star, he had demonstrated his very real and massive power to do so, but sooner or later, as in every family, the son must respond by demonstrating his own strength.

When the blow-off came, it would be triggered, as always, by something vastly unimportant.

"Meanwhile, you have to understand what's happening to me. All that fan mail, the incredible attention I'm getting, my success with the record company—pretty heady stuff for little Julie, you know. And then the little out-of-line incidents. One time I was attempting a cartwheel for the show, fell right on my head, almost knocked out, and without thinking, I said, 'Who says there's only one star around here?' I meant the stars I'd seen when I fell, of course, thought I was being terribly clever and bright, but everybody around the show knowing what the second meaning was," he says.

Then came the matter of the ballet lessons. Godfrey had decided that a certain amount of such training would be beneficial to all the members of his regular group. "I went to the first one, I was being dutiful, nobody else showed up," says La Rosa. "Couple of weeks go by, he's laying out money for the lessons, but nobody was taking advantage of it. So I stopped going too. Then he put up a note on the bulletin board telling us flat out, very clearly, either we show up for the ballet lessons *or else*. The message was very clear. He'd made us—he could break us all, just as quickly.

"One day I suddenly develop family problems in Brooklyn," recalls La Rosa. "They need me over there. I go and tell him about them right after the morning show, I explain what's the problem, and I swear I'll try to get back in time for the ballet lesson, but I want him to understand it's not insubordination on my part—I've got a valid reason. I want to make sure it's all right with him. He says okay.

"As it turns out, I'm over in Brooklyn coping with family stuff until two in the morning. Next morning I go in—I find a note. 'Since you felt your services weren't required at the ballet class yesterday, you won't be needed this morning on the show.' What the hell is that? I go over to his hotel, the Lexington, I call from downstairs, I'm really upset. I know he's there, his Rolls is waiting outside on the street. But when I call upstairs, the secretary tells me no, Mr. Godfrey's not here. So now I'm sure I'm in trouble. What do you do when you're in trouble in show business? You figure you need some muscle of your own, right? And you hire yourself an agent."

It had always been an unwritten rule on the Godfrey shows that performers would not need agents; financial arrangements for the regulars and for guests were made directly, by Godfrey's producer and/or lawyer, without middlemen. La Rosa's newly acquired representative, a seasoned veteran named Tom Rockwell (who also numbered Perry Como among his clients) notified the Godfrey management that he would henceforth act on behalf of the young singer.

"Now it was just a question of when," sighs La Rosa. "Rockwell's letter was mailed, he got it maybe by the end of the week. Monday morning I get to work at the radio studio, I was scheduled for the 10:15 segment; but one of the ways Godfrey would discipline you would be to keep you sitting around there, waiting to go on. It was his show—he pulled all the strings. All morning I sit there waiting, I've got two different songs to do. Around 11:20, just before closing, he calls me up. He announces me, I sing my song."

Quietly, casually, in earshot of an audience of millions, the surrogate father played out his drama of rejection.

"I finish, and Godfrey says to the people out there, 'Thank you, Julie. *And that, folks, was Julie's swan song.*'"

The story instantly became front-page headline news all over the country. A family crisis involving stars; a rebellion by the heir-presumptive, put down by an implacable king.

When eager newspapermen probed for the real reason, Godfrey would merely say that his ex-friend Julius La Rosa had demonstrated a proper lack of humility.

"I remember how it was suggested at the time, in editorials, that if there was ever any doubt about the importance, the impact, the personal nature of television, our locking horns had dispelled it. Nice young kid from Brooklyn, not a terribly good singer—everybody's kid brother—being thrown off the Godfrey show. Who could have believed it would be headline stuff?" marvels La Rosa today.

"Talk about twisted values. I was completely unprepared for what happened—the enormous impact the whole thing had. For years later, people would ask me about it—I'd say, '*Please*, please—forget it, leave it alone.' I never knew what had hit me. I was a callow, inexperienced kid, with no preparation for any of it."

In the years that followed *l'affaire* Godfrey, La Rosa was to be snapped up as a regular star on the Sunday night *Ed Sullivan Show*. The young singer was news; he was hot. If he wasn't the world's most talented performer, that did not matter. Sullivan knew that his presence on the show would boost ratings.

"Again, I wasn't prepared," he says. "I felt like saying 'No, not thirteen times a year for all that money—please, let me go up to the mountains, let me do shows, clubs, let me learn what I'm doing first—order me back then.' It was crazy. Guys with nightclubs offering huge salaries for me to play one week. I knew I had a certain gift, sure, I had a nice appealing quality, 'Gee, he looks like a nice guy, he sounds like a nice guy,' all that. But as for the rest of it, I wasn't prepared. I wasn't any Sinatra, or Dean Martin . . . no way, ever. . . .

"So there were more errors," he sighs. "Millions of people watching me on Sullivan's show, nine times in that first year. I was asked to do some of the most god-awful things. Once they had me singing one of Sinatra's songs— always Sinatra's—'Young at Heart'; they had me in a bathing suit, on a pair of water skis, singing against a rear-screen projection of ocean waves behind me, can you imagine? I did it—all of it—but I was so uncomfortable. Always being trapped into such mistake situations."

Yet another surrogate father for little Julie, was Mr. Sullivan.

The problems of instant success are constant, often overpowering, and for many, terrifying. Witness over the past quarter century the literally dozens of young male and female performers who have been catapulted into the hard, glaring lights of a television studio, introduced to a waiting world, heralded as "stars" . . . and who have just as abruptly vanished from sight, unable to sustain their temporary status as king of the hill.

"You can't really blame the guys I ran up against," Julius observes today. "Godfrey, Sullivan . . . huge public figures. They were the same as the others that television created—Jack Paar, Gleason, even Johnny Carson. TV presented them with enormous power, and if they used it in various ways, that's because they had it to use. Put any of us in the same position as they were, we'd probably do the same. You work for other people, and then one day the miracle happens—bang! You catch on, overnight you're a big personality. You're a Red Skelton, or a Merv Griffin. . . . Overnight you're so big that nobody, not even management, not even the very top people at the networks can tell you anything—because it's you who's up there on top, you are the Man with the Power. So if you start to use all that strength, and swing your club around, that's the way the game's played, isn't it? Who's to say *I* wouldn't have behaved exactly the same way if I'd stayed up there?"

*   *   *

It has taken pleasant Julius La Rosa, that cheerful Brooklyn kid with the good set of pipes, many years of introspection to come to grips with his own particular set of furies. "Sure it hurt then—plenty," he concedes. "All those mistakes I made. But after a while I learned to live with whatever talent I have, and hopefully, not to make those mistakes twice." He shrugs. "But I'm not sure what would happen to me if I ever get a shot at the really big apple spot again. I can only hope that this time I'd be able not to do what so many of those other people have done—to misuse the power. I say 'hope,' because there's that little bird in my ear that says, 'Julius, it's going to happen to you again, you'll see.' I don't know how, I don't know when, or where, but I just have that feeling. It will."

The surrogate son is now in his mid-forties, still youthful, and still very much in show business. He has his own disc-jockey show on a major New York radio station, he is often booked into nightclubs, does TV commercials, and works steadily in music tents. No longer a phenomenon, he is a serious performer, fully capable of playing such complex roles as that of Billy Bigelow in Rodgers and Hammerstein's *Carousel*.

And as for the surrogate father? That big-time star who heard the young kid from Brooklyn singing down in Pensacola, long years ago, and brought him up to New York and the big time, played Svengali, and shoved Julius out into the limelight, to make him a star?

"Last time I saw Godfrey, it was about three years ago," remembers La Rosa. "I was in therapy. My doctor's office was at Ninety-sixth and Fifth, and when you're in therapy, some sessions are perhaps a little more traumatic than usual. Whenever that would happen, I'd walk from Ninety-sixth all the way down Fifth to my office here, fifty blocks, a nice walk, lets you think about everything, no pressure. One day I'm walking that way, thinking, and about forty feet away, coming out of a building, I see Godfrey. Now I don't look so hot, harassed and uptight, but I know I'm going to run into him. So we come together, we both kind of look at each other from the side—'Is it really him?' I could tell he had the same reaction. . . . I put out my hand, and he shakes it. . . . I take his hand and mine over his, and now it's the four-hand shake.

"He didn't look older than the first day I saw him in Pensacola. They talk about Old Blue Eyes? Well, Godfrey, too—he has those incredible, magnificent eyes. 'How are you? You look great—how are you, fine?' It's one of those quick, brief things, and I walk with him a few feet and then I said, 'Hey—

we'd better watch it, or they'll make an item out of us for the papers,' and he says, 'Fuck 'em.' And we walk a little farther, and then we go our own ways. End of story."

La Rosa grins, his familiar cheerful grin. "So after all these years, I guess he's developed some perspective on what happened, too. Funny, whenever people ask me about Godfrey, they always throw in that thing about humility. . . . So they must always ask *him* about La Rosa and humility, too. . . . And I have been told from a number of people that he always singles me out —as the only guy who ever said, 'Thank you.' "

Not exactly a happy movie-musical ending to the story about the big TV star and his find, but, perhaps, a whole lot more *cinéma vérité*.

HAIL SID!
HAIL IMOGENE!

The two men are meeting in a Middle European apartment. One is obviously a courier, and he is being handed a small bag by the visitor. "Here are the diamondss," says the second man. "You vill take them viz you onto the train to Istambul. Ven you arrive at Istambul, you vill valk through the station and out onto the main street. Three blocks avay, a man vill run out from behind a building and scream at you, 'Giff me the diamondss!'"

"Vat do I do then?" asks the courier.

"You *don't* give them to him," says the second man. "Now . . . you vill valk another two blocks and then a very beautiful blonde vill then come up to you and she vill say softly to you, 'Giff me the diamondss.'"

"I don't give her the diamonds," says the courier.

"Yes, you vill give them to her!" says the second man. "That girl vill be *me!*"

The courier does a double take. "Oh, I see," he says, finally. "You'll be in disguise."

"*No!*" says the second man. "I'm in disguise *now!*"

That is not a classic sketch from a Broadway show, nor is it a moment from Mel Brooks' latest comedy film, nor is it something concocted by Woody Allen—although it is generically related to all three.

It is a fondly remembered (one of many) moment from a Sid Caesar–Carl

Sid Caesar and Imogene Coca (Courtesy NBC)

Reiner sketch, a satire of a spy movie performed twenty years ago on a live television program called *Your Show of Shows*, and its only record exists on a scratchy kinescope carefully stored away by the show's producer, Max Liebman.

By now there exists a certain amount of well-justified skepticism about the stuff we used to watch on our home screens in that so-called golden era back then. In the cruel light of two decades' passing, even the finest red wine of drama has a bad habit of turning into vinegar. Light comedy scenes take on a certain antique piquancy, in which everyone sounds like Billie Burke, or Bette Davis trying too hard. When it comes to satiric comedy, nothing is more fragile, or sags faster.

But about Sid Caesar and Imogene Coca, Carl Reiner and Howard Morris, et al., and their Saturday night performances circa 1949–1954, there is good news.

It was great stuff then—and it still is.

Two years back, when Max Liebman put together a compilation of scenes and sketches from those TV programs and called it *Ten from Your Show of Shows*, hard-nosed critics and (proof positive—remember, it used to be free) *paying* customers were unanimous in expressing delight at what had emerged from Liebman's vaults. It was delight mingled with relief—that the idols of our misspent youthful Saturday evenings were still idols, and the talented feet of Caesar and Coca had not turned to clay.

There they were again on the screen, doing their hilarious parodies of pompous Hollywood films—*From Here to Obscurity, Aggravation Boulevard* (read Sunset). There was Coca rising to heaven with wings sprouting, at the climax of a takeoff of a silent film, *The Sewing Machine Girl*. Caesar doing his Italian gibberish as an Italian opera star in *Galapacci*, or presenting us with his ultracool jazz musician, Progress Hornsby. There was the lunatic takeoff of *This Is Your Life*, with a startled Caesar being attacked by his long-lost relative, Howard Morris, who clung to Caesar's leg like a demented leech. A pantomime scene depicting the cast of life-size figures on a Bavarian town clock, all of whom somehow went haywire. A typical husband-and-wife scene between Caesar and Coca—in this one she'd driven the family car through a drugstore window and was attempting to break the news to her spouse as an amusing anecdote. And finally we had Caesar doing his German scientist, the archaeologist Professor Ludwig Von Fossil. ("After many, many years, I have found ze secret of Titten-Totten's Tomb." "What was it, Professor?" "I should tell *you*?")

Two hours' worth; ten gems. But they are merely a sampling, a smorgasbord selection from all the comedic jewelry we were treated to, on all those years of Saturday night delight.

Begin then, by considering the size of Max Liebman's accomplishment. Under his aegis, for ninety minutes a week, *each* week, there came to the TV screen, live, a briskly routined show that contained musical numbers, scenes from opera, elaborate dance specialties, and always the comedy scenes.

The revue form, as anyone who has ever tried to do one will testify, is certainly the toughest ball game in the business. There is no story line on which to hang musical numbers; each and every element of a revue goes onstage and lives (or dies) on its own.

In the long-gone days when Ziegfeld, George White, and Earl Carroll presented their Broadway revues, they sold ticket-holders two hours' worth of entertainment. Into the preparation of a *Follies* or a *Scandals* went months of hard work and rehearsal, and weeks out of town in tryout, where every moment of the revue would be perfected and polished before the producer would allow his cast to face the opening-night audience and the Broadway critics.

Liebman, Caesar, Coca, and company performed a new ninety-minute revue every seven days, all year long.

(And in the process, killed off most of the Broadway shows.)

Liebman had no special secret. But he was gifted with a sense of organization and a sharp eye for talent.

"I'd been doing television all my life without the cameras," he says today, between puffs of his ever-present cigar. During the late 1930s Liebman had staged weekly revues in an adult summer resort called Tamiment. One of his first major discoveries there was a young comedian named Danny Kaye. Together with Sylvia Fine, Kaye's wife, Liebman presented Kaye on Broadway in 1939 in *The Straw Hat Revue,* with much of its material derived from shows that had been done during the summer at Tamiment. That summer camp in Pennsylvania was also to produce other such talents as Alfred Drake, as well as a young dancer named Jerome Robbins, who joined Liebman's summer corps de ballet at age fifteen and stayed until he was twenty-two, and a choreographer. "That summer place was a kind of a laboratory for people who had any kind of a creative urge," Liebman says.

Right after World War II, Liebman encountered Sid Caesar. That young man had emerged from a Coast Guard Service show called *Tars and Spars*

Sid Caeser, Imogene Coca, Carl Reiner, and Howard Morris in "The Clock," from *Your Show of Shows* (Courtesy Max Liebman)

and was in New York looking for a further career in show business. Eventually the two men worked together on a revue called *Make Mine Manhattan*, in which Liebman directed Caesar in comedy sketches.

In the summer of 1948 Liebman was back at Tamiment, producing his weekly revues, when a bright talent agent from William Morris named Harry Kalcheim brought an advertising agency man named Pat Weaver up to the mountains to scout Liebman's show. Weaver had a client who was pondering spending advertising money in the new and highly risky television field. He had planned to return to New York after seeing Liebman's show, but he was so excited by what he had seen that he stayed until 4 A.M., discussing its possibilities. "Pat said to me, 'This is fine,'" recalls Liebman, "But he said, 'Remember, in television you'll have to do it each and every week, a whole new show.' So I told him, 'Come again next week and the week after, because I do one every week.' And he did . . . and I did."

That fall Weaver's sponsor changed his plans, but Kalcheim brought in Admiral, a television-set manufacturer that wanted to sell audiences its sets. To do so, Admiral took the plunge with Liebman and an hour-long revue. The original budget for *The Admiral Broadway Revue* was fixed at a price of

Howard Morris, Carl Reiner, and Sid Caesar in "Strange" (Courtesy Max Liebman)

$15,000 per week. "At that price nobody made any money," says Liebman, "but we all had the itch to get into this new medium." Liebman assembled a group that would be headed by young Caesar, with Imogene Coca, who had also performed with him at Tamiment and had had considerable experience in various Broadway revues. For writing, he brought in Mel Tolkin and Lucille Kallen, two young Canadians; they too were Tamiment alumni.

Carl Reiner, another hopeful with a smattering of experience, was to become a regular, as would the diminutive Howard Morris. Morris later recalled the circumstances of his discovery. "In 1948 I was touring with *Call Me Mister* when a friend told me that someone named Caesar needed an actor he could pick up by the lapels. This was for a television show, whatever *that* was. I went to a studio on Fifty-second Street and met Liebman, Mel Tolkin, Lucille Kallen, and a strange Frenchman. (For a while this guy spoke Yiddish-French to me, and turned out, naturally, to be Mel Brooks.) In any case, Sid walked in, lifted me by the lapels, and grunted—which in those days meant okay."

As for the young, brash Brooks, his appearance on the scene has already been well documented, but the spasmodic nature of his audition bears recalling. "He was hanging around at the time," says Liebman. "Caesar brought him around to the old Broadhurst Theater. Sid introduced us and said to Brooks, 'Do for Max what you just did for me.' And this, believe it or not, was what Mel did. He faced the empty seats and sang, 'Hello, hello, hello/I've come to start the show/I'll sing a little, dance a little/I'll do this and I'll do that/And though I'm not much on looks/*Please love Mel Brooks!*' Whereupon he got down on one knee and made a mammy-type gesture!"

Liebman's assemblage went to work, and the first season of *The Admiral Broadway Revue* appeared on whatever TV screens were operative in those early days. "We finished thirteen weeks," he says, "There were thirteen more to do, but Admiral changed its plans—they couldn't manufacture TV sets fast enough, it wasn't the way they wanted to advertise them for the coming season, so they paid us off and now we were afloat."

Re-enter Pat Weaver, by now a vice-president at NBC, who called Liebman over to a top-level conference. "Pat was sitting with Bob Sarnoff, and he asked me if instead of doing an hour show, I could do a *whole evening*! Saturday night."

Weaver, never one to think small, was envisioning a three-hour Saturday night schedule, one that would bring into the home any and all forms of entertainment that had previously been sold to the public on a cash-and-carry basis, i.e., drama, revue, opera, variety show. "It would be done so that people sitting at home would get a touch of everything that they could possibly see if they'd gone out," says Liebman. "And in the process, to destroy the competition of the movies, as well."

Liebman was astonished by the breadth of Weaver's vision, but not so much that he would back away. "Three hours I couldn't possibly have handled," he admits. "But, with a little gulp, I finally said, 'Well, I can handle an hour and a half.'"

Eventually, Weaver settled for a two-hour schedule, with the first half hour to emanate from Chicago, emceed by Jack Carter. And thereupon *Your Show of Shows* made its debut on the NBC network, in the fall of 1949, under the umbrella title of *The Saturday Night Revue*. A year or so later, the first half-hour show disappeared into the limbo of lost concepts, and until 1954 for ninety minutes each week, Caesar and Coca were to ride the top of the Saturday night ratings.

It was a mammoth undertaking, ninety minutes' worth of live entertainment weekly, one that would call for meticulous planning and management of a rigidly structured operation. Liebman had his own theatrical designer, Fred Fox, and an old Broadway musical hand, Charlie Sanford, as his conductor. "When we walked into the old International Theater, up on Columbus Circle, which they gave us as a studio, to hang the scenery for our first show"—Liebman smiles—"all the stagehands who were there, and were theater guys who'd already suffered through a few of those early haphazard TV disasters, looked at us, and to a man they said, 'Thank God—there are some professionals coming in here!'"

His phalanx assembled, Liebman metamorphosed from a quiet, diminutive chap into a field marshal with an intricate table of organization. Four rehearsal halls were used, each one carefully scheduled. One was for the comedy people. The other three were timed out to allow for the work of the dance team of Mata and Hari, the Billy Williams Quartet, dancers Bambi Linn and Rod Alexander, and singer Marguerite Piazza.

Well organized, true, but all the organization in the world wouldn't have helped make the show a hit had there not been behind the scenes the wildly creative crew of writers, stoking the comedic fires for young Caesar and his co-star Imogene Coca.

Writing, arguing, rewriting, yelling, laughing, improvising—the writers, who would later include such future notables as Woody Allen and Neil Simon, Mike Stewart and Larry Gelbart and Tony Webster, would develop endless variations for their performers. "We were too young—we didn't know how difficult it was!" says Tolkin today. "To create a ninety-minute show each week—my God! Today, for instance, guys get together months ahead of time to plan and write a one-hour comedy special . . . and then they take five, six days to shoot it on tape, before they're through. Then two or three more days in the cutting room to edit and finish. Not us—each Sunday we started fresh, to create a whole new show—from the top."

Tolkin echoes the sentiments of most of the *Your Show of Shows* crew when he emphasizes the all-important talent quotient of the two stars. "Sid grew full bloom," he comments. "I can't imagine him with any less talent than he had when he first emerged on the scene. It was from the pores . . . like some virtuoso kid who could learn to play the piano when he was seven. Both he and Coca—a fantastic combination of talents, with immense ability to cover every facet of stage technique, from pantomime to dialect comedy."

Sid Caesar, Imogene Coca, Carl Reiner in "The Bully" (Courtesy Max Liebman)

Caesar and Coca, with Reiner and Morris, began very early on to accrete into a wildly inventive group, capable of working solo but also ensemble. The same Caesar who could portray the Crazy German professor, or the Japanese samurai in a wild takeoff of a Japanese art-film (*Ubetchu*)—could step in front of the curtain in one and proceed to do a monologue in which he would enact the part of a six-month-old-baby, alone in his crib, commenting on all the adults who were clustered about him. Coca was equally as versatile; she might do a comic ballet turn with the ensemble, sing in an operatic takeoff, or do her delightfully wicked pixie-ish strip-tease routine, in which she never got further than one glove.

"An awful lot of what went into the comedy writing was based on our own personal experiences," says Tolkin. "Remember, all of us had started out very young, making small salaries, but as the show became a big hit—and it was one of the biggest—we all earned more, lots more. So, as we began to acquire new things, we could draw on what happened to us for a good deal of the humor. It's interesting: my relatives in Canada could tell how well my wife, Edith, and I were doing if we did a Sid-and-Imogene husband-and-wife sketch about a couple hiring their first maid. Or buying their first car. Or the tipping problem of the first night in a fancy restaurant.

"In that one, the check arrives, and both of them start arguing about how much they should leave. Coca has her opinion—Sid shuts her up—what does she know about tipping? He then does a big thing about what's necessary—that if there is a white tablecloth on the table, that means 10 percent. An orchestra—15 percent. A maître d'hotel—another 10 percent. Waiters . . .busboys—he starts figuring everything out on the tablecloth. He adds, subtracts, figures it all out—finally, he comes up with the proper figure: eight *cents*! Big laugh, of course. Now, Reiner comes over, the headwaiter. A real monster, the perfect type to show how small men can be embarrassed everywhere by minor officials—again, part of our own experiences. Reiner stands there waiting for the tip. Sid starts to peel off bills from his roll. He waits for Reiner to thank him, but Reiner just continues to stare, haughtily. . . . Sid finishes throwing bills on the table. Nothing. Then he writes out Reiner a couple of personal checks. Reiner stares. Then Sid tosses him his wristwatch! His cufflinks! He offers him his insurance policy! Finally he's absolutely cleaned out. No reaction from Reiner. Sid picks up Coca by the arm and they start out of the restaurant. As they go, Reiner finally yells after him, '*Cheapskate!*'

"Another time," says Tolkin, "Sid and his wife, Florence, and my wife, Edith, and I went to a restaurant, and as we were sitting there, two or three firemen, all wearing slickers, carrying big axes, and dragging a hose, walked slowly through the restaurant, headed for the kitchen. Some kind of a minor smoke fire out back. Nobody paid any attention to them, everybody went on eating, peaceful and quiet. Hilarious scene, right? So three days later we did the whole thing on the show as a pantomime sketch. It worked beautifully."

Inevitably, under such pressure-cooker conditions, there were tensions, both in the preparation of a weekly show and in the performance. "But very little temperament," insists Tolkin. "For that we didn't have the time. We couldn't be competitive—the important thing was to get the show *on*."

Lucille Kallen later observed, "I don't know whether there are any shows today in TV where producer, performers, and writers were as tuned to each other's talents as we were then. From what I've seen since, I doubt it. Coming up with an idea in that group was like throwing a magnetized piece of a jigsaw puzzle into the middle of a room. All the other pieces would come

Carl Reiner, Sid Caesar, and Howard Morris (Courtesy Max Liebman)

racing toward it, each one adding another necessary part. Suddenly, there was the whole picture."

Not that Caesar was himself impervious to strain. As Mel Brooks points out, years afterward, "Sid was the strongest comedian that ever lived. He'd often pick up a steel desk with a heavy IBM typewriter on it, lift it into the air, then set it down. It relieved his tension. One time in Chicago, he picked up a Volkswagen off the street and put it down on the sidewalk—so he could have room to park his car."

There would also be fierce argument. Out on a stroll, Brooks once suggested an idea to Caesar for a monologue in which Caesar's German professor character would discuss how to put the body to sleep. In the process, he would instruct each part of the body to rest, in turn, beginning with the toes, proceeding to the knees, then the belly, etc., up to the heart, and then to the brain. The brain, however, would resist instructions, causing Caesar to lose his temper with it. Caesar resisted not only Brooks's idea, but proceeded to lose his temper over the other man's insistence. As the two men walked down the street, Brooks continuing to nag at Caesar, tempers exploded into an actual fistfight. When it was ended, as quickly as he had lost his temper, Caesar regained it. "He could have flicked me all the way to Chicago if he'd wanted to," said Brooks, "but he simply said, 'Well, if you feel that strongly about it, we'll try it.' I was right and Sid was wrong. The bit was a huge success."

"You see, we all had the right, in trying to come up with comedy ideas, to be idiots," says Tolkin. "Very important. We had the security to come up with terrible ideas, to make mistakes—to draw on our own streams of consciousness and dredge ideas out of it. If we tossed out a lousy idea, everybody would jump on it, build on it, embellish it—and when we argued, which was constantly, I'm sure anybody watching us would have figured we were all ready for the nut house. But the important thing was that we yelled and screamed out ideas, and from them we built great comedy material. Wasn't it the late Sam Goldwyn who said, 'From polite story conferences come polite pictures'? Well, around *Your Show of Shows* we certainly never were polite to each other—and what emerged was improvised, and noisy—but usually funny. We'd stumble onto something great . . . then we'd put it down on paper."

The script was often merely a blueprint; the stars added embellishments of their own. "The basis of Sid's humor," observed Carl Reiner, "came from an internal source: *pain*. Once we were doing a submarine sketch in which I played an officer. I ordered a torpedo fired, then changed my mind. The surprised crew dropped it on Sid's foot. The torpedo was made only of cardboard, of course, but the pain Caesar resurrected on camera was unbelievable. His eyes started to water; I could practically see smoke coming out of the top of his head. I now evaluate all comedians on the basis of their ability to communicate pain. Sid was the best I've seen."

It was when it came to the movies that *Your Show of Shows* developed the cutting edge of satire to its keenest. Tolkin readily admits that one of the crew's prime sources of inspiration was the Museum of Modern Art showings of classic films, to which he and the others often repaired of an afternoon. Nothing in the history of the cinema since the days of Georges Méliès escaped their attention.

Early silent classics such as *The Mark of Zorro* emerged as satiric sketches in which Caesar, dashing madly through old California, slashed, instead of a Z, a large X on his victims. Old-Time morality plays, e.g., *The Drunkard*, produced a full-length pantomime silent sketch with titles, starring Caesar as the drunkard and Coca as his long-suffering wife. "Oh, how exaggerated," chuckles Tolkin. "We wanted to show at the beginning how happy he was. You never saw such happiness in that scene; in his house the canary was singing, the cat had kittens, everything was marvelous. We threw in a silent title in which the doctor told him, '*Any more happiness will endanger your life!*' Then comes the downfall. Everything went wrong. The canary died. The kittens ran away. The stove exploded. He started to drink." Caesar, as the drunkard, began to dramatize his enslavement to the Demon Rum. "In his office he had booze stashed away everywhere. One of the pieces of wood on the clothes tree unscrewed; it had booze in it. He took the typewriter apart; in the roller, booze, which he uncorked and drank. He licked a postage stamp, and got some hidden alcohol out of that!"

There were foreign film takeoffs in which Caesar, a master of dialect double-talk, met the challenge of every tongue. And then there were the backstage musicals, complete with Coca playing the unknown chorus girl named Nancy, third hoofer from the end, just a kid in the chorus. ("What's your name, honey?" "Nancy, sir." "Nancy what?" "Nancy Kidinthechorus." "Well, listen to me, Nancy—our leading lady has just broken her leg and at the last minute you're going to have to fill in for her. Tonight you're going out there just a Kidinthechorus—but you're coming back a *star!*" "I *am?*")

"We did such a job on movie musicals," sighs Tolkin today, "that I'm afraid we helped destroy them as a commercial film form. Some mornings, on Saturdays, when we'd be rehearsing for the night's show, we'd get visitors in, people from the Coast, and they'd sit and watch our musicals and then they'd complain, 'All those jokes you're making about backstage musicals are based on the pictures we're making right now!' It was a case of them literally being laughed to death."

Not even prestigious contemporary film success escaped the Caesar-Coca treatment. "Sid and I went to see *Shane*, which was a great movie," says Tolkin. "You usually can't make fun of something so good. But we decided the thing to kid was that no man could possibly be as brave as the late Alan Ladd had to be. So we did our own takeoff and called it *Strange*. Sid played Strange, and Coca played the frontier kid. In the opening scene, he drinks a barrel of water with Coca watching. 'You seem mighty thirsty, stranger,' she says. 'Have a long, dry ride?' 'No, I had a herring for breakfast,' he says. 'What's your name, stranger?' asks the kid. 'Folks call me . . . Strange.' 'Strange? What's your first name?' 'Very. But you can call me Strange.'

"Five minutes later, he's ready to take on an entire crew of bad guys. She asks, 'Why are you risking your life for us? You don't even know us, you only just met us, and you're already risking your life to take on that gang of cutthroats. *Why?*' And he says, 'Cause we're the good guys, and they're the bad guys!' Next scene, he's in the bar, and everybody's telling him he can't take on the bad guy—the Jack Palance character—and for some reason Strange decides he won't fight anymore. He puts down his gun. Now everybody turns on him, starts to call him yellow-belly, scaredy-cat, abuses him, but Strange stands there, holding a shot glass of whiskey in his hand, taking it all. Finally, one little twelve-year-old kid, played by Howie Morris, of course, comes up and says to him, 'Ahh, you're a coward!' And Strange throws the whiskey right in the kid's face and snarls, '*Nobody* says that to *me!*' "

Classic movies—and classic parodies of them. It seems only fitting that a good many of the Caesar and Coca takeoffs are stored today in the Museum of Modern Art film vaults, close to that same theater where Liebman's writers spent their afternoons, two decades back digging for source material.

For four seasons, Liebman had more than fulfilled Pat Weaver's original plan—to dominate Saturday night prime-time viewing. By 1954 the record book of *Your Show of Shows* had run up statistics at which we must still marvel. "We kept on doing what in essence was a full Broadway show, once each week," says Tolkin. "Somewhere in the neighborhood of 159 ninety-minute shows. And the remarkable thing was, we were all still friends. Maybe it was because we were all too busy with the job of getting the show written and produced. Who had time for arguments—unless they produced a funny scene?"

Then, for reasons that are still obscure and will probably always remain so, a decision was taken up in the NBC executive offices to restructure the Saturday night schedule. Perhaps the ratings were slipping slightly; perhaps the audiences were beginning to take Caesar and Coca for granted. Whatever the reasons, management thinking went like so: if Liebman, Caesar, and Coca had been triumphant as a trio, then by splitting the three, triple success would be guaranteed.

Caesar would now star in his own show, and Coca would have hers. Liebman, the quiet little man who had assembled the talent, nurtured it, and brought it to flower, would now be assigned to produce a series of high-budget "spectaculars," blockbuster specials that would involve Judy Holliday, Steve Allen, Jacques Tati, and other such stars.

For a while, the plan seemed to work well. Caesar became the head of *Caesar's Hour*, taking with him many of the same creative people who had been with him from the start. For his new leading lady, he replaced Miss Coca with the vivacious Nanette Fabray, and she rapidly developed into an excellent partner. From 1954 until 1957 *Caesar's Hour* continued to please the audience.

Miss Coca's solo venture was less successful. Her own show appeared in the season of 1955, but somehow her enormous talent wasn't sufficient to sustain it. Perhaps it was the need for a strong talent such as Caesar's against which she could display all her abilities. In the years that followed, she moved on to other, less grueling work, away from television and back into the legitimate theater, where she has thrived. But three years ago, in an interview with *Esquire* magazine, she remarked, quite wistfully, "You know what I wish for most in the world? That Sid and I could work together again. I'd run twenty miles in sheer joy if I'd hear that we would be able to go back on again. It was the most fulfilling time of my life. Sid and I are alike in so many ways. Neither of us is very articulate. Put us on a talk show and we bomb. But Sid and I could work together. We didn't have to talk. I'd take fifty bucks a week for the chance to work with him again. . . ."

Liebman's "spectaculars," always theatrical, well produced and staged, continued for several more seasons. With the advent of film and tape production, and the moving of so much of television to California, he gradually withdrew from the scene. "It seems to me," he says today, "that the worst thing that happened to television was when they removed the live element from it. They took away the spontaneity, that something that's almost indefinable when the audience knows that they are watching something that is being played right then, at the moment. Sure, they asked me to come out to California and work there, but I just couldn't do it. I couldn't adjust. Too many of my roots were in New York. My business was here, and I was always a New York character."

As for the rest of Liebman's crew of creative types, they are all, to say the very least, successful. Tolkin is a writer for *All in the Family*; Lucille Kallen works steadily in New York. Carl Reiner functions as a producer-writer-director, and also an actor, in films and TV; diminutive Howie Morris is also working steadily, no longer held in midair by his lapels, but as a director. Larry Gelbart is the producer of *M*A*S*H*—and as for the irrepressible Mel Brooks, who once sang on his knees to an empty Broadway theater, must anyone who has seen *Blazing Saddles* and/or *Young Frankenstein* need to be reminded where Brooks is at?

Long since separated, they all look back to their formative years, to that crushing weekly deadline, to the sporadic crises, the constant pressure writing, and to the daily, hourly triumphs, as a truly remarkable period, one that will never, alas, happen again.

"How can you do a show like that every week?" Howie Morris muses. "Everything pointed to its falling on its ass. Well, it went on for almost a decade. . . . That show wasn't stamped out, on a machine, the way they are today."

"I remember once"—Tolkin smiles—"it was maybe the fourth week of *Your Show of Shows*, in weekly *Variety* the reviewer said it was a fine show, but the material was running thin. Can you believe it? Four weeks after we'd started, they said we couldn't keep it up."

For once, *Variety* was wrong.

Why? "What that man didn't understand, because he wasn't backstage with us," says Tolkin, "was the chemistry that was at work. A bunch of people coming together at a certain time in their lives, all of them learning to work with each other—and the results were explosive."

And as for Sid Caesar himself, we have come to praise him, not to bury him.

No longer the kingpin of his own weekly show, he is still very much alive and well. He has starred on Broadway, in *Little Me*, and done films, *It's a Mad, Mad, Mad, Mad World*, among others, toured in plays, and done many guest shots in weekly variety shows.

"I know of no other comedian," Mel Brooks said, "who could have done nearly ten years of live television. Nobody's talent was ever more used up than Sid's. I don't say it wasn't used well. He was one of the greatest artists that was ever born into the world. But over a period of years, television ground him into sausages—one sausage a week—until finally there was little of the muse left. After three years I asked him to break out. I said, 'Enough. Let's do movies.' He wouldn't. Television was the vehicle he knew best, and the thing he loved."

All is far from lost. Thanks to Max Liebman's care in preserving old kinescopes, Caesar and Coca will go on regaling a new generation of viewers with *Ten from Your Show of Shows*, and they will continue to remind the rest of us of how good they were. Just lately, the pair has begun to reappear on the TV screen again, not for ninety minutes, but in clever one-minute commercials for AT&T. Those of us who roared at them each Saturday night must be grateful for small favors . . . and we should applaud Ma Bell for her perspicacity in bringing them both back into our homes, where they were once our most welcome weekend guests.

MR. BURNS,
MISS ALLEN,
AND MR. BENNY

Ralph Levy remembers:

I was on my vacation in Mexico, back in 1951—a well-deserved one. I'd been working very hard for months, doing the Ed Wynn half-hour comedy show here in Los Angeles, and then I began to produce and direct a show with Alan Young, his first comedy show. Both very talented men, but the schedule was a crusher.

I got a call from Harry Ackerman, who was in charge of the CBS West Coast operation, and he asked me to come back from Mexico immediately. Very important. He said, "George Burns thinks he'll go on television, and we want you to be in charge of the show."

I flew back, and we had a meeting. George was there, with his writers, and he had some cockeyed idea for a show, I can't remember what it was, and when he got through explaining it, he looked at me and said, "Well, what do you think, kid?" I said, "I thought it was in very bad taste." Harry Ackerman almost collapsed on the spot. George merely nodded and said, "Oh? Well, we're going to have lunch now, why don't we all come back about one and we'll go to work."

So we evolved the idea for the show: a simple situation comedy with the cut-out set of the Burns's house, and another one for their neighbors, and, downstage, an area where George could stand and talk directly to the audience, to explain about his wife, Gracie, predict what was going to happen, and to comment on his daily life in and around their neighborhood.

It doesn't seem so important now, but you mustn't underestimate how diffi-cult it was for Burns and Allen to have taken that giant step and gone into live TV at that time. Sure, they'd been radio stars for years, but TV meant they'd have to toss away the scripts and perform live. Despite what people think, George is not an ad-libber; every last word of his material is carefully written and rehearsed. He's meticulous about it—I've seen him walking down Sunset Boulevard talking to himself, rehearsing his monologues to perfect every word, each nuance.

Remember, dozens of other performers figured they could do TV. Very few of them survived; TV wasn't just show business—it was an entirely different medium, one that quickly destroyed a lot of reputations. Burns and Allen took the plunge, and they not only survived, they became even bigger stars.

I've always thought that Gracie was one of the finest actresses that ever lived—remember that word, *actress*, it's crucial. True, she played the silliest woman you could ever meet, but she never thought of herself as a comedienne, and George never treated her as one. In fact, there were times in radio, when Gracie was ill, and they'd use somebody like Joan Davis, a comedienne, to replace her—but it never worked properly. Only when a legitimate actress read Gracie's lines did the scenes play.

We did the first six shows of Burns and Allen's new show in New York, from the old Mansfield Theater, and they were fine. Then we came back here to Los Angeles and did the show from here. George had fine writers, and the material was marvelous. It was always character comedy, the best kind. The kinescopes of the old shows are scratchy and very primitive, but the laughs are still there when I run them for people.

By the following year, Mr. Paley had persuaded Jack Benny to try live TV too—evidently the fact that Burns and Allen had gone on and been successful was enough to reassure Jack, so he went to New York and did four live shows, alternating them with his radio show. In 1952 he went on every other week from Los Angeles, and I went to work with him out here, doing both his show and Burns and Allen's, which meant that I was still on that show-and-a-half-per-week schedule. But I was young, and I managed to survive.

Besides, working with such pros was a joy. Take Jack, as a prime example; over the years he had created such a marvelous, identifiable character. If Jack was playing in a straight scene where the waiter came in with the check to

★ 177 ★

present it to him, the audience would start laughing before Jack opened his mouth because they knew he wouldn't pay. That sort of instant identification gave him enormous size. Jack was part of a category of comedians I call the mostest . . . and we haven't got many of those left. Jimmy Durante had the biggest nose in the world and the worst command of the English language. Gracie Allen—the silliest woman. Ed Wynn wasn't just a fool—he was the perfect fool. And Jack was the tightest man in the world, and the most egotistical.

All those people needed a live audience. So what I did was to get the cameras out of the way, put them in the back of the theater, to photograph him from a distance so that he wouldn't even be aware of the cameras. I'd learned a great lesson from Ed Wynn: never let the scenery or the equipment get in the way of the comedy. I told Jack, "The camera is nothing else than another head in the audience." From then on, he went out on the stage and did his stuff. If you ever look at the old Benny shows, you'll be amazed to see how much of it was done by Jack, working by himself in one, in front of a curtain, without any embellishment.

In those days we were a small, tightly knit bunch, no hierarchy of outsiders coming in to tell you what they thought was funny. Benny and his group of writers were such a marvelous team—the guys knew precisely what to create for him, and most of the time Jack accepted it without even arguing. I remember one day, Jack refused to do some line, or a bit of business, I can't remember what it was, and there we were, myself, Sam Perrin, George Balzer, John Tackaberry, Milton Josefsberg, and the others, all of us sitting in the first row of the theater, and Jack stood up onstage and said, "I won't do this—it's not funny." Long pause, and then George Balzer finally said, "Well, Jack— eight of us *could* be wrong." Jack broke up laughing, and that was the end of the discussion.

[Remembering his long years with Benny, Josefsberg wrote in the Writers Guild *News*: "Writing for Jack was a joy, not only financially, but an ego trip. When Jack read your offering, he didn't merely smile or chuckle, he roared. And frequently fell on the floor doubled up with laughter. This is no figure of speech. Jack actually fell down and rolled on the floor in hysterics. We writers had an inside line about this. 'If you don't have Jack send at least three suits a week to the cleaners, you ain't doing your job.'

"Phil Harris summed it up best when he said, 'Making Jack Benny laugh is about as difficult as going to the toilet at White Sulphur Springs.' "]

Hal March, Bea Benaderet, Gracie Allen, and George Burns (Courtesy Ralph Levy and CBS)

We had other arguments. Once we did a show—I'm sure it was one of the funniest we ever did, where Jack's old Maxwell was stolen and he called the Beverly Hills police. He asked the operator for the number of the Beverly Hills police station—she told him it was an unlisted number. That sort of thing. Eventually, he came to the police station, it was beautiful, wall-to-wall carpets, hanging crystal chandeliers, all nonsense, but the set told the whole story. I cast the scene, and we had a reading in the office; I hired Lyle Talbot, the old movie star, to play the desk sergeant. Jack got me aside after we'd read the scene and he was very unenthusiastic. He argued with me about my casting. He didn't want my actors, he wanted his old gang, people like Frank Nelson or Mel Blanc, people whom he always used to do comedy bits. We got to the

Ralph Levy, Rochester, and Jack Benny (Courtesy Ralph Levy and CBS)

point where I challenged him on it, and I said, "Look—I'm your producer and your director on this show. You can fire me right now, but as long as I'm producing and directing, this is the way it's going to be." Jack got furious and he left.

We rehearsed the show, and then we did it—live—and that scene was a smash hit, mainly because the actors played it straight, and didn't caricature the comedy. Now Jack never came into my control booth. He always stayed away, in fact I wasn't sure he even knew where it was, but after the show that night, he managed to find it, he came in and he said, "Well, Ralph, I just want to tell you—it feels marvelous that I *didn't* have to tell you 'I told you so!' "

Another time Jack's petulance took over. That petulance wasn't just part of the stage character he projected, he was capable of it as a person as well. We

Jack Benny and Bob Hope (Courtesy CBS)

had another minor blowup of some kind, and this time he decided not to speak to me directly. During rehearsals, he would send his secretary to me and she'd say, "Mr. Benny wants to know if he could have a cup of coffee now." Or "Mr. Benny wants to know if this is where you'd like him to play his violin." If I was in the control booth, giving directions, I'd speak on the talk-back and say, "Jack, would you mind moving about two steps to the left?" He wouldn't answer; he'd just do it. Really petulant . . . in complete contrast to George Burns, who blows his top over something, yells, and then ten minutes later he's forgotten what he said, because he's rid of it.

Finally, after about two weeks of this, Jack's secretary came in and said, "Mr. Benny wants to know if you want to play golf." I said, "Tell Mr. Benny my clubs are at my house, and I don't have my car with me, but I'll play if he wants to drive me over." Jack picked me up, drove me to my house. Silence. I picked up the clubs, and we went to Hillcrest and played eighteen holes—and he never said one word to me, I never said one word to him.

Then we went inside the clubhouse, and sat down with George Burns. George made some sort of a joke, and Jack broke up, and so did I, and right away we were talking again, and it was as if we'd never had an argument at all! Forgotten. . . .

Such a sensitive man. I don't think he knew the names of two people backstage, or in our crew, but come Christmas, he wanted to buy everybody a present. Most people in his position would send their secretaries out to shop. Not Jack. He'd make up his own list; he'd ask me, "Now, the fellow on the camera, number one, who's sort of bald . . ." He knew every single face, but no names.

I did a lot of other shows at CBS then. I produced the pilot of *I Love Lucy*, and another one of *Corliss Archer*, and *I Love Luigi*, and then I went on to do pilots for *Green Acres* and *The Beverly Hillbillies*, all of which were successful and had long runs. But they were not the same as working with Ed Wynn, or George and Gracie, and Jack. These people were from another era of show business; one in which you took literally years to build your comedic character. I used to have dinner every Wednesday night at Fanny Brice's house; for two or three years, that was a standing date. When Fanny died she was still working on a new comedy character, a Pennsylvania Dutch girl. She hadn't quite refined it to her own satisfaction and yet she'd been working for years on it, just as she worked for years to create Baby Snooks. I remember somebody once told me that Flo Ziegfeld once asked Fanny to do

The business of writing comedy is not funny: Jack Benny and staff (Courtesy CBS)

a comedic ballet, and she told him she would in two or three years, after she'd studied dance twice a week for that time, so she'd know what she was parodying, or making fun of! That's the sort of preparation those people put into their work. And it's certainly the reason why Jack Benny was successful on television.

It's very, very different today. The Burns and Allen show and Jack's show were essentially one-man operations. Nowadays there are literally dozens of people grouped around TV shows, and to get a comedy idea past them, you have to run a gauntlet. And in those days we were enjoying our work. I don't go walking on sets anymore, to visit people the way we used to do. It's not fun anymore. One guy's there saying, "You're going overtime," another guy's there saying, "You're over budget," everybody's tensed up and nervous. Oh, sure, we had plenty of our own crises, but they were usually constructive ones, based on doing the best possible show we were capable of.

I remember when George Burns went from two years of live shows into film. A very logical move, because that meant they could have the show in a film can and sell it again and again, but the difference was that now it was George's money, not CBS's. So George, who never had had to worry about anything, now began to worry about things. I would get calls, any time of day. He'd call and say, "I understand that if we have our reading at 3:30 instead of at three, we don't have to pay overtime," or things like "Ralph, I understand that you could have gotten such-and-such an actress for less money if you hadn't called her in on Monday." "Ralph, why are you using three-inch nails to build the set when you only needed two-inch nails?" One day he called me at the Brown Derby, where I was eating, about something or other, and I finally blew up. His offices were at the Hollywood Plaza Hotel, and I told him I'd be right over. I stamped in there and went down the hall to his office and I told him what he could do with his show, and his family, and his house, and then I stamped out and headed back for the elevators. As I stood there waiting for them, I heard George behind me, saying, "Ralph?"

I turned around and I walked back about fifty yards to him, and he said, "I'm a naughty Jew." And he never in his life opened his mouth again.

Lovely people.

And there's one myth about Jack Benny I'd like to scotch now. He's supposed to have been a guy who relied solely on his writers to get his laughs for him. As a matter of fact, one of the funniest lines that Fred Allen pulled, during those years when he and Jack were having their famous feud on the radio, was "Jack Benny couldn't ad-lib a belch after a Hungarian dinner." [It was actually written by Harry Conn, one of Benny's original writers.]

Well, I was with Jack once when he was sitting in a restaurant, quietly eating dinner, and a nice midwestern lady came up, a complete stranger, and she said, "Please excuse me, Mr. Benny, but could I ask you a question? I've been studying the various people who are comedians, and I notice that most of them are either Jewish or they're Irish. Is there some reason for that?"

Jack sat there for a moment, and then he looked up at her and said, very sweetly, "Madam—have you ever met a funny Lutheran?"

"WILL YOU
SIGN IN, MR...?"

It appeared on CBS in February, 1950, and its first showing on the TV tube was, to be charitable, a mess. If there were any mistakes to be made, they were made that night, up to and including a panel of "experts" that consisted of two gentlemen who both were named Hoffman! (One was an ex-governor of New Jersey, the second was a psychiatrist. They were joined by Louis Untermeyer, the poet, and Dorothy Kilgallen, the Broadway gossip columnist.)

The original notion for the show had been suggested to its producers, Mark Goodson and Bill Todman, by one of their employees, Bob Bach. At the time, Goodson and Todman were radio quiz-show producers earning a steady but unspectacular living by producing such uncomplicated efforts as a half-hour appeal to the public greed called *Winner Take All*. (There is an apocryphal legend concerning the day that Bill Todman, hurrying across Fifty-second Street from CBS's 485 Madison Avenue headquarters to the radio studio, dropped a coffee percolator—one of the many so-called prizes that were bestowed on contestants—en route. Whereupon Goodman Ace, the father of *Easy Aces*, leaned out a window to call, "Hey Bill, you dropped your script!")

In those primitive days there was no time to prepare, nor was there production know-how available. The second airing of the show, two weeks later, was little better than the first. Sans rehearsal, what reached the audience was a half hour replete with contestants stumbling across stage, hesitant interviews, and cameras that refused to stay still. But in 1950 most production was being conducted under such hit-or-miss conditions; small wonder that the death rate of new program ideas was so astronomical.

The show received a reprieve from CBS. The essential notion Bach had come up with, that of a series of anonymous guests who would appear and face a panel of "experts" who would then attempt to discover through a series of questions the visitor's *modus vivendi*, still seemed to hold promise. And the gimmick of a "mystery guest," who would emerge, after the panel had been blindfolded, sign in, and then, by any means, usually vocal, try to stump the panelists, was to become an audience-pleaser.

A desperate program of retooling was needed, and fast. A new director, Franklin Heller, was persuaded to take over the third show. A potential sponsor would be watching. So far, said buyer had been unimpressed by what he had seen.

"In those days, nobody knew much about production," recalls Heller. "But I knew one thing. Everybody was fascinated by the technology of this new medium. People would come to the studios to watch the cameras and the cameramen, switching lenses and zooming in and out; they paid very little attention to the *shows* themselves. I figured that once I could get those cameramen and their flowered sports shirts controlled and fairly immobile, then we might be able to let this show emerge."

Heller hurried over to the old Maxine Elliott Theater, from which the show was telecast, and proceeded to draw up a floor plan—something nobody at CBS had yet thought to do. He then worked out a simple production scheme that involved stationary cameras and a slightly redesigned set, where nobody would stumble on or off.

The physical production was spartan-like: a dais for the master of ceremonies, John Daly; a long covered table for the four panelists; another chair for the guest; and one blackboard, all of it backed by simple gray-velour curtains. The under-the-line cost to CBS and Goodson-Todman (i.e., physical production, props, etc.) was, and would remain for many years, a minuscule $300 per week.

As for rehearsal, Heller and his retooled production scheme were permitted precisely one hour's worth of setup and run-through before the actual air time.

On went that third show, and during the make-or-break airing the control-booth telephone rang; it was Chicago calling. The potential sponsor, a manufacturer of a squeeze-bottle deodorant named Stopette, was on the line. "I like the show!" he said. "I don't know what you did to it, but I'll buy it!"

What's My Line?, 1950 (Courtesy CBS)

From that night in 1950 until October, 1967, *What's My Line?* would remain a fixture (and a very profitable one) on the CBS network. Its successful rebirth and an ensuing seventeen-year run would make it the cornerstone of a major television empire for Messrs. Goodson and Todman, who in the ensuing years would produce many more variations on the original theme: *I've Got a Secret* and *To Tell the Truth*, among others. But their *What's My Line?* seems to have developed a sturdy life of its own. Even after it left the CBS network in 1967, the show was to reappear elsewhere, on a five-times-a-week syndication basis. Twenty-five years after its debut, those tapes are still being shown somewhere tonight.

MAX WILK

The cast of panelists was remarkably stable. Daly stayed on throughout as master of the questions. In the early years, behind that durable set piece, sat Bennett Cerf, the genial publisher-raconteur; Miss Kilgallen; Arlene Francis, the actress; and a gag writer named Hal Block. (Miss Francis had been acting on the stage and in a few films before TV, but she cheerfully concedes that it was *What's My Line?* that made her famous. "I made a picture once at Universal called *Murders in the Rue Morgue*," she says. "When I was very young, of course. Years later they used to revive it at the Rialto, on Times Square, and whenever I came on the screen, usually threatened by the villain, the guys in the audience used to yell, '*What's my line, honey?*' ") Block's spot as house wit was filled in years to come by such reliable ad-libbers as Fred Allen, Tony Randall, Peter Ustinov, Jack Paar, Henry Morgan, Buddy Hackett, and Ernie Kovacs, Steve Allen, Mort Sahl, et al., all of them flipping good-humored gags as they concentrated on third-degreeing a seemingly endless stream of contestants with oddball occupations.

And then there were the "mystery guests." It would be far more simple to list the names of the celebrities who have *not* appeared on the show over all these years than it would be to list those who did. On the occasion of the show's twenty-fifth anniversary, in May, 1975, a special commemorative review of its career was presented over ABC. For ninety minutes, with kinescope clips from all their past shows as source material, Goodson and Todman concentrated on a parade of "mystery guests" over the years. What made the program so remarkably poignant was not so much its durability but the glimpses of so many celebrities who have vanished from the scene since 1950, after the nights when, to tumultuous applause, there "signed in" Gracie Allen, Jack Benny, Paul Muni, Maurice Chevalier, Gypsy Rose Lee, Mrs. Eleanor Roosevelt, Buster Keaton, Ed Wynn, Bert Lahr, Barry Fitzgerald, Senator Everett Dirksen, Noel Coward . . . and the rest.

The mammoth impact of television as a selling force is nowhere more amply demonstrated than by the story of the genial old white-haired gentleman from Kentucky who showed up one night, some years ago, with the ostensible purpose of attempting to stump *What's My Line?*'s panel of experts.

"We rarely accepted obvious commercial 'plants,' " says Frank Heller, "but this fellow came in through Toots Shor, the famous restaurant owner, who was a good friend of John Daly, our host. He'd passed along material on the old man to John, who gave it to us. There were pictures and biographical stuff—we looked it over; he was a lovely, courtly Kentuckian whose occupation

★ 188 ★

seemed to be that he made and sold his own fried chicken. We called him up down there and checked him out, and he sounded marvelous, quite a unique southern character, so we booked him on the show.

"He arrived wearing a white suit and sporting a silver-headed cane—little beard, glasses. Marvelous. I don't remember whether or not the panel guessed his occupation, but at any rate, there he was, on CBS, telling the whole country about his special recipe for fried chicken, and how he did it all in his own kitchen, and when it came out, how it was really finger-lickin' good. The audience loved him. When it was time to go, he got up and bowed to the panelists, very courteously, and waved good-bye to the audience. That was it. He went back to Kentucky, and we didn't think much about him. After all, we'd had many other effective contestants over the years.

"Except, of course," Heller adds, wryly, "that within a few months after that, Colonel Sanders Fried Chicken stands began to blossom all over the landscape, and eventually, it became one of the major franchise businesses of this era. A couple of years later, a man named Brown, in Louisville, Kentucky, who was one of the original backers of the Colonel's chicken, was being interviewed by *The Wall Street Journal* on the origins of this vast new empire, and he cheerfully admitted that while the Colonel had a pretty good recipe, the whole shebang would never have gotten off the ground if Toots Shor, up in New York, who was Brown's friend, hadn't managed to arrange to get Colonel Sanders onto *What's My Line?*

"I also hate to add," says Heller, "*nobody* ever suggested that we buy a single share of stock in that finger-lickin' chicken."

And yet another performer—this one the singer Pearl Bailey—can give *What's My Line?* credit for inadvertently making her into a Broadway star of the first magnitude.

A few years back, it seems that both Miss Bailey and Mr. David Merrick, the eminent theatrical producer, had been scheduled one evening to appear as mystery guests; on some nights, the show did have two. "But nobody had had the nerve to tell Merrick that he was going to appear first, and that somebody else would be on next-to-closing," says Heller.

"That particular night, our producer brought Merrick into the control booth, and left him sitting there with me. I spent a few minutes explaining the game to him, showing him where he'd enter, all that technical stuff, and in the course of conversation, it came out that he would be going on right after the first commercial. Merrick caught on immediately—he said, 'I thought *I*

was the headliner here tonight; who's supposed to be the second mystery guest?'
I told him that it was against the rules for me to divulge to absolutely anybody
else who that would be—and I could tell that Mr. Merrick was beginning
to work up a head of steam.

"Just at that moment, in walked Miss Bailey herself, accompanied by a
young agent from the William Morris office. She'd been on the show before,
and as anybody who's ever been near her will tell you, she's absolutely the
nicest human being you've ever been around. Merrick wanted to know who
she was, and I told him. Well, he figured out that she was to be the second
mystery guest, and he obviously wasn't too impressed with her—or me. I went
over to Pearlie May, and I took her aside, and I said, 'Pearlie, you've been on
the show before, and it's no problem for you, but we have this big Broadway
producer here, and he's a little nervous about going on—do you think you
could go over and reassure him, and kind of keep him happy?'

"She thought that was a marvelous idea, and she went over and started
honeying up Merrick and sweet-talking him, she landed on him like a feather
comforter, and he never knew what hit him. So, then he went on the air, and
did his spot—but he didn't leave backstage—he hung around waiting for
Pearlie May to come on. She did her appearance, and she was her usual marvelous self—and then, when the show was over, everybody went out to the Oak
Room at the Plaza for supper. While they were there, Merrick leaned over to
Pearlie May and said, 'You know—I just had an idea. I have a show running
called *Hello, Dolly!*, with Carol Channing, and she's about to leave. How
would you like to replace her?' "

Miss Bailey got a long-term contract, Mr. Merrick's show received a new
lease on life, and that William Morris agent who accompanied the lady to the
Sunday night show went into his office the next morning an overnight hero.

Several years later, Miss Bailey was asked by a reporter how it had all come
about, and she was reported as saying, "Well, honey, I don't really know. But
it was so funny, I was the mystery guest on *What's My Line?* and somebody
over there introduced me to David Merrick, and that's about it."

A decade or so later, Heller smiles. "I guess if you're called 'somebody' by
Pearlie May Bailey," he remarks, "you really *are* somebody."

In the twenty-five television seasons since that first question-and-answer period, the TV audience has been treated to an endless procession of look-and-
sound-alike imitations of *What's My Line?*, all of which have emerged hopefully, and then, sometimes within short weeks of their premieres, vanished

into the limbo of lost quiz shows. What do you recall of *Jukebox Jury?* Of *Who Said That?, It's News to Me, Place the Face, Two for the Money, Who's the Boss?, Where Was I?, The Name's the Same, Make the Connection, Down You Go, Leave It to the Girls, This Is Show Business,* and/or *It Pays to Be Ignorant?* There have been literally dozens of such half hours, concocted by hopeful entrepreneurs expecting to cash in on the lasting popularity of that tantalizingly simple original Goodson and Todman concept.

They're gone. But somewhere tonight, on some local station near you, there's a contestant still signing in, to challenge the panel to define his vocation. Is it really possible that the working population of these United States can contain such an endless supply of pigeon-trainers, sail-hemmers, feed-bag sewers, date- and prune-pitters, ladies who stitch baseballs, wedding-cake icers, railroad track walkers, bumper-sticker printers, tugboat pilots, animal grave-diggers, sod-planters, etc., etc.?

For twenty-five years *What's My Line?* has answered that rhetorical question affirmatively. If it takes all kinds of people to make a world, then it's certain that most of them have at one time or another scrawled their John and/or Jane Hancocks across that blackboard, and, in the process, transformed Mark Goodson and Bill Todman into two citizens with one simple occupation: money-coiners.

"PEACE":
Dave Garroway

In those frenetic early years of TV's infancy, when noisy extroverts and brassy ex-vaudevillians, down-home howlers and Catskill refugees all dashed out in front of the cameras and fought to grab the audience's attention, to keep Ma and Pa's itchy fingers from flicking the dial to another channel, Dave Garroway's weekly show was an oasis of talent . . . and quiet.

Serene in a witty half-hour musical revue that entertained, pleasured the people, and constantly talked up to them, Garroway was the first "personality" to take advantage of the intimacy of television. As the host and participant in *Garroway at Large*, he was no aggressive weekly door-to-door salesman; rather, he was a friendly, amiable visitor to the living room, a wanted guest, completely at home in your home.

Tall, quiet, given to understatement, with large glasses that gave him the mien of an amiable owl, Garroway, an instinctively shy person, was never at his best in front of a live audience. But when it came to establishing a tight one-to-one rapport with the people on the other side of the TV tube, he was to have few equals.

Garroway began his career as an NBC pageboy in New York, but after World War II he moved to Chicago, where he became the host of his own radio show, *The 1160 Club*, on which he played jazz records and chatted.

By 1948 Chicago had become a thriving television center, with a series of original program concepts emanating from the NBC studios. Under the aegis

Dave Garroway with J. Fred Muggs and Phoebe B. Beebe, *Today* (Courtesy NBC)

of production executive Jules Herbevaux there would come *Kukla, Fran and Ollie*, a pioneer live daytime serial called *Hawkins Falls*, an improvised show called *Studs' Place*, which starred Studs Terkel, and eventually, in 1949, the uniquely original half-hour musical revue *Garroway at Large*.

Charlie Andrews, who was to become Garroway's writer and close friend, began his career by selling occasional pieces of material to the radio disc jockey. The two men developed a fine comedic rapport, and when Herbevaux persuaded Garroway to take his first shot at television, it was logically Andrews who was called in to assist in developing some sort of a concept.

The first effort designed for Garroway's talents by producer Ted Mills was a long-forgotten effort called *Contrasts*, in which Garroway was to muse on the various opposites of life: black and white, loud music and soft, the cube versus the round ball, and so on. Needless to report, it was scrapped promptly after its first outing, and fortunately thereafter emerged the most ingenious and inventive *Garroway at Large*.

To describe a good revue is like giving a menu for smorgasbord: you get a list of the elements, but none of the total effect. "Songs and dances, little comedy routines, a lot of visual humor, all of it held together by Dave, who worked without any audience," remembers Andrews, a taciturn man who a quarter century afterward still functions full-time as a television producer. "It was a very daring experiment for those times, believe me. We operated out of a very small studio, with no room to set up or reset our scenery, nothing could be moved, or flown upward. So we had to improvise our own technique. I said, 'Well, let's just pan from one set to another—Dave can *walk* from place to place, and introduce the numbers, and the scenes, and the people,' and the whole thing became a sort of musical *Our Town*, not because we ever intended it to be, but because we had to."

Garroway at Large, with its amiable cast of regulars—Jack Haskell, Connie Russell, Cliff Norton, and Betty Chappel, soon caught and held tight a large audience. From the beginning, Andrews was the lone writer, responsible for devising program material each week. "Today there'd be five writers," he remarks, ruefully. "But who had a budget for such lavishness? I was getting about $150 a week—by the time we finished, I'd gone up to $250. But for a guy who at the time had never seen a hundred-dollar bill in his life, that seemed like a huge paycheck, believe me."

Invention, rather than largesse, was the spirit of the show. "Everybody pitched in to work up creative ideas," he says. "The crew, the cameramen—whenever somebody suggested an idea, we'd try it. Nobody was out to knife anyone else, the spirit around that studio was terrific. Television was brand-new, you could do any damn thing you wanted to, and nobody could tell you, 'No, don't do that, it won't work,' because nobody knew anything. So there was this burst of creativity around NBC because there was so much room to burst."

Strolling through the proceedings, chatting with his cast, occasionally commenting on the proceedings, Garroway was the pleasant escort through a relaxed half hour that tried to expand the horizons of this infant medium. "Not that any of that stuff would be too remarkable today," concedes Andrews. "In those days, if Connie Russell picked up a picture frame with a picture of Jack Haskell in it and sang a song to her fellow—and then we'd dissolve through to Jack Haskell, live, in the picture frame, and he'd start singing back to her— well, that was a fantastic effect for then. Today it's been done so many times since that if anybody suggested such a transition to me, I'd toss him out of my office. But in those days, it was innovative, believe me." And someday, perhaps, it will be again.

Garroway's crew indulged in other imaginative stagings. If a sequence in- volved a patient in a dentist's chair, then the camera would become the audi- ence itself, sitting in the chair, with Cliff Norton, as the dentist, peering into the home viewer's mouth, chatting away as he worked on his mute patient. "I got that notion when I was having my own teeth cleaned," says Andrews, "and then one of the cameramen suggested that we distort the shot so that Norton's face would loom up as he leaned in . . . and then we used a sparkler to flash—that was supposed to be his drill. Vivid as hell. . . ."

One of the program's most admired devices was the sign-off, in which, to the strains of his theme, "Sentimental Journey," Garroway would say a few fond closing words, bid his audience a gentle adieu, and then hold up his hand to declare "Peace." After which, the credits would roll, over a final visual joke. If, a moment previously, a girl had just finished singing "Black Coffee," a torch song dealing with lost love and late-night caffeine addiction, then, as the credits rolled, the audience might see a shot of milk being poured into a cup of black coffee, and the milk spilling down all over the studio floor. "This program came to you from Chicago," said the NBC voice, "the neatest studio in the world."

"That came to be known as 'the milk-bottle ending,' " says Andrews. "Our trademark. We'd have Dave saying things like '. . . from Chicago, the friend- liest city in the world,' and he'd turn around and we'd show a knife sticking out of his back. One night we actually cut a piece of cable in front of the camera and went to pitch black as if all the lights had blown, and Dave said, '. . . from Chicago, the darkest studio in the country.' "

Simultaneously with his chores on *Garroway at Large*, Andrews moved into the preparation of *Studs' Place*, an even more innovative program concept, a half-hour show that took place in Terkel's mythical corner bar and grill, where all the denizens improvised their dialogue, sans any memorizable script. In these rigidly structured times, such a program idea would instantly turn any network executive's hair white. But in 1950 the stakes were less enormous, with ample room to experiment. Andrews would sketch out the episode's action on a couple of pages and then present his actors with a rough draft of the proposed plot. "We'd rehearse, with everybody improvising dialogue, about such a situation, say, as Studs fighting with his wife because she was spending too much on groceries—and then I'd stand back and let the actors take over. All I did from then on was to tell them whenever I thought they were getting boring—then they'd move on to something new."

Somehow, the technique worked. The charm of *Studs' Place*, and it was considerable, was enhanced by the sense that what was happening on the home screen was actually taking place, as it took place, with spontaneity. So skillful were Terkel and his fellow performers at their improvisation that they were able to project as real people, never actors. And remember, all this took place a thousand miles or so away from the Actors Studio in New York, the home of improvisation.

Congoleum-Nairn was the original and well-satisfied sponsor of *Garroway at Large*, and stayed with the show for three years. Then Swift & Company, the meat-packers, took over, but were soon caught in a commercial bind that was not due to the show's popularity, but to the elementary state of television's technology. "Somehow or other," says Andrews, "in those days the advertising agency brains had forgotten that our show was sent around America on kinescope. So when you did a program selling Easter hams, that kinescope might not get to Cleveland until, say, the week after Easter, when they didn't want to sell any more hams. Thanksgiving turkey sales pitches would get to California maybe two weeks or so after the holiday—if at all. They canceled, and that left us stranded in Chicago."

Not for long.

High up in the towers of Radio City in New York, an NBC production executive, Sylvester ("Pat") Weaver, was, in concert with a young producer named Mort Werner, planning a bold new concept for a daily morning show to be called *Today*. (The story goes that Weaver wandered into Werner's office one day to ask, "What are the first things you think about when you wake up in the morning?" To which Werner replied, "That I have to go to the bathroom—and what happened while I was asleep." "Congratulations," said Weaver. "You've just become the producer of a show called *Today* and what happened while you were asleep is what it's all about.") Both men began to look around for a host—he would be called a "communicator"—to serve as a genial early-morning low-keyed human alarm clock to the vast yawning populace across the land.

How was the quiet, reserved Garroway selected as the "communicator"? Werner, who was the producer not only of *Today* but also of NBC's *Tonight*, supplies a curiously revealing insight into Garroway's character.

"I didn't really know Garroway at all," he says, almost a quarter century later. "Only what I'd seen him doing on *Garroway at Large*. Remember, at that point I was quite a young man trying to make decisions in an area called television which had just been invented. His name came up, and I finally decided, no, he wasn't right at all, too slow and plodding for what we had in mind. Then I got a call from Chicago. Garroway himself. I didn't even know him. He said, 'I want to introduce myself; I understand you don't really feel I'd be right for the *Today* show.' I told him my intuitive reaction was to go in a different direction. He said, 'Mr. Werner, what do you know about me?' I said, 'Well, I've seen your program. . . .' He said, 'What do you *know* about me?' I began to feel somewhat awkward, because he was right. He said, 'I'll tell you what, Mr. Werner—before you make the decision about whether you'd like to give me an opportunity, don't you think it would be a good idea if we talked to each other?' I agreed that would be a good idea. He said 'Well, I'm in Chicago and you're in New York—what are you doing for dinner tonight?' It ended up with my flying that afternoon to Chicago. Didn't get there until midnight because of the delays. He picked me up at the airport, took me back to his hotel, the Ambassador East, he said, 'I saved some food, I thought you'd be hungry.' He got out two cans of Campbell's baked beans from the refrigerator, and two bottles of root beer, which weren't refrigerated. And he said, 'I hope you like baked beans and root beer.' I said, 'Of course—who doesn't?'

"We ate, and then we sat and talked all night, and I discovered a lot of things about Dave. First, that he was very well educated; second, that he had worked for NBC radio for many years in several different cities as a newscaster and a reporter; and finally, that he'd won the Chicago Open golf tournament, which wasn't pertinent. But I really fell in love with the man on a one-to-one basis. So I came back to New York and I said, 'I've found my host—Dave Garroway' . . . and I learned a great lesson from that experience: not to make snap decisions without investigating."

In late 1951 Garroway was summoned to New York, to be briefed on the details of Weaver and Werner's potential program.

"That was a day I'll never forget," says Charlie Andrews. "We were ushered into Pat's office at the top of the building, overlooking the ice rink below, with the whole New York skyline. I was just a simple midwestern guy, overwhelmed by this enormous office and the view. There was Weaver, immaculately tailored, behind his huge desk, and I sat in the back with all the program people while he started to tell us what he had in mind.

"Pat said, 'Let me describe this concept as we've all been working on it—we've been going at it for over a year, trying to figure it all out. Norman Bel Geddes will design the studio; a huge glass structure, glass-roofed so that the sun can come in; there will be a long balcony up above so that the public can look down and watch the show as it happens. Down below, at a big desk, there will be the "communicator." He'll have every known means of communication feeding into the place. Radio, TV screens, telephones, the lot. If the communicator wants to pick up the phone to call Berlin about something that's happening right then and there, he'll get a direct report, and visually, it'll flash on the screen behind him. Tokyo, Australia, everywhere—he can describe it as it takes place—we'll see it—this studio will be the communications center not only of the world, but of the whole *universe!*'

"Pat went on and on, painting this fantastic picture—and I'm sitting there thinking to myself, 'This is the most incredible damn thing I've ever heard about—please, God, let us get in on it!' Finally the meeting ended, and I was walking down the hall, still stunned, with one of the guys who'd been working with Weaver for the past year, and I said, 'Listen—this is certainly going to be the biggest thing that ever hit television, but I think I missed one little point. It's supposed to start in three months, fine, but exactly where *is* this terrific studio Pat was talking about, with the glass roof and the huge balcony?' And the NBC guy said, 'Oh, nobody's built that yet, so to begin with, we're going to have to share a studio with *Howdy Doody.*'" ("Not only *Howdy Doody,* but *Bob and Ray!*" remembers Werner.)

The Weaver-Werner broad-vistaed vision may have been missing a few tangible details, but *Today* did debut on the air, on the morning of January 14, 1952, with Garroway as its "communicator-host." The show emanated from even more mundane surroundings than originally planned: Werner had arranged for the use of the tiny Johnny Victor Theater, on Forty-ninth Street, which had originally been a showroom for the display of RCA TV sets. ("I wanted a place where people could look in and watch us doing the show—and where *we* could look *out,*" says Werner.) The show's initial impact was somewhat less than solid. "For one year we died on the air," Werner admits. "Just died. But NBC kept us on—Weaver was determined to prove he was right. I discovered that the only way to do the show was to keep changing things. Everything—put on new people, put on a new weatherman, new features—just go, go, go—to the point where one morning I got into an elevator and bumped into a chimpanzee who shook my hand, and I said, 'Let's you and me go back to my office,' and the next day we named him J. Fred Muggs and put him on the show—which got us a cover on *Time* magazine. It was a calculated campaign to make people know we were there."

Eventually Werner's persistence began to pay dividends, and *Today* established itself on firm ground. And (as it is somewhat superfluous to report) the show has remained a fixture in the 7–9 A.M. NBC time slot ever since.

In the same year that *Today* debuted, *Garroway at Large* also returned to the NBC schedule, from a New York studio. Shortly afterward it was retooled into one of the first variety shows to be telecast in Living Color, with the NBC peacock heralding a half-hour visit with Garroway's now-familiar troupe of regulars. Such was Garroway's capacity for work that he was also able to take on a daily fifteen-minute radio show, *Dial Dave Garroway*, while at the same time maintaining his strenuous TV chores, a weekly work schedule that set a record for stamina, to be equaled only by CBS's omnipresent Arthur Godfrey.

Amid all the tensions of the three-hour morning schedule (in those precoaxial cable days, *Today* telecast a third hour that was sent out to the midwestern audiences from nine to ten, New York time), Garroway sat behind the desk and cheerfully managed to keep his cool in the midst of crises, of which there were many. "One morning Dave was doing a dog-food commercial," says Andrews. "Most of the commercials in those days were live. The stagehand brought over a small puppy who was supposed to sit on Dave's desk while he talked about the product. The camera was just about to switch onto Dave when suddenly the puppy developed stage fright and did his business—right on Dave's desk. Everybody froze. The floor manager, a young kid, just stared at it. Not Mort Werner. He grabbed a piece of paper, ran over to the desk, and scooped the mess off Dave's desk, seconds before the red light on the camera went on. Dave went right off into his commercial. Werner, still holding the paper, grinned at the floor manager, and he said, 'Now, sonny, you've finally learned what a television producer *does.*'"

The secret of Garroway's longevity? "He was a tremendous salesman," says Andrews. "Projected sincerity. He was never one of those hard-driving huckster types, who bullied you into buying the product. He *understood*—and that really was his secret. Whether it was a beautiful Rodgers and Hart ballad, or a tube of toothpaste, he hooked you, got your attention, and he kept it, with that remarkable fey sense of humor that he has."

Garroway has been in semi-retirement for some years now, and certainly those of us who fondly recall the innovative pleasures of *Garroway at Large* are much poorer for his absence. "I would very much like to tell you that it was because we were all geniuses then that it all happened," says Andrews. "But it isn't quite true. What is the truth is that we guys who started out in the early days of television had marvelous opportunities—we had so much room in which to move around then—that we were able to take advantage of them. I've worked on a lot of shows since then, but I'm very proud of *Garroway at Large*. It's the best thing I've ever done. Although," he adds ruefully, "I'm equally proud of surviving in this goddamn business—which isn't exactly the easiest thing to do."

Let Garroway provide his own closing.

"I got a lovely Christmas card from Dave this year," says Andrews. "A full typewritten page, which said he'd been concerned with studying the work of Einstein and Newton and a lot of other mathematicians. He set down a lot of very complicated formulae, which were obviously put there to confuse me, and then he said he'd finally worked out a formula of his own, which was written all the way across the page—something an atomic physicist could have created. Dave said that by feeding into that formula—it's called a *quork*—the amount of money that he had to spend at Christmas, the number of people he had to spend it on, the amount of affection he has for all these people, the amount of loyalty he feels toward them, their affection toward him, et cetera, then the *quork* divides all those factors up, and he ends up knowing exactly how much to spend on each of his friends for Christmas. And enclosed was his personal check to me for $4.45."

Andrews smiles. "That's exactly the sort of whimsy we would have used back there on *Garroway at Large*, at the end of our Christmas show. Dave would have demonstrated his formula to the audience, and then said, 'I can't mail it all out, but if I could, you are each entitled to my personal check for a million dollars.'"

For which sentiment, Mr. Garroway, we thank you.

VARIOUS NIGHTMARES
AND HORROR STORIES

Perry Lafferty remembers:

I got into television in the earliest years. I'd been doing a couple of radio shows for BBD&O, an advertising agency, and I was standing in the doorway of one of the executive's offices one day—he was obviously getting bawled out by somebody upstairs, because he was cringing there with the phone in his hand. He took advantage of a beat in the other man's diatribe to say, "I've got just the man for you!" He meant me. That's how I got my first TV job, directing a show called *B. F. Goodrich Celebrity Time*, which starred Conrad Nagel, Kyle MacDonnell, Herman Hickman, who was the Yale football coach, and the basset hound named Morgan whose only function was to sit on the table and stare at the audience.

I didn't know very much about directing cameras, so most of it was learning how to stage all the little stunts that we would dream up for the guests to do on the show. We telecast it from a tiny studio up on top of the Chanin Building on Forty-second Street. In those days they stuck a transmitting "dish" out the window and aimed at Grand Central, across the street. The signal would be picked up at CBS Master Control, over there. No cables—just the "dish" sticking out the window, high up.

That was in 1948. That year, Arthur Murray decided he was going into television. He and his wife, Kathryn, were to do an *Arthur Murray Party*. Remember, she'd say, "Put a little fun in your life—try dancing!" Their show lasted a long time, almost ten years, off and on. Arthur was an absolute dynamo of a

Arthur and Kathryn Murray, *The Arthur Murray Party* (Courtesy NBC)

man, opinionated and arbitrary, but one of the greatest promoters I've ever encountered—a great showman and, needless to say, a great dancer. So this was going to be my big chance. I'd learned enough about the machinery to take the plunge as a producer-director.

So I went through the most elaborate preparations for that show you can imagine. I'm a terribly meticulous guy, and in those days, as insecure as I was, I overprepared. I worked four months getting it all ready. Hired dancers, set up the show's routines, blocked out all the shots, got everything planned out. The first day of rehearsals, the first hour, we're all there, and I said to the pianist, "All right, now hit the opening music. . . ." I said to the choreographer, "Have the girls start across the stage in position." And Arthur Murray suddenly said, *"Hold it!"*

Everybody stopped, and I looked at him, and he said—out of a clear blue sky—"You know . . . I don't really think I should go on television this summer. . . ."

He meant it. He went off the air before he went on the air!

So my debut as a director-producer had to be postponed awhile.

Kay Kyser and Ish Kabibble, *Kay Kyser's Kollege of Musical Knowledge* (Courtesy NBC)

Eventually, in 1949, I did get another show, with Kay Kyser—*Kay Kyser's Kollege of Musical Knowledge*, which had been a hit for years on radio. We

Russell Arms, Giselle McKenzie, Dorothy Collins, and Snooky Lanson, *Your Hit Parade* (Courtesy NBC)

had two writers who came in to help produce the show for television, Bob Quigley and Eddie Lawrence. These days Quigley is a very successful game-show producer, and Eddie, who's also a very successful painter, is the television comedian "Old Philosopher." Wonderful, crazy guy. I remember when he first met Kay, who for years had been a hit on radio shows with that deep southern accent of his, standing up there doing the intro's to songs—that was all he had to do. Eddie said to Kay, "I know who wrote '*evenin' folks, how y'all?*' but tell me, Kay, who wrote '*So long, evabuddy*'?"

In those days your television career was very diverse; you didn't do anything for very long. I did comedy shows with Victor Borge, and Imogene Coca, and I had a spell on *The Lucky Strike Hit Parade*, and eventually I got into hour-long dramatic shows. The one I worked the most for was Robert Montgomery's hour show on NBC.

I believe it was Brooks Atkinson who once wrote, "Live television is the art of the possible," and I'm sure that about sums up those days in TV drama. We were always dealing in crises.

One time Bob Montgomery talked James Cagney into doing a live TV show, I believe it was his only one. A very lovely show called *Soldier from the Wars Returning*, by Robert Wallace, about a sergeant in the grave detail, in charge of bringing bodies back to their homes for proper burial.

Cagney had a long scene in the play with an actress named Audra Lindley, in which the two of them are seated in the garden at night, quiet, with crickets going, and he had this marvelous monologue about life and what it meant. Cagney really was a magnificent actor, and there was nothing much to do in this scene except let him do it. It was two pages long and I had a few reaction shots of Audra, but mostly I merely held on Cagney's face. Well, we were on the air, and he got three quarters of the way through it, and he was coming up to the climactic paragraph that ended it . . . and if you've been a director long enough, you can see the invisible curtain come down over an actor's eyelids that means he's not seeing anything—he's gone blank, gone up in his lines.

There was nothing I could do. It was one of those terrible moments. Audra couldn't say anything because this was his inner feeling that was being poured out to her—she couldn't speak. I tried to make some cuts with the camera, I improvised some shots, maybe only five or six seconds, which doesn't sound very long, but try timing it on your own watch. I cut to her face. I cut back to him thinking. I flipped to a tighter lens, cut back to her face, back to Cagney—I was desperately improvising.

Then I saw the curtain go up in his eyes again, and I knew he had it. He went on and finished the speech, finished the show without a flaw.

Next day, one of the New York television critics raved about the show. Especially that monologue toward the end. "James Cagney could teach all these new-fangled television actors a thing or two about the value of silence. Not unlike Beethoven's Fifth, with the pause at the end of the first four notes. . . ."

What happens at times like those—if you're the director—is that you sit up there in the control booth watching your life flash past your eyes, and you think of your unemployment check . . . and how long it will take to get downtown to the line.

THE CAPTAIN
AND THE KIDS

Cherubic, soft-spoken, amiable, the exact antithesis of the frenetic android types who serve as television "hosts," Bob Keeshan is the caretaker-in-residence of five weekday hours of valuable CBS-TV prime network time, fifty-two weeks a year. He must be doing something right every day—he's been at that same location for over twenty years.

Bob *who?*

Children (and more than likely, you yourself, if you've been one since 1955) know Keeshan somewhat better as his alter ego, Captain Kangaroo. For over two decades now, he's been the cheerful father figure, stage manager, and star of that charming, intelligent, and instructive CBS children's show that bears his stage name.

That daily morning hour, from eight to nine, shines like a good deed in a naughty world of network news, inane chat shows, syndicated reruns of antique sitcoms, frenetic grab-the-prize-grab-the-prize! game shows, and noisy third-rate assembly-line cartoons. It's a well-known industry truth that CBS might have long since moved the Captain, his good old friend Mr. Greenjeans, his various live animal pets, his puppets, games, and music, off to some limbo-like and less valuable time slot, and thus convert that 8–9 A.M. real estate into some far more lucrative venture, such as NBC's immensely profitable *Today*.

But in these times, when the press and public take turns in badmouthing TV, we must give Mr. Paley and CBS their fair share of brownie points for behaving with a certain amount of integrity when it comes to Captain Kangaroo.

"Oh, I know that our time spot has been coveted for a long time." Keeshan grins, puffing on a pipe in his modest West Fifty-seventh Street offices, deep in the CBS production center. "Dick Salant, who's a top CBS executive, is quoted by Sally Quinn in her book as admitting that fact. He's even said it to me. 'If I could only get your hour. . . . But I don't dare put myself onto the firing line against the mothers of America.' "

Paley, Salant, et al., are very wise men. Keeshan's show is an institution, one that involves Children, Home, and Mother—a formidable trio, and in a fickle business as chancy as TV has proved itself to be (just this past season, the majority of the "new" thirty- and sixty-minute turkeys having been beheaded long weeks before Thanksgiving) you don't fool around with success.

And after twenty years, nobody can argue that Keeshan hasn't been that.

Let us consider the Captain. He maintains his steady, tortoiselike pace across an electronic scene that is filled with the wreckage of dozens of failed "kid-vid" shows—those Saturday morning abominations that noisily and incessantly peddle plastic toys and sugar-crammed breakfast food. His daily hour remains a model of what parents would like TV to be. And he's been at it, with relatively the same format, these twenty long years.

For such extraordinary longevity, there certainly must be an explanation. Perhaps more than one?

Keeshan has some answers. To begin with, there's the factor of his competition. "We've always been on opposite *Today*," he says. "But that's an adult show, and a totally different audience. So we don't have to do what other shows do, which is to try and knock off the opposition. Then, more importantly, within our show, we don't really think of it as a show, but we do think of it as a *visit*. It's low-key, it's an understatement—it tends to wear better than other shows. And we have always tried to serve our audience. We respect them, and we respect their intelligence, and their potential good taste, and we program accordingly. That's enhanced our position, because it's recognized by parents. So we've always had the support of thinking parents."

Quite a departure from the programming standards utilized by those faceless Fagin-type hucksters who utilize children's viewing times as a personal merchandise mart for their shoddy wares.

Keeshan smiles. "I don't know what anybody else's experience may have been with CBS, but for me, it's always been a good one. I can remember back when I had no commercials whatsoever on the show, and a sponsor came in, and he proposed a totally unsuitable product for the program. I had no right to say it, but I did—I insisted I would not have that product on *Captain Kangaroo*. The advertising agency said, 'Who the hell is *he*?' They weren't going to take any of that nonsense. It finally went all the way to Frank Stanton (then the head of CBS) and he said, 'Well, Keeshan's absolutely right. That commercial does not belong with that special audience he has in the early morning.' And that's been the CBS attitude all the way, ever since the beginnings."

The Captain's beginnings were, in retrospect, most accidental.

It was back in 1944 that a very young Bob Keeshan was accepted as a pageboy at NBC, in Rockefeller Plaza, a traditional launchpad for dozens of young men seeking a career in broadcasting. The U.S. Marines interrupted his civilian life for two years, and he returned to NBC in 1946, working days at the studios and attending night school at Fordham. "In those days, there was no television at all, it was radio," he recounts. "The whole NBC building was devoted to radio, but by 1947 there was a little office up on the sixth floor where a few men were involved in television. The executive in charge was an ex-vaudeville booker named Warren Wade, and he had Owen Davis, Jr., with him, plus a staff of four or five—and they were the entire department. In 1947 nobody at RCA believed that television would ever become a major force for a long time to come—their most optimistic projection was 1956 or so."

There were a couple of pioneer TV shows on—John K. M. McCaffrey and *The Author Meets the Critics*, and *Tex and Jinx McCrary*—but very little else. One of the standby NBC radio shows featured an entertainer named Bob Smith, who did a show for kids on Saturday mornings with a character named Howdy Doody, so called because that was his constant greeting. Keeshan, assigned to page duty on NBC's fourth floor, eventually began to help out with odd jobs around Smith's radio show.

One momentous day, Warren Wade conceived of a plan to transfer Smith and Howdy Doody to the infant NBC schedule for TV: a show in which Smith would co-star with a large puppet created especially for the home viewers. "It had to be Bob," says Keeshan, "because in those days you couldn't get anybody else to work in TV. If an actor was making a living in radio or the theater, he was being paid—which certainly wasn't the case in TV. In that medium, there wasn't even a union yet."

The first *Howdy Doody* telecast took place (historians please note) on December 27, 1947.

Bob Keeshan as Captain Kangaroo (Courtesy CBS)

"And I missed the first show," mourns Keeshan. "They'd said, 'You get off at five, we need somebody to come and help pass out the prizes to the kids, we have props we need carried on—would you come in and help?' I agreed—but on that particular day we had a real snowstorm, eighteen inches or so, and I couldn't make it into the city from Forest Hills. But the following week, January 3, I was there—and that's when I made my TV debut."

By the end of January, 1948, *Howdy Doody* appeared on NBC's flickering screen three times a week, an hour a day, and Keeshan's career took an upward swing. "Somebody thought, 'The kid doesn't look right in a page uniform, we really ought to dress him up'—so they gave me a clown costume." By March the show was rescheduled to half an hour each day, and Keeshan was now provided with makeup suitable to his running character, who was dubbed Clarabelle the Clown.

He worked days as a page, then appeared afternoons on TV as Clarabelle, after which he removed his makeup and hurried downtown to his night classes at Fordham. His newfound career, while flourishing, offered little financial reward. "Every day, Bob Smith would slip me a five-dollar bill out of his own pay," he says. "But eventually Bob got tired of putting out his own money each day, and persuaded NBC to give me a deal. Warren Wade agreed to put me on salary—$35 a week—but he insisted that for that much money, I'd have to become a film editor and learn to edit film as well! I balked at that—what did I know about editing film? They said, 'You'll learn—you'll learn!' I refused—I had enough to do without that! Finally they reluctantly made the deal with me—and I was a salaried TV performer."

By the spring of 1948 *Howdy Doody* was an established NBC attraction, its juvenile audience limited to metropolitan kiddies whose parents and/or friends were affluent enough to afford ownership of one of the new ten-inch TV sets. Now the corporate heads of NBC decided to test the waters, to discover the extent of their puppet star's audience. It being a presidential year, somebody craftily devised the notion of Howdy running for President. "Since nobody knew anything about the drawing power of television," remembers Keeshan, "it was decided to offer a *Howdy Doody for President* button to anybody who'd write in. One day I was in Bob Smith's office and a young man dropped by after the show and said, 'I've been put in charge of this whole campaign, handling the mail and distributing the buttons, but I really don't know how many buttons we'll need. How many do you think it should be?'

"Bob didn't know, and Marty Stone, who was Bob's manager, suggested

Buffalo Bob Smith and Howdy Doody (Courtesy NBC)

maybe 10,000 buttons. The NBC guy was dubious. 'Ten thousand? Do you think we can get rid of that many?'

"To make the story interesting, I should tell you that the NBC man was named Sarnoff, Robert Sarnoff, and this was his first job around the place." Keeshan smiles at the recollection of the future boss of RCA haggling over a supply of tin buttons. "To get to the point, we went on the air and made the offer, and within three days we already had 14,000 requests—and nobody knew what the hell had hit us. In a matter of six weeks, we gave away over 100,000 of those *Howdy Doody* buttons—and that was in a period when there were no sets!

"You see, in those days, anybody who had a set in his living room could expect a bunch of kids from the neighborhood to drop in each afternoon—and it was the same with Milton Berle and his Tuesday night show; television shows were a home entertainment event."

Working conditions for performers were, to be polite, primitive. *Howdy Doody* was telecast from a third-floor NBC studio, from 5:30 to 6, and so tight were production facilities that within sixty or seventy-five seconds of the show's sign-off, a second NBC show would be transmitted from the same studio. "We'd go off at 5:58.30, and at 6, the cameras would have been turned around to the other side of the studio, and the crew would start telecasting a musical show with Johnny Andrews and his people.

"I'd been in contact with George Heller, who was the secretary of AFRA, the radio actors' union, and he was part of what was called the Television Authority, TVA. They wanted to set up a contract for performers, regulate rehearsal schedules and working conditions, all those basic things. George would ask me about what I thought was needed, aside from wages. I said, 'First of all, I'd just like a dressing room.' See, in those days, I had a choice. I could make up in the men's room on the third floor, or they'd taken a closet, literally a closet, and they'd put in a couple of tables and some mirrors and a chair or two, and they informed us all—everybody working on the third floor in TV—that it would be our communal dressing room." Keeshan can still wince at the memory. "That sort of thing was what I thought were the issues. They seem silly now, but they weren't then. As a result of my working with Heller, when the authority took over, he came and handed me Card ⚹1. Which I've always been proud of, thinking that in some way, maybe I was the first television actor. One who never had worked in any other medium, but came in and worked in video *first*. . . ." He smiles. "I still have that card. TVA, ⚹1."

Howdy Doody thrived and soon became an American institution, one that would spin off huge profits for the network and for the producers, if not for the performers. Kinescopes of the show were sent out to stations across the country; then, in 1950, the midwest and eastern networks were joined by cable, and the audience grew even larger. "By that time, everyone was saying, 'Maybe we were wrong, this medium is really taking off.' In 1950 there must have been between 15 and 18 million sets out in the country, and the growth was incredible. We had a union now, AFTRA (American Federation of Television and Radio Artists), actors were coming into the medium, there was money to be made, and radio was rapidly dying. . . ."

Two years later, Keeshan, as well as most of the *Howdy Doody* regulars, became involved in a salary dispute with the show's management, with the result that two days before Christmas, on December 23, he and the other dissidents were replaced. "Proving," he comments, "that nobody was indispensable, because the show went right along with an entirely new cast."

CBS beckoned. "We auditioned a show for them. I played a clown, and we had puppeteers, and did a lot of the things we'd done on *Howdy Doody*. The show turned out to be absolutely dreadful. We still have that pilot here." Keeshan chuckles. "It's called *Billy Buttons*, and we pull it out every few years and take a look at it. It never got on the air, but we get some laughs every time we run it. . . ."

By the fall of 1953 Keeshan found himself again gainfully employed, this time at ABC-TV, in a minor New York–based effort called *Time for Fun*. "I did that show for two years, another clown character—this time a very gentle non-slapstick sort of a guy who sat on a park bench with his cocker spaniel and talked to the kids. He was called 'Corny the Clown.' He was very popular— I still get mail from people who remember Corny. But I was convinced then that there was an audience early in the morning from seven to nine that would want a kids' show." In November of 1954 the ABC program manager, faced with a sudden opening in his morning schedule, decided to allow Keeshan to try and fill it. "He called—it was on a Friday morning—and asked me if I still wanted to do the show. I said sure, and he said, 'Okay, you've got the hour eight to nine.' I asked him when. He said, 'This coming Monday morning.'"

Another performer might have been reluctant to dash into the battle at such instant notice. But, as Keeshan is the first to admit, he was a quarter century younger, possessed of energy, optimism, and the fires of youth. "We started with nothing, literally nothing," he muses. "But we worked all weekend, designed a set, had one built. I had a producer friend working with me, and we ran down to Brooks Costume and got some costumes, spent the weekend picking up props and writing material, and Monday morning we were on the air with a show called *Tinker's Workshop*. Five days a week, eight to nine!"

Nobody in ABC's management had too much faith in Keeshan's hurried creation, until the ratings that began to come in showed a sizable audience, one that would grow steadily. "We were on opposite *Today* and CBS had Jack Paar on a *Morning Show*, and yet in eight weeks we were showing double their rating in New York. That was when CBS began to notice us, I guess; and when Jack Paar began to get restless in the spring of 1955, they approached us about coming over to do another show for them, from eight to nine."

★ 213 ★

In the summer of 1955 CBS auditioned five other shows for that time period, trying out such performers as Frank Luther, the singer, and Jerry Colonna, the bemustached veteran of Bob Hope's radio shows. But Keeshan's concept, which involved an hour-long visit with a gentle character known as Captain Kangaroo, seemed the most attractive, and in August CBS made the decision to try it out for a few weeks beginning in October.

The fact that *Tinker's Workshop* was still thriving at ABC, which did not choose to release either the vehicle or the performer, presented the sort of problem that only a creative talent agent with the gifts of a Solomon can unravel. In this case, Keeshan's agent, Marvin Josephson, emerged with a *modus vivendi* for all parties concerned. ABC retained the format of *Tinker's Workshop* and Keeshan became a free agent. *Tinker* has long since folded, but for the past twenty years Keeshan, Josephson, and CBS have all thrived. In spades.

"We went on the air on October 3, 1955, with substantially the same show we do today," continues Keeshan. "Lumpy Brannon is Mr. Greenjeans, Gus Allegretti, who plays most of the animal characters—Peter Birch, who was our original director, and is still at it. We've turned over producers in the past twenty years, but not that often. As for staff, well, we've trained dozens of people in the course of working on the show. Our production people came in as clerk-typists, or production assistants, or whatever, and as they learn their jobs, we move them on up to become associate producers, producers, and even executives...."

Keeshan feels no competition whatsoever from the later arrivals on Public Broadcasting, such trail-blazing shows as *Sesame Street* and *The Electric Company*, and *Zoom*, which shine like good deeds on Channel 13. "Why should I?" he beams, like a proud parent. "They're all staffed by my people. Jon Stone, who's the executive producer at Children's Television Workshop, started here as a production assistant. Sam Gibbon, who created *Electric Company*, started here as an assistant director; and David Connell, who's their vice-president in charge of production, started here in 1955 as a clerk-typist. We have almost twenty people who have gone over there from *Captain Kangaroo*."

Over the years, then, the staff of Keeshan's show could be considered members of a long-term TV academy in children's programming. "You bet," he says. "None of our people are ever out of work. It's great training. There's no other show I know of in television that can take a production assistant and teach him everything—because we do everything here. We do everything in a technical sense; we do everything in a program sense. We're a variety show with guest stars [some of whom lately included Imogene Coca, Lucy Arnaz, Eli Wallach, and Clifton Davis], we do some dramatic scenes, there's always some comedy—and in the technical department, with visual material and film, and trick-shot effects, a production assistant gets to learn to work on everything that's available in the medium."

Has his program changed over the years? "Technically, yes," he admits. "Today's children are more mature—they've been exposed to so much more around them, and on TV, and they're quicker to learn *because* of the medium. So our technology has changed and become more complex than in the early days. Every so often, just for the fun of it, we'll run an old kinescope of one of the shows we did back in 1956, before electronic tape recording came along, and it's always a shock how different the show looks.

"In 1956, I would chat with Bunny Rabbit, at the desk (he was played by Gus Allegretti), then I'd go to the garden to talk to Mr. Moose—also Gus. I had to stand there and 'pad'—fill in time—until Gus had gotten up from the desk, around the back of the set, into the garden, and climbed into his Moose outfit, and then was ready to talk to me. I'd be out there alone for maybe thirty to forty-five seconds. Today I can talk to him in one place, then go to the Moose in the garden, split-second timing, all done on tape and edited later. Today we do a show in the studio, and what with the taping of all the various segments, it may take us three hours to do what used to be done in one hour, live.

"But, in terms of the philosophy of the show, and our approach to the kids," he says, firmly, "we haven't changed that at all. Nor do we ever intend to."

Considering the size of its output, the Keeshan unit's accomplishments are even more formidable. Current production of his daily shows has been stabilized on a schedule calling for 120 new hour shows per season. Of that number, perhaps 80 will be well enough received to be repeated. The remaining 60 hours will be supplied from holiday shows, Fourth of July, Washington's Birthday, Christmas, Thanksgiving, et al., shows that can be repeated each year. "At this point," he says, "we have a library of close to 500 shows put away in the warehouse, and some of them are based on such subjects as our American history. We go out and shoot them live, using historical backgrounds—and they become standard pieces of our schedule."

The advanced technology of TV production has eased his chores somewhat and has also provided Keeshan with one other important side benefit: more sleep. "In those early days when I was on live," he sighs, "I'd be out of my house in Babylon, Long Island, to make the 4:20 A.M. train—every day, because we had to be in the studio at six in the morning. That," he says fervently, "is something you never get used to, believe me. Unless you were a farm boy, or an insomniac—and that I was not. I always lived in terror of oversleeping. For five years I used to have three alarm clocks, plus a telephone service that would wake me up. The real problem was getting to bed. If you're getting up at 3:30 in the morning, what time do you get to bed? You're always up before dawn. . . . I'd get in here, do the show at eight, then in forty seconds we'd turn around and repeat the whole show again, for the midwest. Then off the air by ten—two hours of live programming, *six* days a week, from Monday to Saturday. And always that nightmare . . . if I don't get in, who'll do the show? Without the Captain, there *was* no show.

"It was a tough grind," he adds, superfluously. "I'd stay around here until two, rehearsing the next day's show, then I'd have conferences, then I'd go home and take a nap. But remember, in those days I was much younger; I was only twenty-eight when I started as the Captain. I don't think I'd be able to do that today."

The times may have changed, the techniques may have become sophisticated, but one thing remains constant: the high quality of the Captain's daily show. Perhaps he is not drawing the largest possible audience to CBS each morning, but he does continue to maintain his original high standards.

"I think the writing has a lot to do with that," he explains. "In this business there's a lack of respect on the part of producers toward writers. I can't think of a show that's been successful where I couldn't point to the writing. I don't care who the star is—a star can get all the credit in the world for being a great personality and for doing a great job, but basically, the writing has to be there. If the actor does a good enough job, then you, the audience, will not be really aware of the great writing. But as a producer, I think I've always respected writers, and that, to me, is where it begins; you have to have a good script before you do *anything*."

In this era of the *auteur* school, in which the total film is considered primarily the vision and execution of the director (Fellini, Hitchcock, Robert Altman, Mike Nichols, Mel Brooks, and so on) what Keeshan is propounding is a somewhat old-fashioned concept: namely, *the play's the thing.*

He nods. "You bet. It's what makes theater, it's what makes motion pictures, and," he adds, waggling a Captain Kangaroo finger for emphasis, "it *has* to be what makes television."

High praise for the craft of writing, from a performer whose relaxed, casual manner toward his cast and his audience so often seems to be almost ad-lib and improvised.

"Sure, it may look that way," he concedes, "but most of the time, I'm not ad-libbing. There's always dialogue set down, and it may look ad-lib, but it's not. The one thing I will not do is to go out with a script that's not right. If I don't like a script, and we're close to studio time, then I'll say, pull the script and let's do another, because the worst thing in the world is to go into a studio and start rewriting when you're there. It's not only expensive, but you end up with a bad show, no matter how much you do."

And let no one assume that writing his show is an easy job. Writers for *Captain Kangaroo* are not born, they're made. Most of the time they come up through ranks, working at any and all production jobs, and eventually, when they know the show and its workings, they can put their accumulated knowledge to work and try writing. Keeshan grins at me. "If we brought *you* in cold, with all your experience writing for television, and asked you to turn out a script, it would probably take you six months to learn what the show was all about, before you could get the proper feel of writing for the Captain."

So get up early tomorrow, switch away from Hughes Rudd and Jim Hartz and John Chancellor and all their bad news, over to CBS, and you'll see the Captain as he ambles onto your screen, wearing the inevitable cap, charming his audience, and starting their day off with some laughs, a few songs, a book or two, some poems, a lesson, and a whimsical adventure. Just as he has each day since that first season two decades ago. And later on, tomorrow afternoon, he'll put on his civilian clothes, and resume his civilian life. "I have a marvelous life," he admits. "I'm not really recognized on the street, or in most public places. I can go into a restaurant and have dinner without being bothered. I'm a relatively private person; I *enjoy* my privacy. My kids have never had anything to do with show business. We had an anniversary party last year at F. A. O. Schwarz—people came from all over on a press junket, and I asked my twenty-two-year-old daughter to come and serve as a hostess. It was the first time she'd ever been exposed to the press, and they kept asking her, 'What was it like to grow up with your father a TV star?' She said, 'Gee, I never knew. I never thought about him as being an actor—or Captain Kangaroo—or anything like that.'"

Keeshan lights up his pipe and beams through the smoke. "You see, I don't really *look* like the Captain at all," he says. "On an airplane, after looking at me for half an hour, maybe the stewardess will come up and say, 'Captain! I watched you when I was a little girl!' "

He may not look much like Captain Kangaroo when he strolls down Fifty-seventh Street, headed for the commuter train that will take him home to Long Island, just as it has done for the past two decades. But he'll be back tomorrow, promptly at eight, and when he returns, he *will* look like Captain Kangaroo.

And in a world replete with failures, closings, shut-downs, and people who don't show up on time, if at all, it's somehow quite reassuring to know that you (and your kids) can count on the Captain.

EYE OPENERS
AND CLOSERS

Mort Werner remembers:

I came to New York in 1949 at the invitation of CBS. In those days I was a successful operator of small radio stations in California. In towns like Ventura and Santa Barbara, where the words "disc jockey" hadn't been invented, and the small radio station was the corner drugstore of communications.

I went up to CBS and had a disastrous interview. I left and walked down Madison to see my old friend and boss, Pat Weaver, who had been at Young & Rubicam; but he had just quit there to go with NBC as head of television programming. We talked, and I said, "I'm in the radio business in California, but if there's anything that comes up in the future that you think I can do better than anybody you know, call me, and I'll come right back."

I didn't hear from him for about six months. One day the phone rang, and Pat called me back from California—a six-week consultation job to find out what the problems were with a show NBC had called *Broadway Open House*.

I walked into that with absolutely no knowledge of anything, but I quickly observed that nobody else there knew any more than I did, because in 1950 they were all finding their way.

A lot of people, even network executives, have forgotten there once was such a show, on from 11:30 at night. [The show made its debut in 1950 with Morey Amsterdam as the first host, but he was replaced by Jerry Lester, with

Wayne Howell, Jerry Lester, Milton Delugg, and Dagmar, *Broadway Open House* (Courtesy NBC)

a regular cast that included announcer Wayne Howell, singer David Street, a dancer named Ray Malone, a musical group led by Milton Delugg, and a tall, ample lady named Dagmar, whose function was, at first, obscure.] It was on a very limited network; we had no cable hookups then, and we sent it out on kinescopes. The show wasn't totally unrehearsed, but it was damn near so. What happened was really *Hellzapoppin*. Anything went, it had to, because the show, which started as an hour and then went to ninety minutes, was on five nights a week. No performer could be on the air that much and memorize any lines. So you couldn't possibly have writers doing sketches, or stand-up material—we didn't have TelePrompTers, and it ended up with everybody ad-libbing. Jerry Lester clowned around and did all the sketches and songs and "bits" that he'd ever worked up in all his years of nightclubs and vaudeville. We did it from the Hudson Theater on West Forty-fourth Street. Kate Smith did her show there every afternoon, we came in at night. We went on at 11:30, live, with a live audience. Problem—how do you fill up the Hudson with people at that hour?

We used to get our NBC pageboys to go drag in an audience from out on the street. At that hour of the night, you got all sorts of characters, drunks, pimps, anybody!

Jerry was unique—the very first of his kind on TV. Rowdy and wild—and funny. Sometimes terrible and wild, but there he was, keeping it all going. He infected the whole crew with his craziness—they captured the public's fancy. All of them running around the stage, doing musical numbers and impromptu bits; fortunately for us, it was fairly clean stuff. Sometimes it got a little off-color, but never enough to offend. Remember, in those live days, you had absolutely no control over what went out over the tube. And he had that remarkable Dagmar who sat there on her stool, looking beautiful. [Hitherto an obscure hopeful, née Jennie Lewis, who was hired to decorate the premises at $75 per week. By the time she left the show she had become so popular a cult figure that she commanded $3,250 on her next engagement.] Eventually he got her to talk, and they'd do nursery-rhyme poetry bits together, and bingo, she became a big star. Every morning, people would talk about her. Once that happened, it made her, *and* the show, a hit.

That was a very exciting period in my life. Television was such a brand-new medium—I don't really know how the Pilgrims felt when they landed in Massachusetts, but we were in somewhat the same position. We had to construct a whole new business, and we went ahead and did it, from the ground up. You made instant stars—Jerry Lester and Dagmar were prime examples of that. Of course, Milton Berle was already on with his Texaco show, but his was a weekly hour, remember, with writers and a lot of production. Ours was an impromptu ninety-minute madhouse that opened up a whole new late-night audience.

Eventually the show went off. It was followed by another show—but not for a while. CBS took over with *The Late Show*—old movies. I went to work to prepare *Today* with Pat. We brought in Garroway and we began in 1952, and for a year we struggled to make that show into a success. In those days everything was completely unstructured; we were constantly setting precedents. We did *Today* from that tiny studio in West Forty-ninth Street, and in the early years we even began to have arguments with the unions about the type of show we were doing.

For instance, we hired a girl fresh out of college, Estelle Parsons, and she served as Dave Garroway's secretary. Then the actors' union came in and complained—they said she really wasn't his secretary, she was an actress, and they insisted on making a test case out of her being subject to their jurisdiction. They also wanted our weatherman to be considered an actor!

I fought back. It finally went to an arbitration. I presented my case. I said, "Estelle Parsons says to Dave Garroway, 'Dave—the weatherman's on the phone.' If he *isn't* on the phone, then she's an actress." They all looked at me. I said, "But if he *is* on the phone, which he is, then she's *not* an actress!"

End of my case. I won my point. The unions weren't being difficult; they just didn't know. None of this had ever happened before. And, later on, Estelle Parsons certainly did become an actress.

Now it's 1953. I was somewhere down in Florida, on vacation. I got a telephone call from Pat Weaver. He wanted me to come back. The late-night situation had changed, the telephone company had installed lines that linked up stations—we could now telecast on a much bigger network. CBS was still showing all those late-night movies, and Pat figured it was time to go out and try to pick up some of that audience. So I came back and we found a new host for a show that was to be called *Tonight*. Steve Allen, who was doing a local NBC show out of New York. We added two bright young kids named Steve Lawrence and Eydie Gorme . . . and we went on the air.

My first instructions to the *Tonight* writers were: Let's not try and be the funniest people in the world—*let's get talked about on the commuter train tomorrow morning.* "Did you see what Steve Allen did? Did you hear what he said?" That sort of thing. The minute you got that going, it was like a party line—tell-a-friend. It goes wham, and away you go. Whenever you get talked about, your show clicks. Just as true today. Archie Bunker goes on CBS, people start *talking* about the show, it becomes a smash hit.

We had no set formulas then—and we were fortunate, there were so many places from which we could draw talent. There were still a lot of nightclubs around the country, and we could discover bright young people who had potential, put them on at night and see what they could do in front of the audience. [For example, Andy Williams is only one of the impressive parade of comics, dancers, singers, authors, and so on, who have subsequently auditioned for the vast insomniac *Tonight* audience in the past two decades.] And the only thing that mattered then was get the show on, every day, live.

There I was, doing *Today* and *Tonight*. Some schedule. I did nothing but work. Once in a while I'd meet a friend on the street, get to talk for a minute before I hurried on to the next rehearsal—but socially I never saw anybody. When you do a show that early in the morning and that late at night, you're

Skitch Henderson, Steve Allen, Eydie Gorme, and Steve Lawrence, *Tonight* (Courtesy NBC)

going all the time. My wife, Jill, used to ask me what the devil I thought I was proving . . . but that's another story. On that job, you never went home during the week. We had a hotel, one of those West Forty-fourth Street fleabags, we'd get off the air at the Hudson after *Tonight*, take an hour break, have a production meeting that would last until about 2 A.M., set up tomorrow's show, then I'd go to sleep, be up at around 5 A.M. for *Today*, go up to that studio and set up. . . .

I've reached a different stage of my life now, where I can sit back and think, "I did that for five years? *Five* years? Incredible!"

Jack Paar as emcee of *Bank on the Stars* (Courtesy NBC)

Tonight went along fine with Steve Allen—he was a college graduate, a well-trained guy who did a good job driving the train, keeping the show on the tracks. In 1956 Steve went on to do his own weekly nighttime hour, once a week. In 1957 NBC replaced Steve with Jack Paar. He was a very different type than Steve, a very witty, cynical guy, knowledgeable, made a lot of headlines, got the show talked about constantly—but he knew how to drive that train very well.

[Jack Paar once said: "TV interviewers often don't listen to the guests they are interviewing. They ask a question and then sit with an absentminded expression trying desperately to think up their next criticism, regardless of its bearing on the answer their interviewee is giving.

"They are never at a loss for words, however, since they use the expression 'That's wunnerful' to cover almost any contingency. Once I saw a program which had as its guest a patient in an iron lung. The announcer asked how the iron lung worked and the attending nurse explained its operation, saying that if the electric power should go off, the patient would die.

" 'Oh, that's wunnerful,' beamed the announcer.

"But perhaps the best example of the nonlistening interviewer is Les Paul's story of an interview on a Hollywood TV station with Cornelius Vanderbilt, Jr., the globe-trotting journalist. The interview got off well enough and was progressing nicely, when the announcer asked Vanderbilt about his most exciting experience.

" 'It was during World War II,' the journalist said, 'and I was covering the fighting on the Russian front. One day I was captured by the Russian troops. I was thrown into an armored car and driven wildly through the night to an unknown destination.

" 'When I was dragged out of the car I was stunned to see we were at the Kremlin. My captors hauled me into that forbidding bastion, down a long gloomy corridor, and finally hurled me to the floor. Looking up, I saw Stalin glowering down at me!'

"At this point, Vanderbilt stopped for breath in his harrowing story.

" 'I see,' said the nervous announcer. 'Do you have any hobbies?' "]*

Meanwhile, I worked on another of Pat Weaver's concepts: *Home.* That began in 1954. Arlene Francis was our hostess, along with Hugh Downs; they were a fine team, Arlene is very witty and bright, but I think we made some

---

* From *My Saber Is Bent*, Trident, 1961.

★ 225 ★

production mistakes. We built a huge studio and equipped it with an elaborate camera, set up a revolving set—with many areas—and maybe the whole thing was a bit overproduced. What eventually emerged was too much of what I call a "New York show," a bit too brittle and smart. It went on for about four years, we took it out of New York and toured it all around the country, trying to get it closer to the audience out there. The original concept for *Home* was to do a television version of a women's magazine—and in that I think we succeeded.

By the time *Home* went off, Pat Weaver had left NBC, and so had a lot of the other people who'd worked with him in starting and producing those shows, including me. I left to go to work for Henry J. Kaiser. I built television stations for him and handled his advertising. The first show I bought for him was a film series from Warner Brothers called *Maverick*, which was a huge success. By the mid-fifties you could see filmed television coming down the pike; that was a business I didn't know anything about, but I wanted to learn.

Then I went to Young & Rubicam, to head up their TV department. Being in advertising gave me a chance to look at television from the point of view of the sponsor who buys programs. Up to that point, remember, I'd been mostly inside studios and conference rooms; I wanted to find out what it was like on the other side of the business.

Then, in 1961, I went back to NBC. Just in time for Jack Paar to quit *Tonight*. I'd been gone for four years, and the minute I returned, Jack walked into my office to resign. I'd hired him before I quit NBC—and he left when I got back! So my first assignment was to find another host for the show.

I stewed and stewed, and kept thinking about this problem: where could we find another such guy? Finally I began to think about the backgrounds of the three guys who'd been our nighttime hosts, and that gave me a hint as to what might work for the replacement.

Eventually, I made a presentation to Bob Kintner, who was then my boss. I had an easel, and I opened up with a picture of Jerry Lester. Jerry Lester, who, prior to *Broadway Open House*, couldn't be called a star. He'd worked in clubs, saloons, all over; but when he went on NBC late-night, bingo—he was a runaway hit. The next picture I turned over: Steve Allen. Disc jockey, all night radio in L.A. CBS brought him here, tried him out on different shows, nothing much happened. We put him on the *Tonight* show—*he* was a runaway hit! Now to the third host. Jack Paar. Got out of the Army in 1946, where he'd been a comedian, goes on radio as Jack Benny's summer re-

Buddy Hackett, Jack Paar, and Alexander King, *Tonight* (Courtesy NBC)

placement. Came to New York, did all sorts of other shows, quiz shows, daytime shows on CBS. Out of work, living in Bronxville, needs a job, he goes on *Tonight—he's* a runaway hit!

Now the parallel was becoming slightly eerie. I said, "Gentlemen, I have found another failure for you." A midwestern kid, used to be an announcer, then a writer for Red Skelton, now he has a quiz show called *Who Do You Trust?* I flipped over his picture. Johnny Carson. Became the biggest star of them all.

Don't ask me to explain it, but it's a fact. All of those men who had no real impact elsewhere turned out to be stars when they took over *Tonight*.

Today is one of the few live shows left on the air. Everything else is either tape or film, and nowadays everything is produced to a formula, and carefully structured. Even sports. Take baseball. It's a totally different game than it was years ago. Nowadays the manager gives the sign to the catcher, who gives it to the pitcher—when a hitter gets up to bat, he's told what to do . . . it's a committee decision, so the game is really programmed. As a matter of fact, I've suggested to our sports department that if they really want to get a special event, why not have one of our Saturday or Monday night baseball games go on the tube totally unprogrammed—let the players play their game without any instructions. You'd get every sportswriter in the country writing about that!

But when I think back to those early live days, I wonder to myself, how the hell *did* we ever get it done—and get all those hours of television on the air?

KUKLA, FRAN
AND OLLIE

Fantasy has never been too sturdy a commodity on television. Beneath the hard glare of those bright, white lights, its imaginative essence shrivels away and often becomes merely foolish. That clear, cold camera eye manages to reduce the most antic of whimsical personalities to that of a limp, witless showoff.

No wonder, then, that nervous television network executives in search of mass audience have long since come to rely on sitcoms *à la* Father-is-a-dope, cops-and-robbers, doctors-and-patients, shoot-'em-ups and chase-'em-down-before-the-closing-commercial as the most reliable means of selling products.

But . . . once upon a time, way back there in the primitive, live-TV days before all the factory-type assembly-line schlock proliferated, the home viewers were fortunate enough to be able to share one small and delicious fantasy world on NBC—one that opened up each night at seven and presented a half-hour visit with a hilarious group of characters whose nightly antics were a source of continual pleasure.

And, most remarkably, only one of those creatures was human.

Her name was Fran Allison.

The rest of the cast of *Kukla, Fran and Ollie* (happily, they are alive and well and thriving still) is physically much smaller than Miss Allison. They represent the considerable talents of puppeteer Burr Tillstrom. But such is the magic of the interplay between his crew of puppets and Miss Allison that throughout the long run of the show (it began in 1947) nobody has ever thought of her as being anything else but a larger Kuklapolitan.

"Fran," says Tillstrom, "has always believed."

Tillstrom's troupe of hand puppets made their professional debut at the 1939 World's Fair, in New York. He then became one of TV's earliest pioneers, having worked at Chicago's first station, WBKB, before World War II. "Kukla and Ollie used to appear as a sort of entr'acte in another marionette group," he says. "They'd be announced by a very straight announcer type. I used to get Kukla up to heckle the announcer; out at the World's Fair, at the RCA exhibit, there were all sorts of lovely actresses and models, acting as hostesses to explain this new medium of television to the people. Eventually I began to use them to work with the puppets.

"Then, just before World War II, I was selling bonds outside WBKB, and Fran showed up, as a guest. At that time she was 'Aunt Fanny,' on the old *Breakfast Club* radio show, and they'd asked her if she'd come and talk to Kukla and Ollie. They met her and instantly hit it off, and afterward we all became great friends. Fran laughed at everything—she was a marvelous audience and she always has been."

After the war, when TV went commercial, NBC took over WBKB. There were some three thousand television sets in Chicago, but most of them were in saloons and taverns. "They wanted television to be brought into the home," says Tillstrom. "They decided that the Kuklapolitans would be just the right choice for that, so we were contracted to do thirteen weeks on daytime television. They asked me if I wanted a writer. I'd always ad-libbed, and the only thing I could think of, quite frankly, was how could I turn the pages of a script with both my hands busy? So I'd said I'd love to work with a pretty girl, someone who preferably could sing. Somebody asked, 'How about Fran Allison?' That was on a Thursday. Monday we called Fran. Right away she said, 'Sure! Sure, honey!' She never asked how much money—that's the way she is. She just asked, 'When do we start?' Monday afternoon we met, we sat in a drugstore, had a cup of coffee, started talking about what we wanted to do, shook hands, went on the air for the thirteen weeks, and stayed on—from October 13, 1947, for the next ten years." (The thirteen-week cycle was a programming holdover from the days of radio. It was strictly an economic plan, i.e., to divide the year into four thirteen-week cycles.)

There has never been a prepared script since. The special pleasures of *Kukla, Fran and Ollie* all those evenings at 7 P.M. were enhanced by the

Kukla, Burr Tillstrom, Fran Allison, and Ollie, *Kukla, Fran and Ollie* (Courtesy NBC)

show's improvisational quality. "We always had a rough idea of where we were going," Tillstrom says. "We learned to let the show go. If it wanted to go a different way than we'd planned, then we'd let it go. But somehow we learned to wind it all up in half an hour—that became instinctual.

"In the beginning, the Kuklapolitans were strong enough characters," he says, "but they didn't have any life histories. So Fran would stand up there and chat with Ollie, and Ollie would say, 'Fran, I love your hair.' She'd thank him, and he'd say, 'You know, my mother used to wear her hair something like yours,' and Fran would say, 'What's your mother's hair like? I'd love to meet your mother,' and she'd ask questions, and I'd never thought what

Ollie's mother was until that moment—and then Ollie would make up what his mother was, and suddenly, that whole history emerged, on the air."

Over the years of interplay with Fran, a considerable body of knowledge, now familiar to its fans, has emerged about Tillstrom's creatures. There has always been Kukla (the name derives from the Greek word for doll), the somewhat harassed bald-pated leader of the crew, a truly gentle character, long-suffering, who hides his teddy-bear qualities beneath a thin veneer of braggadocio. Most of his problems are with his long-nosed, single-toothed dragon pal, Ollie, who was born at Dragon Retreat, in Vermont, where he attended Dragon Prep. Traditionally, dragons breathe fire. Not so our old good buddy Ollie. One of his ancestors once swam the Hellespont and, in the process of making the trip, took in too much water, thereby drowning the family's hereditary talent.

Others in the mini-repertory troupe include Madame Ophelia Oglepuss, a grand dame with operatic pretensions, whose ample poitrine throbs violently whenever she attempts to hit high C above C. Her gentleman friend is a debonair southern blade named Colonel Crackie. Then there is Fletcher Rabbitt, whose chore is to handle the Kuklapolitan fan mail, but whose major problem has usually been his long set of ears, which refuse to stay upright. The stage manager of the Players is Cecil Bill, possessed of a unique language all his own, a gibberish that runs *"Tooie-ta-tooie-ta-tooie"* (fortunately translatable to Fran and the rest of us by Kukla and Ollie). There is also Ollie's female niece, the young Dolores Dragon, who over the years has grown from noisy infancy into an obstreperous and quite typical teen-age dragonette. Mercedes is a rather spoiled brat friend of Dolores.

Last, but certainly never least, there is a slightly demented lady, the beloved Buelah Witch, who soars back and forth across the stage on her broomstick, usually just arrived from a cross-country jaunt above Indiana, screeching "Hello, dear!" to the world as she comes in for a landing. Buelah, an adventuresome soul, was once arrested for buzzing Michigan Boulevard on her broomstick—and in New York she once flew much too low over the UN Building. "Picked up for that by Interpol, I guess," says Tillstrom.

The scenery and props for *Kukla, Fran and Ollie* have always been minimal, and the show was produced in a tiny room in the NBC studios in the vast Merchandise Mart. "We made up television," Tillstrom observes, a quarter century after the fact. "There was no influence to teach us, we weren't conforming to anything. California never bothered to develop any television techniques—they just adapted films to television. But Chicago in those days was a very special place. [From the NBC Chicago studios came such other early trail-blazers as *Garroway at Large, Studs' Place, Hawkins Falls,* and *Ding Dong School.*] It's not that I'm opposed to film—it's the strongest influence in television today, but it has changed television. The technical aspect of those filmmakers is so beautiful, but they make up with tricks for the hollowness inside. What they've developed is two-dimensional. It goes across the screen on a flat surface; it doesn't reach into you. Live television and live-type television still comes out through the screen and reaches the audience. I believe television should be an intimate thing—you're not playing to a lot of people, you're playing to *one*—*ones*—in different places everywhere. And the instant you have that as a guide, you approach things with a much more intimate style."

That was part of the special magic of *Kukla, Fran and Ollie,* the intimacy and the improvisation. From that gentle interplay between Fran and her Kuklapolitan friends came literally endless comedic situations, none of it contrived, all of it based on character, which, as any good comedy producer will tell you, is the very best kind. Some evenings, there could be arguments based on Ollie's temperament, and personality clashes between him and the others. Buelah might be engaged in a mother-daughter contretemps with her mother, Mrs. Witch. There was also a constant series of experiments designed to do something constructive about Fletcher Rabbitt's drooping ears, starch having proved to be of no help very early on. Ollie often upstaged everybody with his insistence on demonstrating his loyalty to Dragon Prep with fight songs, and a "pep rally."

And then there was always singing. "Music has always been very important to us," says Tillstrom. "We might improvise, but we always know what songs we're going to do, and how." With the considerable assistance of Jack Fascinato, their long-time composer and accompanist, the Kuklapolitans specialized in all manner of vocal performance. Not only would Madame Oglepuss treat the audience to frequent operatic recitals, but also Buelah Witch (she is named after Beulah Zachary, the show's original producer, and please note the different spelling, it is intentional) had her own school song, one she'd learned years ago at Witch Normal—an institution to which she is certainly as loyal as Kukla is to his. There have also been full-scale productions of operettas. One such memorable evening involved the presentation of Gilbert and Sullivan's *The Mikado,* in which each member of the troupe essayed a Japanese character; there was another night when the Kuklapolitans put on a performance of *Saint George and the Dragon*, and Ollie spent a considerable length of time disposing of his type-cast prey, Kukla, whose death scene was a classic piece of overacting.

Fascinato also supplied the original music and lyrics for the show, starting with the show's theme song ("Here we are/back with you again/Yes by gum and yes by golly/Kukla, Fran and dear old Ollie."), the various school fight songs, the duets between Buelah and Fran, the familiar exit music ("My mother is calling me, tra la/my mother is calling me/so I will have to go and see why mother is calling me!") *

It is nearly impossible to synthesize in flat prose the unique flavor of what took place all those nights within the minuscule Kuklapolitan world. It's not that Burr Tillstrom's delicate blend of wit and sharply observed characters loses in the description; it's simply that one had to be in front of the TV set, watching it all, believing in it, participating while it was all happening. "Television is special," insists Tillstrom, "not like any other entertainment medium." And he has been proving that point ever since the first Kuklapolitan popped up in front of the tiny set of curtains. To try and tell somebody who hasn't enjoyed evenings with Kukla and Ollie, who hasn't lived with Buelah and Fran and inhabited their small world, is much the same as describing a magnificent dessert you ate last night. How does one explain a superb soufflé?

When, in the mid 1950s, *Kukla, Fran and Ollie* departed from the NBC nighttime schedule, its passing was mourned by certainly as many adults, perhaps far more, as the small fry for whom incautious observers may have thought the show was designed. "I don't think we ever intended it for kids," says Tillstrom. "Not for them alone, at least. We've always assumed that *this* family was for the whole family."

He has been behind the curtain, Svengali to his creations, for four decades now, but he shows no visible sign of slowing down. ("Only my feet," he says, grinning. "Can't stand up on them for as long a time back there as I used to.") He teaches at Holland College, in Michigan, and he and Fran and the bunch have never stopped making live appearances, doing commercials and guest shots on television.

And now, as Ollie might say, for the really terrific news! Arrangements

* Copyright Vera Nova Music, 1947.

were completed for the return of *Kukla, Fran and Ollie* to TV on a regular basis, beginning in the fall of 1975, on a syndicated basis all over the country.

Once again, we shall be treated to evening visits with them, the night will be filled with Kuklapolitan solos, duets, and the shrill cry of "Hello, dear!" as Buelah and her broom descend on us. All the small ones, plus their larger friend Fran, will once again be back where they belong—on the small screen, where they live.

Things can't be all bad.

PAT WEAVER

Sylvester L. Weaver—over the years along Madison Avenue, in and about Rockefeller Center, and out at the Beverly Hills Hotel coffee shop, where breakfast is a ritual part of the TV bourse, where shows are bought and sold over toasted English muffins, he has always been "Pat"—is an angular, cheerful gentleman. He is also one of the very few legendary figures who remain from the days of commercial TV's gestation.

Pat is a thinker, a planner, and a terrific salesman. If the mark of a great salesman is that he can sell you smoke, then Pat will leave you gasping for a reorder.

Except that he's never been in the smoke business.

Weaver would make an ideal subject for one of the Italian Futurist painters who specialized in personifying motion; he is a man perpetually traveling, always in pursuit of the broad horizon ahead.

If you're looking for Pat, it seems that he has always just been here and gone, nipped out to the Coast, paused for a few days in Palm Springs, went up to San Francisco, no, now he's in London for meetings, sorry, he's somewhere in France in conference.

Remarkably, this day, he is paused in mid-flight in Manhattan, having spent several long days in consultation with his associates; meetings at which a vast new entertainment project involving a pay-television system is being

Pat Weaver and Dave Garroway (Courtesy NBC)

designed. "Something I've been at for over ten years," he concedes. "But now, it's going to happen. Its time has come."

Today's network executives discuss TV programming with such negative terms as "audience demographics," "middle-brain America," "penetration factor," "personality acceptance," and "Is this for the bluejeans, or is it for the Geritols?" Concepts are aborted daily, being proven by computerized testing as "potentially weak in the numbers." Weaver, who literally hand-made NBC into a major TV network years back, can hold his own in any rhetoric session, but with one basic difference. Firmly committed to the high road, he has always thought in terms of making the medium live up to its potential. Pat has always been a planner on a very bold scale, a man enraptured (and enrapturing) with possibilities.

★ 237 ★

There have been other fearless leaders in TV; network executive suites have housed many others who could, at the onset of each new season, promise the audience and their bosses the moon. Palm Beach, La Costa, and Palm Springs are filled with such discards, most of them richly pensioned off. ("Nothing," goes the saying around TV, "succeeds like failure.") But Weaver, with his dreams, his blueprints, and his grand design, led NBC into the Canaan of corporate profit. Even his most captious critics cannot fault the man's accomplishments at 30 Rockefeller Plaza. If, at this point in a somewhat random history of the formative years of TV, all those who worked with and for Pat haven't sufficiently footnoted his impact on American viewers during those early years, then we can briefly rerun through a few of his accomplishments.

He brought Max Liebman and the rest in to produce the Caesar-Coca Saturday night extravaganza *Your Show of Shows*. With Pat's enthusiastic backing, Fred Coe developed *Philco Playhouse*, and drama began to flower in the one-hour form. He nurtured a revolving stock company for star comics into *The Comedy Hour*, and *The All Star Revue*, presented the lady of the house with a "magazine-type" show called *Home* (one that did not insult or condescend to Ms., years before Women's Lib), he opened our horizons to *Wide, Wide World*, and he conceived of a top-drawer series of musicals, comedies, and drama, *Producer's Showcase*, for which the word "spectacular" was appropriate. For years, NBC thrived on the dividends from his presentation of Mary Martin in *Peter Pan* and Gian-Carlo Menotti's *Amahl and the Night Visitors*, and, for the posterity-minded, Weaver nudged the network into producing *Wisdom*, which afforded us hour-long exposure to the minds of such giants as Bertrand Russell and Sean O'Casey (years before Public Broadcasting took on the I.Q. franchise). *Garroway at Large, Ding Dong School*, and *Kukla, Fran and Ollie* thrived during his reign. On NBC radio, Weaver's concept for *Monitor* lasted for many seasons, and even now, we have only to switch on *Today* and *Tonight* with Johnny Carson, both of which were nurtured into life while Pat ran the shop at NBC, and which still spin off massive profits, to prove what a shrewd judge of programming he has been.

If he is now of an age when most of his confrères have gone to pasture, Pat Weaver shows no signs of being a Sun City resident. He is still lean and energetic, possessed of his daily enthusiasms, and he remains a man obviously still in love with the collective insanities of show business.

He was infected with the virus at an early age. "I was born in Los Angeles, and I grew up with all the movie people around," he explains. "When I was a kid, I would be down at Santa Monica, on the beach by Crystal Pier, and I can remember picking up Rudolph Valentino's medicine ball and handing it back to him when he'd dropped it. I got to see pictures being made, and as I grew up, I became a movie fan. I went east to college, and in the four years I went to Dartmouth, they'd change the bill at the local movie house each day, and I never missed a movie except when I was sick or out of town. And," he adds cheerfully, "I still came out of Dartmouth Phi Beta and summa cum laude."

Weaver's brother was also stagestruck. Nicknamed "Doodles," he was taken by his career into the business as a comedian. (Years later, when "Doodles" attempted a half-hour TV show of his own on NBC, the eminent wit Goodman Ace tersely reviewed the effort: the caption on his critique read, "Oh, Brother!")

But young Pat headed for the more secure world of advertising. He became editor of the Advertising Club magazine in Los Angeles, wrote jokes for it, and then found himself a job with the local CBS radio station. "In 1932, there was an experimental TV station there, up on the roof," he says. "They played old movies—which in 1932 were old movies! I'm not saying that back then I foresaw what was going to happen, because I really didn't, but I was fascinated by both the audio medium, radio, and by the audiovisual, which was movies.

"Movies were very limited then. I was always trying, even in radio, to push the medium forward and expand it. Back then it was fairly primitive; and I began to see what could be done in movies as well." He shakes his head. "It still seems to me such a waste, the way picture people have never tried to use that medium with any intelligence."

In a pragmatic dollars-and-cents commercial arena not known for much more than sales pitches, Pat soon developed into a thoughtful and articulate speaker and writer.

(Jack Paar, the ex-host of Weaver's Tonight, and a man not well known for his warm feelings toward ex-bosses, once wrote: "I have always admired Pat Weaver. He was one of the most creative executives in television . . . and I have been awed and baffled by his mastery of those twin weapons—the meeting and the memo. Pat's conversational style was a particularly deadly executive weapon, since no one understood it. His small talk was larded with such phrases as 'A fortuitous concatenation of circumstances,' 'contiguity discounts,' 'the pluralistic nature of twentieth-century culture,' and 'cybernetic civilization.' All of this sounded wonderful while Pat was expounding it, and it wasn't until you had left him, teetering precariously on his Bongo Board, with arms outstretched like a crane about to take flight, that you realized you hadn't understood a word he said.")

Volubility has certainly been one of Weaver's strong points, especially in terms of those famous NBC interoffice memos. (Paar is especially fond of one that he insists went: "Between Marathon and today, if you're used to thinking in terms of galactic clusters, which to me immediately sets you aside as somebody that is moving forward toward mutancy, there isn't much change.") But the simple fact remains that the Weaver rhetoric was not your standard advertising-agency chuffa-chuffa gobbledy-gook. The man was, and still is, attempting to elevate the human condition.

Another friend of Weaver's, a man who has dealt with him on an intellectual level over many years, Goddard Lieberson, late of Columbia Records, puts it precisely. "Pat," he says, "is probably the only true visionary who has ever headed up a television network, then or now."

Confronted with such an accusation—even more damaging in this confused, know-nothing era of TV management—the man pleads *nolo contendere.*

"Absolutely," he admits. "I came to New York in the middle thirties to produce the Fred Allen radio show, and very quickly I became supervisor of program product at Young & Rubicam, the advertising agency which put on that show. Later, I became head of the whole thing, but I was already both a creative man and a manager, also a thinker—that is to say, a guy who was really concerned about the world and its future. Even to the point where, long before we got into World War II, I was already committed to anti-Axis action, and I joined Nelson Rockefeller about a year before Pearl Harbor, working on pro-democratic propaganda, to be broadcast to the Latin-American countries. That was the other side, the citizen-of-the-world side of me—because what I really was doing was to generate a philosophy that I still have, absolutely. I believe totally in the fact that communications are the way we're going to bring about a mutation in the human condition, and make us from tribal idiots, certainly preadult fools, eventually into the first civilized adult society. *Only* through communications," he says, firmly, "and you can't do that if communications aren't better than they are now.

"And it also won't work, talking about people in a democratic society— unless, first of all, you can get them to listen. Which means, in effect, that you have to use entertainment, all the showmanship devices available, to *get* their attention."

So, when Weaver was summoned by General Sarnoff in 1949 to take over television at NBC, he came equipped with the same philosophy that has underscored his thinking ever since. "I thought then that you'd get into this medium because it will do good for society," he says now. "Your mission would not be just to make money, and it is not just to entertain people and it's not just to sell goods, and it's not just to have social influence, and it's not just to elect people to political office—because even then, the 1948 elections, the first that had been televised, had shown us what a power TV could be in that arena—all of those things are part of the medium's charter—but I thought, the real thing here is a power greater than print, which can change society, and shape it for the better—and it isn't even going to be hard to do it!"

As for the endless stream of single-spaced memos that began to issue from Weaver's office suite, in which he outlined his vision of the future (the official name was "Operation Frontal Lobes," and the mass of material would fill endless bound volumes), Weaver makes no apology. He was attempting to communicate his own enthusiasm, and more often than not, he did.

"You got your creative people in," he says, "and even though you had to make jokes about it when you talked about something that was to be an exciting new step for mankind"—one of his oft-quoted slogans was, "Let us dare to think and let us think with daring"—"you really *did* get them excited, because all people, and particularly creative people, really do want to have a better world, and would like to play a role in making it better. They don't really want to be in it for the money, or for the applause, or for the ego—they really *do* want more than that. And therefore you can get to them and you can make them work harder, work better, really outperform their talents!"

It was far from a haphazard and random blueprint that Weaver applied to his new job at NBC. Those bound volumes of memos were based on what he calls "a grand design," and it was to serve the network well for quite a few seasons to come.

"In that grand design," Weaver recounts, "entertainment was used to get the people to watch the medium and to get caught by it, but the end would be that we would inform them, enrich them, enlighten them, to liberate them from tribal primitive belief patterns."

The sugar-coating of the pill was simply accomplished. "We used comedy at 8 P.M., practically every night, in order to dominate the audience. We put on people like Berle, Bob Hope, Dean Martin and Jerry Lewis—and then, at nine, we'd let the audience flow on to shows with more substance. Take the *Philco Playhouse* that Fred Coe was producing. It followed *The Comedy Hour*—Fred's show was so good that it would probably have held up against tough competition from CBS, anyway, but it was a great help to *Philco* that it inherited that huge, huge comedy audience. We did that as often as we could—and it usually worked."

Weaver's critics, and he was to develop many, have often leveled the charge against him that his greatest successes, shows such as the Caesar-Coca Saturday night extravaganza and the venturesome *Wide, Wide World* and the opulent *Producer's Showcase* series, were produced with no regard to cost, and that the leakage of red ink that drenched the NBC books as a result were sufficient cause for his dismissal years later.

Weaver shrugs and, for once, becomes terse. "Baloney," he says. "We were immensely profit-oriented, always, and we made fantastic money for General Sarnoff. It's quite true that the RCA people [the parent corporation of NBC] didn't like my methods. After all, I knew how they operated from having worked around NBC all those years as a Young & Rubicam agency man, and I knew the kind of red-tape stuff that they thrived on." (Was it not the late Fred Allen, an acerbic observer and Weaver's old friend, who once described an NBC vice-president as a man who arrived at a desk each morning to find a molehill of mail on his blotter, which he proceeded to turn into a mountain by lunchtime, and reduced it back to the original molehill by 5:30?)

"I spent lots of money, sure," he says. "Everything they needed to make the show first-rate, the performers, the producers, the writers, everybody involved —but I gave them all that money because I knew we'd get it all back. And despite what you may hear from others," he adds, pointedly, "the network did."

In 1956 Weaver resigned his job as chairman of the NBC board, to be succeeded (unsurprisingly) by Robert Sarnoff, the General's son. In tandem with Robert Kintner, Sarnoff took over the operation of the network. Industry wits suggested that above young Sarnoff's desk should be placed a motto reading "Somebody up there likes me." Whether or not NBC enjoyed affluent years thereafter (and it did, until lately), it was the end of an exciting, venturesome era for the network, and there are those who insist that ever since Weaver departed, NBC's programming has slowly and steadily slid into shapeless mediocrity. In November, 1975, a behind-the-scenes palace coup took place in RCA headquarters, one that resulted in the abrupt resignation of Robert Sarnoff. *Sic transit* the executive.

As to the state of television, circa 1976? The optimistic Weaver displays his first signs of deep depression. "I think it's disgraceful what's happened to it," he mourns. "And I don't only mean in entertainment. Take the way news is marketed. Back in the days when I was in radio, the way information was handled was marvelous. With shows like *World News Round-up*, radio gave you a sense of what was going on around the world. The lead stories weren't simply fires and murders and all the kind of stuff which dominates TV news today. Think about all the commentators radio gave you, men like Elmer Davis and H. V. Kaltenborn, men who had been around a long time—when they spoke, you listened. They weren't just young reporters standing in front of a mobile-unit camera. When I got to NBC, I made them put on commentary, which the news department hated—but I insisted. We had people like James Reston of the *Times*, Marquis Childs, both Alsop brothers—anyone we could find who was an observer of both weight and standing, no matter what he said, I didn't care—I wanted him on. Then we went and hired Chet Huntley, who brought some perspective to the hard-news stories . . . but nowadays that whole concept is a thing of the past, and I firmly believe the TV audience suffers because we don't have it."

One of Weaver's most compelling and prestigious concepts was the hour-long series of interviews called *Wisdom*, and it is the one whose departure from TV he mourns the most. "That was my pet idea," he says. "I went to England myself and got Bertrand Russell to appear on the show. If I'd left it up to the news department, they'd never have put it on the air. They didn't believe in it, and they resented it because I started out by saying, 'Fellows, the interviewer on this show will be a faceless nobody—*Bertrand Russell is everything*. We want him, we want Sean O'Casey, we want Edith Hamilton talking about ancient Greece—we're recording history for the audience.' We got it on, but we still didn't do nearly enough. I tried and tried to get that concept extended—I went back to them and said, 'Fellows, I want a moving van that is in effect a mobile studio, and I want it parked at Idlewild Airport, and I want somebody over there grabbing people as they come off the plane, and making them come in and do a half hour for us, if they will.' In other words, if you had a way whereby you could say to a Bernard Baruch or a John Dewey,

'Look, gentlemen, it really isn't that much trouble—we will have the studio here, just step inside it and give us a half hour of your time so we can record you and your ideas for the future generations!' "

Weaver shakes his head. "I got most of the ideas I had onto the screen—but that one I never got done, and it's always bugged me that it got away from me."

True, there were other meaningful ventures produced on NBC throughout those years, such shows as the multi-episode *Victory at Sea*, which was the history of the U.S. Navy during World War II, and there was the long-departed *Project Twenty*, which explored a multitude of historical aspects of America and its origins. "They were fine, but I wanted to do even more venturesome things," Weaver says. "For instance, a history of the Roman Empire, in depth. It wouldn't be all that difficult to do, but I couldn't get anybody to go along with that. Someday, I promise you," he says, grinning, "I will. You see, I just believe in those things."

Most of the talented producers, directors, and creative associates who happily followed Weaver's plans in those very early days are no longer involved in today's television, except, perhaps, as the rest of us are—as sporadic, disillusioned viewers. (The latest statistics available indicate that, for the first time in many years, commercial television is losing significant numbers of viewers: proof positive that at last the audience is watching the home screen less, and enjoying other pursuits more.)

"All vanished. Fired. Gone," mourns Weaver. "Take the writers we developed. I don't blame them for having all moved into other fields. In those days when Fred Coe or Tony Miner and all the other creative producers were giving us hour-long dramas, twenty years ago, do you realize that there were *eleven* live hour dramas on NBC each week? The medium could attract talented people then—we had so many. But nowadays, if you're a writer, and you sit down and you have to think of writing an episode for some cops-and-robbers potboiler—and that's what most of the hour shows are—then you've got yourself a whole different world. So who can blame the creative community for leaving television and going into the theater, or to books—or to the motion-picture business, which," he adds, somewhat balefully, "isn't all in such good shape either, these days."

So, alternatively, can we look forward to a renaissance on the home screen, if and when Mr. Weaver's scheme for pay-TV becomes a reality?

"Oh, absolutely!" he says, rising from the chair on which his lanky frame

★ 244 ★

has been sprawled. Perhaps the vistas that surround us are momentarily depressing, but the man's optimism refuses to go away. "Not that I haven't been in business with this system half a dozen times before, and had something come up that stopped it," he concedes, "but right now, I can tell you this—I spent the whole day in meetings, and I'm way up. Things look great for it—and I assure you, when it happens, the thing will go like gang-busters!"

Weaver glances at his watch. He has another appointment waiting, and then, after that, he'll be off again, back in motion tomorrow, still working on the grand design, and, what is more remarkable, still hopeful after more than forty years of travel through the cynical world of mass-communication.

He grins. "I just hope I've left you on an upbeat note."

Which is what he's done to the audience whenever he's had the chance.

That same audience which is waiting (not so patiently) for Pat Weaver to get the renaissance of TV started.

NEXT TO CLOSING:
Lucille Ball

By the mid-fifties live television production was booming, and boomtown was New York, where literally dozens of dramatic and comedy variety shows were being telecast to the home screen each week. Night after night, authors, actors, and production crews shuttled from studio to studio, rushing crosstown to rehearsals, up- and downtown to meet deadlines, and, as soon as one show was finished, up to a production meeting for the next one.

Not only were there the seemingly endless supply of half-hour comedies and mysteries (remember *Martin Kane, Private Eye; Ellery Queen: Man Against Crime*; and *Rocky King, Detective?*) but the roster of one-hour dramas is remarkably impressive.

Call the roll of *Robert Montgomery Presents, Kraft Television Theatre* (which brought to its audience a total of 650 plays in the eleven years of its tenure), *Armstrong Circle Theater, The Kaiser Aluminum Hour, The Pulitzer Prize Playhouse, Studio One, Philco-Goodyear, The Hallmark Hall of Fame* (it remains the sole survivor of that era that is still today alive and very much kicking, thank you), *The U.S. Steel Hour, Playwrights '56, The Best of Broadway, The DuPont Show of the Month,* the CBS low-budget experimental *Camera Three,* Albert McCleery's *Matinee Theater* (which presented three years' worth of daily hour-long drama for five days a week, beginning in 1955 from Los Angeles, but had its origins in New York), *Seven Lively Arts,* and the long-

Lucille Ball, Vivian Vance, Desi Arnaz, and William Frawley, *I Love Lucy* (Courtesy CBS)

vanished but far from forgotten Sunday afternoon review of the arts hosted by Alistair Cooke, *Omnibus*.

Then television underwent an abrupt change of face. Within a few short years, by the end of the fifties, most of the business was headed westward, to new studios where filmed and taped entertainment would be the order of the day, and of the night. Videotape had made it possible for the medium to record itself for posterity, and profit. Today, all that remains of all those early Manhattan-made hours of live comedy, variety, of the singers and dancers and actors who strutted and played out their brief moments before the live TV cameras are files of yellowing TV scripts in warehouses, and some very blurred kinescope recordings.

The metamorphosis from live to film was, although few observers in the 1950s were realistic enough to concede the point, inevitable. It is not too easy to pinpoint where the change began (the hows, being mostly economic, are much more obvious), but if you were paying close attention, you might have noted the first stirrings of revolution as early as 1951, on an improvised theater setup on a movie sound stage in Hollywood, where a tall red-headed comedienne and her husband, a cheerful chap with a thick Cuban accent, were trying out an experimental comedy concept.

Go back to the relatively peaceful fall of 1949, when Ed Wynn was bravely starring in his first, trail-breaking comedy television half hour, for CBS, in Los Angeles. It was a makeshift show, but it was in good hands; young Ralph Levy had learned enough about television production in New York to be able to direct Wynn's show successfully, and Wynn had recruited Hal Kanter, a first-rate comedy writer (he was later to write and produce the highly original *George Gobel Show*), to provide him with scripts.

"Out here in California, when it came to television," says Kanter, "the general attitude of people around town was one of pure dislike. Motion picture people were sneering at TV—except as possibly a minor publicity vehicle on which to exploit their films. Twentieth Century–Fox might let somebody like Linda Darnell go back to New York to do a walk-on guest shot on *The Kate Smith Hour*, say, but purely to get a plug for one of Fox's current pictures. But otherwise it was very difficult to get studio star talent to appear on television. Not only did the film people look down on TV as a sort of freak child of show business, but when it came to the other performers here—people who supposed video might just possibly be the golden infant that would grow up to be Hercules, they stayed away too. They were mostly concerned with what they would look like on television. And they were absolutely right. The lighting was appalling, particularly treacherous for ladies."

There were, however, some adventurous local talents who were willing to appear with Wynn on that first season of California television's infancy. One young lady singer who had made a considerable reputation in radio with Eddie Cantor agreed to do a guest shot. She perched herself on Ed Wynn's perambulating piano and sang cheerfully while he wheeled her back and forth across the stage. (Typical of Wynn's brand of humor was the introduction written by Hal Kanter and Leo Solomon for her. "It was a showboat set, with people entering and going up the gangplank. Ed came on and asked the ticket-taker if dinner was being served on board. 'No,' said that chap, 'if you wish to eat, you must dine ashore.' 'Dine ashore?' screamed Ed. '*Dinah Shore?*' And on she came," recalls Kanter. "Which is what, in those days, we called a real entrance.") That was Dinah Shore's first TV appearance, and after it, she never once looked back to radio. Twenty-six years later, she is still available on your screen, singing and blowing kisses, and adding to CBS's (and her own) store of corporate profit.

And then, a few weeks later, there were two other guests on Wynn's show. A red-headed comedienne who had made a number of films, and her husband, a young song-and-dance man who specialized in babalu-type numbers. "She wanted to come on television to find out what this medium was all about," recalls Kanter.

A quarter century later, it seems obvious that the lady and her husband were very quick studies. In the space of a year or so after Lucille Ball and Desi Arnaz did their guest shot (she essayed a silent movie takeoff in which she wore a black wig as Cleopatra, and she and Wynn held up their dialogue on hand-printed cards for the audience to see) she and Desi were to launch a TV project that would have a most powerful impact on the infant medium.

They would essay a half-hour comedy show of their own in 1951, to be called *I Love Lucy*, and within a very few years of that show's success most live television producers, performers, et al. would follow their trail to film. (There were several other L.A.–based half hours contemporary with *I Love Lucy*, such shows as Joan Davis's *I Married Joan*; *Ozzie and Harriet*; *The Stu Erwin Show*; *The Alan Young Show*; *Oh, Susannah!* et al.—but in terms of longevity and impact, the Ball-Arnaz shows remain the untouchables, not to be confused with the later Desilu shows of the same name.) The business would fold up its New York tents and travel westward. Ever since, a steady supply of half-hour sitcoms has poured off Hollywood's assembly lines with the monotonous rhythm of a General Motors factory output (and little more originality).

Lucy is still on—and so is Miss Ball.

Twenty-five years after the fact, the lady herself, she of the red hair, the wide eyes, and the terrific legs, sits in the living room of her comfortable Beverly Hills home. Her voice, now that she is no longer engaged in those weekly screaming matches with Desi, Bill Frawley, Vivian Vance, and Gale Gordon, is deep and surprisingly gentle. She is a very beautiful woman who does not resemble a

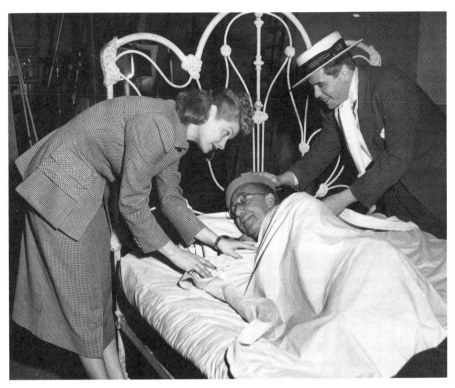

Lucille Ball, Desi Arnaz, and Ed Wynn (Courtesy Ralph Levy and CBS)

pioneer woman in the slightest—a pioneer who helped induce an entire entertainment medium to move away from New York—but the truth is indisputable. After she and Desi showed that it could be done, the gold rush to film began.

How did it all come about? As she tells it, the saga seems simple enough. "CBS had asked us to try a comedy show. I'd done one on radio called *My Favorite Husband* and they wanted something like that," she says. "We tried for months to figure out what sort of characters we wanted to be, and we couldn't find anyone to come up with an idea that fit. It was all stuff about Hollywood couples, and so far as I could see, a Hollywood couple has no problems in the eyes of the audience. If they have a big house, a car, a swimming pool, and live in California, tell me—what's their problem?"

What the lady was looking for was some sort of a family comedy about unaffluent people, with large helpings of domestic squabbles along the way. "The man would be the master of the house, and she would be a scatterbrain—but wily enough to get her own way, in a comedic sort of fashion," says Miss Ball, thereby articulating a golden rule that has remained commercially viable on TV screens ever since 1951.

Once a script had been prepared, there arose the problem of finding her a leading man. "I said, 'Desi.' They said, '*Desi*? Nobody'd believe *that!*' I said, 'What do you mean—nobody'd believe? He *is* my husband!' They said, 'Yeah, but . . . *American* domestic comedy.'"

To prove their point, the couple took their proposed show out to play vaudeville dates, performing the domestic comedy sketches and interspersing the material with song and dance, at which both were, it is somewhat superfluous to add, expert. She could sing. He could sing. The comedy came naturally to both of them; his dialect nicely complemented her sense of low comedy. "They loved us," she says. "I guess that proved the point. More trouble. Now they wanted us to go to New York and do the show. It would be seen outside New York on kinescopes, but produced in Manhattan. I said, 'No! No kinescope!' I said, 'For Chrissake, we started this thing so we could be together, and we could stay home and get away from Desi's band business!'—which was very lucrative, but Desi had been out touring with his band for five years—then he'd been in the Army for three and a half years—that meant we'd been married for ten years, and together for maybe a year and two months in all that time.

"So I said, 'Look, Desi, I'm going to do it with you, I will not go to New York, and I will not do the show on kinescope.' He said, 'What *are* you going to do it on?' I said, 'I want to do it on *film*.' He said, 'That doesn't make sense. That's not television.' I said, 'Look—we'll do it for a year or so, and if it bombs, then at least we'll have something like home movies—to show to our kids.'"

The executive wing of CBS was not enchanted with Miss Ball's proposal. They thanked her for suggesting it, and went on to other problems. "So we borrowed $5,000," said Miss Ball, "and became owners of our own idea."

(Are you listening, Horatio Alger?)

"That's when the pioneering began," she says. "It had never been done. We had to find facilities. We went and rented space at the old General Services Studio and figured out a way to set up a theater. The audience was the big thing; we always knew we had to have one to play to, and that meant building a special stage in which there'd be proper exits for the audience onto a main thoroughfare. Desi had to go to the fire department, the police, all the authorities, and find out exactly how our studio could be set up."

Then came the problem of filming the performance itself, on 35 mm. cameras. "We didn't know what we were doing, where we were going; we were experimenting on everything," she recalls. "Nobody had ever filmed a show before simultaneously on three cameras. Luckily, we had a very great intelligent gentleman named Karl Freund, a cameraman who had been with UFA in Germany, and who'd come here to Hollywood and worked for years. He'd already retired—he made an awful lot of money during the war on some inventions of his own. We went to him and asked him how to do this, and he said, 'I'll tell you how you can do it, and I want to do it with you.'

"One night he brought us out to his house in the valley, and showed us a system he'd invented for us, one that could film simultaneously on three cameras, and then, when the show was over and the film was developed, you could sit in the cutting room and his machine played back all three shots simultaneously, so you could cut from one shot to the other. I said, 'What the hell is *that*, Karl?' And he said, 'It's a three-headed monster that's going to save our lives.' Which it did. You saw the close-up, the medium, and the longshot—all on the machine, at the same time. We used that machine ever since—and practically all the shows that are done today are still using Freund's device."

The *I Love Lucy* pilot was shot, with the couple, supported by William Frawley and Vivian Vance, with Marc Daniels as the director, grappling with the various technical problems that arose every ten minutes or so during production. When it was finished and shown to CBS, the same executives who had turned it down in its primary stages were quick to recognize their unfortunate error and, being nothing if not resourceful, arranged for it to appear on their network, with Philip Morris cigarettes as its original sponsor.

"We experimented with everything—except our writers, who were marvelous," says Miss Ball. (She refers to Madelyn Davis and Bob Carroll, Jr., whose association with her has been primary and permanent.) "As we went along, we were working nine days a week—no Sundays off, Saturday nights. We sat there day and night, night and day, rehearsing and filming, for months and months. Gradually we got our schedule down to five days a week, and then four. It was ours, we owned the show . . . and then the whole thing just snowballed. Desi turned out to be a fantastic businessman. A showman, a gambler, a try-anything-and-see-if-it-works type. Desi would never hire anybody until he had done the job himself, to see what it entailed. He didn't know how many people he needed, how many technicians or what, until he'd seen exactly what the work entailed

William Frawley, Vivian Vance, Lucille Ball, Desi Arnaz, and Maurice Chevalier (Courtesy CBS)

—then he'd go find the right guy for it. Sure, we made mistakes, but we've had people who've stayed with us for more than twenty years."

Miss Ball has always been known for her bedrock candor. "I've been very lucky with the use of nepotism," she says, smiling. "Why not? If you have a nepot around that's worthy—*use* him, or her. . . . By the way, what the hell exactly *is* a nepot?"

A dictionary is produced from her library, and it reveals the word is derived from the Italian *nepotismo*, which is "nephew," and the expression refers to the practice of hiring relatives to do one's business. "Goes a long way back before the Italians," observes Miss Ball. "Started with Moses, I'm sure. And I'm a firm believer in it."

In her own career, there has not only been husband Desi, but after the two divorced and she remarried, her current husband, Gary Morton, became a basic part of her production team. "He studied five years before he took over," she says. "My sister Cleo worked with us—and so have my kids. Everybody pulled his weight, too."

The Desilu saga through the fifties and early sixties is well known—how from the one basic acorn of *I Love Lucy* the Ball-Arnaz team grew literally dozens of other successful ventures. How, in years that followed their first success, Desilu became so affluent that the firm took over physical ownership of the old RKO studios as its own base of production. "It was Desi himself who was the one who got tired of it all," Miss Ball admits. "At the beginning we had our own five-year plan, and then we had another, and then another . . . and it never stopped. By then it was too big."

I Love Lucy, with its endless permutations on the misadventures of Mr. and Mrs. Ricardo and their close pals, Frawley and Vivian Vance, is still showing somewhere on a screen at this moment, dubbed into practically every known language. In the years since Miss B. and Mr. A. borrowed that original $5,000 with which to launch their first half hour, there have been literally hundreds of other carbon copies of their solo-flight concept. You've seen them on your screen—the ones that got past the "pilot" phase, flickered into a few weeks' life, and more often than not disappeared to molder away in someone's film vaults. But *I Love Lucy* and its successor, *The Lucy Show*, in which Miss Ball carried on with Gale Gordon as her leading man, have prevailed, and obviously will prevail, as long as there is the electrical power for your set.

Is there one reason for this extraordinary longevity?

"It must be that people have always identified with her," says the star, without hesitation. (She has obviously answered this question many times.) "I kept the character the same because I liked her, and I knew her, and I dug her. Even though the cast changed, and the format changed, she was always kept in the same vein. I always played straight, and let the others in the show get the laughs. Didn't mind it a bit. So Lucy never really changed much. And for all those years, she has to have connected with the audience —the kids, the parents, the grandfathers and grandmothers, the deaf people, the bedridden ones in the hospitals, the foreign audiences—they all know her and they all love her. She's easily understood, even when she's translated into other languages. Everywhere she plays, they dig her."

In the past several seasons, Miss Ball has been very busy with the film of *Mame* and with assorted appearances on various TV specials. She's had time to reflect on the enormous impact her shows have had, but she's more interested in the future. "Yes, we were together, it was successful, it was a pioneering wonderful experience that we are proud of, and yes, it was at the very beginning and yes, a lot of people have copied it, and yes, a lot of people have fallen beside the wayside, and yes, it did interfere with the movies, but once it got started, it just couldn't be stopped." She shrugs. "It was progress—and I guess that's our whole story."

It all sounds so ridiculously simple as Miss Ball sits in her opulent Beverly Hills living room this pleasant afternoon and talks about a unique form of trail-blazing—that cottage-industry mom-and-pop type of production in 1951 that changed the entire format of what was once live television. But, as any professional who has come within twenty feet of a TV operation will fervently point out, nothing that was accomplished by Miss Ball and Mr. Arnaz over the years was that easy. An enormous amount of hard work and talent and effort and careful planning went into the thousands and thousands of assorted feet of "*Oh, my goodness, Loosy, what're you doeen now?/Oh, Ricky, I can't tell you exactly but will you do me a favor and just grab this lever here and pull so I can get down?*"

"Of course," she admits ruefully, "there's a certain amount of confusion with the people about how I look now, as opposed to 1952. I can be in the supermarket shopping, and people constantly come up to me and say, 'My, you've lost a lot of weight since last week!' And there are always those characters who insist on telling me all about the show they saw last night—the *entire* plot—as if I'd forgotten it . . . which I have."

Back in 1950, an enterprising distributor brought to the ten-inch screen the two-reel Hal Roach comedies of another pair of great comedians, Stan Laurel and Oliver Hardy. Ever since then, those two-reelers have been shown so often on TV that, in the parlance of the film business, the sprocket-holes of the film have worn out.

So it is with *I Love Lucy*. All those half hours, hilarious classic comedy situations that they are, remain right up there, running along with Ollie and Stan. Pretty good company for a comedienne.

"Yes," she concedes, "I admit I would just as soon be doing it still—except, at my age, I got feeling a little sorry for my poor writers, who were trying to come up with new ideas. And I also began to feel a little alone out there, at my age, acting silly."

And then, without too much hesitation, she quickly adds, "Although, if I could do three movies right now in the Lucy character, I would—so I guess I don't feel *that* silly!"

She laughs. Suddenly, it's that old familiar loud, piercing boy-are-we-in-trouble-wait-till-Ricky-finds-out-what-a-mess-we-made laugh.

And thank heaven, it's still Lucy.

Which, in this year of 1976, where most of what flashes across the screen is forgotten before the second commercial break, is very reassuring.

FINALE

As the home screen became larger, going from ten-inch to twelve-inch, and then to the mighty seventeen-inch, so did the handwriting on the wall that predicted the imminent end of live TV programming.

Television audiences in the mid-fifties were beginning to laugh at filmed half-hour comedies, and they were also being made aware of their set's enormous potential as a mirror of real life.

It was 1954, and in Washington, D.C., senatorial hearings were scheduled that involved Senator Joseph McCarthy, of Wisconsin, and the United States Army. It was McCarthy's contention, which he intended to prove, that the Army was riddled with Communist infiltrators.

"Those Army-McCarthy hearings were getting an enormous amount of attention in the press," recalls Robert Kintner, who at the time was head of ABC–TV programming. "One night I was home and I thought to myself, why don't we put it on television? So I went to my office next day and I said, 'Get permission to go into the hearings with television cameras.'

"McCarthy was all for it. I don't think he had the vaguest idea what was going to happen to him. From then on, we televised the thing every day, and as McCarthy and Joseph Welch, the Boston lawyer, began to grapple with each other in that hearing room, it drew enormous attention. Remember, in those days, the two other networks were just beginning to program their daytime soap operas. We didn't have any on ABC, so it didn't matter to us what shows we preempted. We went on from the opening gavel to the closing, every day, five days a week, and we took over an unbelievably large audience. People all over the country stopped listening to their radios, and watching the soaps, and stayed glued to what we were showing them on ABC.

"I used to get calls from executives at NBC, crying and saying, 'Would you take those goddamn hearings off? We're getting calls from all over asking us why *we* don't put them on!' And I said 'Well, why don't you lose some money for a change and put them on?'

"The end result of those hearings on television is now history. The huge power of television coverage of live news events was demonstrated beyond any doubt—much, much stronger than any sort of live entertainment programming that could be done from a network studio. The mass impact of those hearings really did destroy McCarthy's career; after his confrontation with Welch, he began to go downhill very rapidly.

"What that taught me," says Kintner, "was that the networks would have to look for some other sort of programming, other than the shows that were on at the time. So I went in and talked to Leonard Goldenson, who was running ABC, and I suggested that we make a deal with a movie company, to supply us with product for our daily programming. Leonard, who knew the movie business better than I did, said he didn't think it would be very productive, since the studio bosses had such closed minds about television.

"And he was right. We went out there and called on everybody—from the bosses at Metro right on down the line to Columbia. Harry Cohn was the rudest of all of them. I remember he said something like 'You dumb young son of a bitch, you won't get any of my stars, you won't get any people—*you* can't make films! People want the companionship of the theater, they want the idea of going out of the house, they want their movies the way they *are* —not on TV!'

"The others were a little more polite, but just as negative. Nick Schenck at Metro was polite, but flat out against the idea. Spyros Skouras at Fox discussed the idea, but in the end he turned us down cold. Finally we come to Jack Warner. He was having a bad time at the studio keeping his production going, and he came around to our way of thinking, and eventually we made a deal. We arranged to make four filmed series—it would all be stuff like *The Roaring Twenties* and *Bourbon Street Beat*—action adventure. They weren't very good at first, but gradually they caught on.

"Then I went and talked to Walt Disney about coming on TV. He said he thought it was a hell of an idea, but he didn't want to part with any of his feature films because he wanted to use them himself, if he ever went on television, to promote Disneyland. So out of that discussion came the afternoon *Mickey Mouse Club*, with Walt as the master of ceremonies, five days a week. He was reluctant to appear on the show at first, but later on, Walt told me that he was so glad I'd insisted that he do it. Up to the time he went on television, even though he was the man who'd made *Snow White* and all those other great films, nobody knew who he was, or what he looked like. But from that time on, he could go anywhere, and be recognized—it meant getting a cab at the airport, or the best table at any restaurant!

"Then I said, 'Let's go after the backlogs of old feature films.' I went everywhere but I couldn't find anything to buy. I finally got some English pictures from Rank, put them on Sunday nights, and when they didn't go over, that of course proved to everybody that showing features on television wasn't a good idea.

"Well, they didn't go because they were British, and they were second-rate, and they didn't have the proper promotion." Kintner smiles. "The idea was good, and out of it came *Saturday Night at the Movies*, on NBC. [Mr. Kintner moved to that network to preside over its programming in 1957.] In terms of producing profits for the network, that was the greatest smash hit that's ever been on TV." (In the early summer of 1975 NBC concluded a deal with Paramount to televise *Godfather* and *Godfather II* on the network for a total price of $15,000,000. So much for Harry Cohn's clouded crystal ball of 1954.)

And what about the early, live days of television? "I think it was great for the beginning of the medium," concedes Kintner. "But I certainly don't think there was enough product, enough production know-how and ability to program for the home—where people want constant service, hour after hour. Those early shows like *Studio One* and *Robert Montgomery Presents*, *Philco*, *Kraft*, and all the others—they simply couldn't survive today. Film shows would knock them off very fast. Those shows didn't have any dimension, no movement—they were mostly talk. They were fine for their own time, but not for today."

Mr. Kintner's thesis is buttressed by the pragmatic views of Perry Lafferty, himself a veteran of the live TV days in New York, who for a decade was the

The Kefauver Hearings, 1951 (Courtesy ABC)

head of CBS's vast California production. "Starting with Jack Warner and his film shows," he remarks, "the live TV shows were doomed. The New York shows were all essentially anthologies, a different story each week with a different cast, subject to the absolutely rigid limitations of an NBC or a CBS four-walled studio. Film was used so minimally that it literally was not used at all. One show where I had an airplane crash in the Pacific, we did the whole thing live from Brooklyn studios, except for one film clip of eight seconds, of a plane hitting the ocean. Truthfully, you just couldn't turn out thirty-nine good plays a season on the eleven or twelve weekly anthologies. The writers were simply unable to provide that much material.

"So what did Warner and the guys out here in California do? They started with guys running up and down the streets, in cars, with guns, shooting at each other, and chases, and they introduced a lot of Troy Donahues and Tab

Hunters bare to the waist, and little by little, the television audience began to slip into the viewing habit, because with action adventure stuff like that, you really don't have to think. Usually, when you saw one of those early *Studio One* shows, or a *Philco-Goodyear*, you had to think a little, it wasn't purely escapist entertainment, the playwright was making some sort of a point. But with the stuff that began to be turned out here in California—which rapidly took over—no thought was necessary."

"One of the problems with those early live shows," adds Kintner, "was that they'd go on the air and they'd become very successful, but in those days there was no concept of cost control. A hit show such as the one Sid Caesar and Imogene Coca did on Saturday nights simply skyrocketed in price each year. When we made the move to filmed shows, the film companies could deliver their films at a specific, guaranteed figure. With a live show, everybody had a budget, but nobody paid too much attention to it.

"But the real reason why live programming ended is that we found out that the medium *sold* so well—so fast," he says. "All the big sponsors, the soap companies and the cereal manufacturers and the automobile makers, jumped in to sponsor shows. The medium got away from itself by its ability to *sell*. The truth is," Mr. Kintner concludes, "that if the advertisers hadn't discovered how potent a sales medium television is, there wouldn't be a network going today that could support commercial programming of *any* kind, live, or film, or taped."

Twenty-odd TV "new seasons" have flashed across the tube.

And now?

It was in the mid-sixties that Newton Minow, then the chairman of the FCC, coined the expression by which he described commercial television as "The Waste Land."

Today the vast panorama seems even less hopeful.

"Three years ago, I got out the list of the shows in the Top 15 from 1955," remarks Perry Lafferty, "and do you realize that in twenty years, the forms remained exactly the same? Ed Sullivan, Red Skelton, *Gunsmoke*—nothing had changed one whit. *All in the Family* is exactly the same form as Lucille Ball's original show, and if you want to go back further, the same as *The Stu Erwin Show* or *Ozzie and Harriet*. The form is identical—all that changed was the content. That's why people keep asking me in interviews now, 'What do you see? What trends do you see coming up in TV?' and I say, 'I don't see any changes in the forms. There are the franchised forms that have always been there—the cop, the marshal, the private eye, the lawyer who saves you with his law book, the doctor who saves you with his scalpel, the other guys who save you with a gun. The good guys—they're allowed to do something. They have the franchise.'

"Then there are the nonfranchised forms that never succeed. Since *Route 66* up to the time of *The Waltons*, there never has been a successful non-franchised form. In other words, whenever they did a show about a guy who didn't have the right to carry a gun, wear a law badge, or use a scalpel, not one succeeded. *The Waltons* came along right after Vietnam, when everybody was obviously craving a return to the old values, and it's a fairy tale, one that's laid back in the Depression. But it satisfied the audience. Others tried to copy it, *Lucas Tanner* on NBC didn't succeed, we even tried with *Apple's Way*, and it failed. I can give you a whole list of shows that have failed that are not franchised. I'm not going to count *Bonanza* or *Little House on the Prairie*, because a rifle and a pistol and/or people against nature is implicit in those forms. Even Ben Gazzara's show *Run for Your Life*—he had a dread disease—so there has to be jeopardy in those dramatic forms, or they don't work. Ever since *Route 66*, *The Waltons* is the sole exception.

"And as for variety shows," he adds, "they are absolutely the same as they always were. Red Skelton, or Dean Martin, Carol Burnett or Flip Wilson. You find that whoever runs those shows had to be a person the audience loves. We've been lucky; we've just discovered a new such person. Cher Bono . . . and she's the only new one around. But the *form* of even her show remains exactly the same.

"So what am I saying to you?" asks Lafferty. "Pity the poor creative community in television. Pity them all because they've tried everything and this is all that works—the same old forms. I'm not talking about specials, I'm not talking about mini-series—I'm talking about the major part of our schedule —prime-time nighttime weekly series, week in and week out. What's new?" He shrugs. "There's nothing new."

One of the few remaining "creative" types who still function as a television dramatist is Reginald Rose, whose contributions to the medium began back in the early fifties when he wrote *Twelve Angry Men* for *Studio One*. His assessment of the current scene is, if possible, even more cynical.

"What television has done, and has learned," he remarks, "is the same thing that food manufacturers have learned to do, and that is to make everything plastic, and to make people need and enjoy and demand plastic. You go into McDonald's and what everybody wants to know beforehand is that they can walk into one, anywhere, and get exactly the same food, at any time. They're all the same, whatever chain you go to, the same hamburgers, the same fried potatoes, the sodas—everything—so you know in advance what you're going to get. You know you're eating plastics. You see the kids today demanding it. It's what they want—they have to get it or they're not happy. Kids won't eat anything else unless they're from very special families who insist upon introducing something at home to the kid such as snails. 'Eat this, you're going to like it,' and so forth.

"The TV audience has been conditioned to want what it's watching, and it makes things a helluva lot easier for the television networks now, because they don't have to change the shows much, if at all," says Rose. "All they have to do is to change the actors' costumes."

Back in 1961 Jack Paar, who was at the time one of the major personalities of the medium, somewhat cynically remarked, "Practically everybody seems to be complaining about TV except the people, who go on staring at it as if hypnotized."

These days, Paar finds nothing improved.

"I think it's very sad, what happened," he mourns. "I did try to do worthwhile things on my shows, to go to Africa, say, and to interview Dr. Schweitzer —and I tried hard to communicate my own enthusiasm for good things. But the public that supports stuff like that isn't large. You do it, and nobody watches, and then the program executives start telling you to go out and find a new rock group to fill the time and attract viewers."

Paar is in semi-retirement, as are so many of his contemporaries. "I found that I could never be good if the show was being taped," he says. "Tape wouldn't allow me to be me.

"Creativity isn't something you can operate by survey, or by committee. Can you imagine Beethoven, or Bach, or George Gershwin working under the aegis of a committee? 'Fellows, here's this *Rhapsody in Blue* I've been working on. How do you like it?' 'Well, George, it needs a little something down there at the end—we're not sure the audience will go for that section.'

"It wasn't the heads of the networks that were at fault," Paar insists. "Pat

Weaver and Mort Werner from NBC, Hubbell Robinson and Harry Ommerle at CBS—they were all guys who really wanted to do good things, I'm sure of that. I never met any one of them that I heard suggest that he felt the audience out there was twelve years old, and that we should pander to them. Never. Every time we talked about a new show idea, we went into it with enthusiasm, hoping to make it great.

"But what happened was that the audiences didn't respond. For that, I have to blame *them*, quite a bit. Their lack of response—how they sit there and accept bad shows. We really should have *led* them more.

"Eventually, when those network guys got their heads beaten a bit, can you blame them for losing their enthusiasm? In order to survive, they had to give the audience what they *thought* it wanted. Then Jim Aubrey came along at CBS with his theory—give them the lowest possible denominator, the worst stuff—and his theory worked. It made money, lots of it. And that was the end of it, as far as I'm concerned.

"What's ahead?" mourns Paar. "I don't see any renaissance possible. Since it's a medium today that's operated strictly by survey and committee, then tell me, how the hell can a renaissance get started under those circumstances?

"I'm afraid," he says, "television will never get better. And it makes me very sad to recognize that."

Over the years, television has conditioned us to absorb the message in sixty-second hunks.

So for a summing-up on the passing of live TV, the postmortem should not take longer than the traditional one-minute spot.

Here, then, lies live television. Born commercially in 1947, it flowered for a few frantic years, and with the coming of videotape it passed away.

It grew very fast. Probably too fast for its own good.

It spawned phalanxes of fresh creative talent—writers, actors, producers, and directors. Some of them it burned out in a matter of weeks. Others thrived and grew. None of them have remained in television—the medium spurned its own progeny so thoroughly that its very best have long since departed for films and the theater.

At its peak, it was a gawky, frenetic, higgledy-piggledy fire-when-ready-Gridley medium, which substituted talent and energy for controlled structure. And since TV proved to be such a valuable sales tool, it obviously needed the guiding hands of accountants and economic theorists, slide-rule wielders, polesters, advertising agency thinkers, and other such noncreative types to straighten out the whole rag-tag mess. Which they did. And when they were finally done with live TV, everything was all laid out. Flat.

As a medium, it's possible that it might even have survived on videotape— except for Gresham's immutable law (California statute ⍟76-009), i.e., *Bad television shows inevitably drive out good.* And the MCA/William Morris Agency law of TV economics: *A live TV show is over and done with at the end of the hour. But a filmed TV series goes back into the film can, to be sold again . . . and again . . . and again . . . and . . .*

But it was fun while it lasted.

Wasn't it?

INDEX